AFGHANISTAN

The New Great Game

AFGHANISTAN
THE NEW GREAT GAME

Edited by

Alok Bansal

Foreword by

Ram Madhav

PENTAGON PRESS LLP

AFGHANISTAN: The New Great Game

Edited by Alok Bansal

ISBN 978-93-90095-49-0

First Published in 2022

Published by
PENTAGON PRESS LLP
206, Peacock Lane, Shahpur Jat,
New Delhi-110049
Phones: 011-64706243, 26491568
Telefax: 011-26490600
email: rajan@pentagonpress.in
website: www.pentagonpress.in

Printed at Aegean Offset Printers, Greater Noida, U.P.

Dedicated to
My friend, Shakti Sinha
who conceived this book, BUT left for his Heavenly Abode
before taking it forward

Shakti Sinha
(11 May 1957 – 4 October 2021)

Shakti, one of the foremost scholars on Afghanistan in India, lived there for many years and built lasting relationships. He could feel the pulse of Afghanistan and relate to its people. A renowned bureaucrat, Shakti was known for his academic rigour as well as administrative prowess. He served as Private Secretary to Shri Atal Bihari Vajpayee when he was the Leader of Opposition, and subsequently, the Prime Minister of India. He served in the World Bank and later with the United Nations Assistance Mission in Afghanistan and for UNDP in Afghanistan as Strategic Policy Advisor. He also served as Chief Secretary of Andaman & Nicobar Islands. He worked in a number of think tanks, starting with the Observer Research Foundation and then with the Institute for South Asian Studies at Singapore. He was the founding member of the South Asian Institute for Strategic Affairs (SAISA) and was its Director for a number of years. He was also a Director at India Foundation and subsequently, served as Director of the Nehru Memorial Museum and Library. He was selected by the Gujarat Government to be the first director of the Atal Bihari Vajpayee Institute of Policy Research and International Studies at MS University, Vadodara. He was also involved in setting up the Delhi School of Public Policy and Governance at Delhi University. He authored the book *'Vajpayee: The Years That Changed India'* and his most recent *'One Mountain Two Tigers: India, China & the High Himalayas'* and edited many others.

CONTENTS

FOREWORD

Afghanistan is a tragedy, not today after the US withdrawal, but has been for decades. It became a playground for the superpowers who played their wild games of geopolitics of the most opportune variety. The people of Afghanistan hardly mattered in these geostrategic machinations; if anything, they have been victims for only the last four decades.

When the Soviets invaded the country in the 1980s, the Americans decided not to sit quiet. They activated their agencies and pumped in millions of dollars through dubious channels to the rebel warlords to fight the Soviet 'occupying' force. What later became famous as "Charlie Wilson's War" had resulted in a decade of strife, misery, and extreme poverty for the people. It was the American agencies that were responsible for the rise of the Islamic fundamentalist Mujahideen rebels who fought pitched battles with the Soviet forces first and then with what they had left behind, the Najibullah government. Najibullah was finally dethroned and dragged onto the streets of Kabul and killed in the most grotesque manner in front of thousands of people. His chilling murder in public was telecast by some foreign broadcasters too.

After a decade-long occupation, the Soviets, under President Mikhail Gorbachev, decided one fine morning to quietly retreat leaving the people at the mercy of the warring Islamist Mujahideen rebels and a beleaguered Najibullah government. Having accomplished their mission of throwing out the Soviets, the Americans too quietly withdrew until the monster created by them in the form of an Islamist terror outfit returned in a decade to haunt them on their own soil.

At the receiving end of the Afghan conundrum this time, the Americans were forced to return to Afghanistan in the early 2000s after the al-Qaeda sponsored the 9/11 attacks that killed thousands of American citizens. What was a strategic intervention for his father a decade earlier became an ideological war for George Bush Jr. after 9/11. Thousands of groups and billions of dollars found their way into Afghanistan once again, this time not clandestinely but publicly. Bases were set up, interrogation centres sprang up, and the Bush-Cheney duo declared that bringing democracies to the lawless lands of the Middle East was their mission.

However, once Osama bin Laden, the mastermind behind the 9/11 attacks on America was killed in a highly secretive and praiseworthy operation in 2011, the Americans lost their appetite for their ideational agenda. President Obama announced the withdrawal of the American forces from Afghanistan in 2011; President Trump initiated the withdrawal process by indulging in a highly controversial negotiations exercise with the Taliban leadership at Doha with Qatar as the midwife. Finally, Biden bit the bullet by actually withdrawing the American forces.

A lot of debate is going on in America and the rest of the world over the clumsy manner in which the withdrawal of US forces was done and the way Afghanistan was returned on a platter to Taliban religious extremists. Biden tried to demonstrate false courage by insisting that the mission had been accomplished with the elimination of Bin Laden and he would not sacrifice any more sons and daughters of America in futile wars like the one in Afghanistan. However, that is not going to put an end to the debate, which will continue to rage for many years to come. The American action will face scrutiny once its consequences come before the world in a glaring way in the coming years.

Two countries that should not escape this scrutiny are – Pakistan and China. Gorbachev and Biden concluded twenty years apart that Afghanistan was an unmanageable terrain and efforts to bring in an orderly and democratic regime there were bound to end in failure. Both seemed to put the blame on the people of Afghanistan whereas the real culprits are the two countries themselves. Left to themselves, the Afghans would heartily cherish a liberal and democratic dispensation. They have demonstrated their democratic commitment in the last two decades abundantly. The last two decades saw the maturing of a democratic political process that had provided representation for different sections of Afghan society, including women in large numbers. It would be unfair to put the blame on the people of Afghanistan for a failure the onus for which rests elsewhere.

That brings into focus the role of the above-named two countries. Pakistan has always treated Afghanistan as its backyard, which is critical for its strategic depth in its conflict with India. It played a crucial role in promoting Islamic hard-line groups in Afghanistan and became a safe haven for terror groups of all hues. It is no secret that the Mujahideen and their successor avatar, the Taliban, are funded, sponsored, and supported by Pakistan's agencies.

Similarly, the role of China too has been critical to the rise of the Islamists in Afghanistan. Deng Xiaoping had actively supported the American overtures in the 1980s and 1990s in Afghanistan when the Mujahideen were being armed, funded, and encouraged by the CIA and other Western agencies. Chinese weapons flowed freely into Afghanistan to settle scores with the adversary in the neighbourhood, the Soviet Union. In the last few years, China seems to have re-entered the Afghan theatre by actively supporting the Taliban. In fact, apart from Pakistan, China was also another country, which did not withdraw its diplomatic staff from Kabul after the Taliban takeover. Its ambassador is actively collaborating with the Taliban leadership after the American withdrawal and providing necessary support for the ragtag regime.

However, the real victims of these power plays, the people of Afghanistan, continue to suffer silently. Most of the democratic leadership has dispersed helter-skelter to different countries. Many of them, especially the women politicians, were rescued by America and are living in camps there. Any discussion about the future of

Afghanistan should keep the people and the democratic leadership at the centre. Dismissing the fact that democracy does not suit that country would be a mistake. Democratic ethos comes naturally to some countries; it needs to be nurtured in others. There is no better alternative than democracy to provide space for human aspirations like freedom and liberty.

This volume, initiated by Shri Shakti Sinha, an erudite scholar and expert on Afghan affairs, had to be completed by Capt. Alok Bansal, another erudite scholar of Pakistan and Afghanistan affairs. I am sure this compilation of articles by eminent scholars would throw light on Afghanistan's future and, by implication, the future of peace and stability in the region and beyond.

Most importantly, it focuses on the future of the ordinary people of Afghanistan.

10 December 2021 **Ram Madhav**

PREFACE

Taliban's returning to power in Afghanistan is undoubtedly one of the biggest humanitarian disasters of the decade. So was the sudden fall of government in Kabul that it left the Afghan population stunned. Many of them had experienced Taliban rule earlier and this was evident from their desperation to get out of Kabul, which had been surrounded on all sides by the Taliban. The large crowds that flocked the Kabul International Airport, trying to board aircraft bound for any destination out of Kabul, clearly showed their apprehensions and concerns. Not only were the Afghans stunned, most of the members of international community including the global powers and international community were also shocked by the rapid developments in Kabul. Unfortunately, many of the countries had their own geopolitical interests to look into, consequently, their voices against the unfolding humanitarian disaster, were also quite muted. Some of them were even quick to issue the Taliban, certificates of good character.

In India there was a sense of bewilderment. Some wanted to open communication channels with Taliban, so that India is not completely left out of Afghanistan, whereas others felt it would amount to supping with the devil. Consequently, New Delhi's reactions were also quite muted. One needed to look at various questions, whether Taliban would give up its radical Islamist ideology? Whether there can be any meeting point between a secular nation like India and a theological state governed by a radical Islamist outfit like Taliban. Will Afghan population and especially those, who have looked up to India, be happy with India providing legitimacy to Taliban. What about the rights of women, children religious, ethnic and sectarian minorities? How does India provide succor to Afghan population, which would face starvation during the impending harsh winter? Will India's disengagement be China and Pakistan's gain? Can the resistance to Taliban be revived? Why did the US leave Afghanistan so abruptly and why are Iran, Russia and Central Asian Republics still talking to Taliban? These and many more question needed answers, which were not readily available in the public domain.

Rajan Arya, the publisher, approached Shakti Sinha, our common friend and one of the leading experts on Afghanistan, to come up with a book that could answer most if not all of these questions. Unfortunately, as soon as Shakti started working on this idea, the cruel destiny snatched him from us. In the early hours of 04 October 2021, just a few hours after communicating with us, Shakti left for heavenly abode. Consequently, Rajan, who was extremely distraught, felt that in order to honour Shakti's memory, this book must come out and approached me to take this project forward. Shakti had already approached some of the contributors, we decided to approach others and come out with the book expeditiously, so that the curiosity generated by recent developments could be quenched. I also felt that the book must contain a strong component of important factors for a common man to understand the background of current crisis.

The book has been written in a very short timeframe with each chapter written like an essay. The avowed objective being to reach out to the readers while the incidents of Kabul, are still fresh in public memory. This would hopefully allow them to understand the "new great game" being played in Afghanistan and its neighborhood. At a time when there is clamor in India for reaching out to Taliban, this would enable the readers to make up their mind if it is the right steps that India needs to adopt.

I am grateful to all my authors from India, Afghanistan and Pakistan, who are at this moment living in different parts of the globe, for their painstaking efforts and meeting the deadline. It was an absolute pleasure working with them and going through their manuscripts. All credit must go to them for penning such informative chapters in such a short time. Shortcomings, if any, are purely due to my oversight on account of a tight timeline and other commitments. I would like to acknowledge my gratitude to Shri Ram Madhav, who kindly consented to write the Foreword, despite his grueling schedule. His Foreword provides the proper perspective to the book. I am also grateful to my colleague Deeksha Goel for going through and editing this vital component.

It would not be out of place to acknowledge the efforts taken by some eminent experts on the subject, who took a quick look at the book and endorsed it despite their busy schedules. I am grateful to renowned journalist and Member of Indian Parliament Shri MJ Akbar; former Indian Ambassadors to Afghanistan, Shri Amar Sinha and Shri Gautam Mukhopadhaya; former Military Advisor in the National Security Council Secretariat of India, Lt Gen Vinod G Khandare, PVSM, AVSM, SM and Professor Rohan Gunaratna, the Director General of Colombo based Institute of National Security studies, for their valuable endorsements. This book would not have seen the light of the day, but for the invaluable support that I received from my colleague Soumya Chaturvedi, who not only wrote an important chapter, but also helped me with the editing, proof reading and even giving ideas for the cover. Above all I owe this book to Shakti, who I had known for close to four decades, for conceptualizing this brilliant book.

I hope that the readers will find the book intellectually stimulating and it will answer some of the questions that must have been rising in their minds after watching the painful events that unraveled in Kabul.

Alok Bansal

List of Abbreviations

AFM	American Feminist Majority
AFP	Agence France-Presse
AFPAK	Afghanistan-Pakistan Region
ANA	Afghan National Army
ANDSF	Afghan National Defence and Security Forces
ANSF	Afghan National Security Forces
ASWJ	Ahl-e-Sunnat Wal Jamaat
BRI	Belt and Road Initiative
CIA	Central Intelligence Agency
CPEC	China-Pakistan Economic Corridor
CTBT	Comprehensive Nuclear Test Ban Treaty
DRP	De-Radicalization Program
ETIM	East Turkestan Islamic Movement
FATA	Federally Administrative Tribal Areas
FATF	Financial Assistance Task Force
FBI	Federal Bureau of Investigation
FMCT	Fissile Material Cut-Off Treaty
FOB	Forward Operating Base
GWOT	Global War on Terror

HM	Hizbul Mujahideen
ICRC	International Committee of the Red Cross
IMF	International Monetary Fund
IMU	Islamic Movement of Uzbekistan
IS	Islamic State
ISAF	International Security Assistance Force
ISI	Pakistan's Inter-Services Intelligence (Directorate)
ISKP	Islamist State Khorasan Province
ISPR	Inter Services Public Relations
J&K	Jammu & Kashmir
JCIB	Joint Counter Intelligence Bureau (ISI section)
JeM	Jaish-e-Mohammed
JIB	Joint Intelligence Bureau
JIM	Joint Intelligence Miscellaneous
JIN	Joint Intelligence/North
JIT	Joint Intelligence Technical Division
JIX	Joint Intelligence X
JSIB	Joint Signal Intelligence Bureau
JU	Jamaat-e-Islami
JUI	Jamiat Ulema-e-Islam
KP	Khyber Pakhtunkhwa
LeT	Laskhar-e-Taiba
LoC	Line of Control
MAK	*Maktab al-Khidamat*
NATO	North Atlantic Treaty Organisation
NBC	National Broadcasting Corporation
NPT	Treaty on Non-Proliferation of Nuclear Weapons
NSA	National Security Adviser

OGWs	Overground Workers
PDPA	People's Democratic Party of Afghanistan
PoJK	Pakistan-occupied Jammu and Kashmir
QUAD	Quadrilateral Security Dialogue
SDGs	Sustainable Development Goals
TAPI	Turkmenistan-Afghanistan-Pakistan-India
TNSM	Tehreek-e-Nafaz-e-Shariat-e-Mohammadi
TRF	The Resistance Front
TTP	Tehreek-e-Taliban Pakistan
UN	United Nations
UNAMA	United Nations Assistance Mission in Afghanistan
UNDP	United Nations Development Fund
UNGA	United National General Assembly
UNOCAL	Union Oil Company of California
UNOCHA	United Nations Office for the Coordination of Humanitarian Affairs
UNSC	United Nations Security Council
US	United States (of America)
WASO	Winter Aerial Surveillance and Observation

Contributors

Captain Alok Bansal is Director, India Foundation. He is also the Secretary General of Asian Eurasian Human Rights Forum. He was the founder Executive Director of the South Asian Institute for Strategic Affairs (SAISA) and a visiting professor at the Pakistan Studies Programme at Jamia Millia Islamia. He has been the Executive Director of the National Maritime Foundation and has also worked with IDSA, and CLAWS. A former naval officer with over three decades in the navy, he specialises on South Asia and has published many books and articles on the region.

Colonel Harjeet Singh is an author as well as defence and strategic analyst based in Chandigarh. He holds an M.Sc. and M.Phil. in Defence and Strategic Studies from the University of Madras. He has written many articles, monographs and reports published in various professional journals. He is well-known in military circles for his erudition and perspicacity of analysis. Amongst his publications is the book *Understanding Operation Enduring Freedom: Afghanistan 2001-2014*.

Dr Omar Sharifi is Assistant Professor in the American University of Afghanistan, Senior Research Fellow and Kabul Director of the American Institute of Afghanistan Studies and Research fellow at the University of Minnesota. He is Asia Society Fellow and member of Afghan 21 Young Leaders Forum. From 2006 to 2008, he studied Cultural Anthropology at Columbia University in New York under a Fulbright Fellowship. He also received a fellowship, through the Rumsfeld Foundation at the School of Advanced International Studies

(SAIS) at Johns Hopkins University. He completed his PhD in anthropology from Boston University in 2019.

Professor Harsh V Pant is Director, Studies and Head of the Strategic Studies Programme at Observer Research Foundation. He holds a joint appointment with the Department of Defence Studies and King's India Institute as Professor of International Relations at King's College London. He is also a Non-Resident Fellow with the Wadhwani Chair in US-India Policy Studies at the Center for Strategic and International Studies, Washington, DC. He has been a Visiting Professor at the Indian Institute of Management, Bangalore; a Visiting Fellow at the Center for the Advanced Study of India, University of Pennsylvania; a Visiting Scholar at the Center for International Peace and Security Studies, McGill University; and an Emerging Leaders Fellow at the Australia-India Institute, University of Melbourne.

Saaransh Mishra is a graduate in Political Science, Media Studies and International Affairs from Ashoka University, with a keen interest in human rights, security and economic sanctions. Having previously interned with media outlets, coupled with his credentials in global affairs, he wishes to pursue his work at the intersection of media and global policy in the future. As a Research Intern at the Observer Research Foundation, New Delhi, he has written extensively on Afghanistan and West Asia. He is currently working as a Research Associate at the Observer Research Foundation, New Delhi, tracking the developments in Russia & Eurasia.

Ajay Singh is a renowned writer and defence analyst who has authored five books and over 250 articles. Besides his interests in military history and geopolitics, he also writes short stories, and screenplay for films and television.

P. Stobdan from Ladakh has been a student of the Eurasian affairs for a long time. He has been closely following the Himalayan affairs, particularly the India-China boundary issues. He is currently a Senior Fellow at Delhi Policy Group (DPG), New Delhi. He is also on the Advisory Council of Oxus Society for Central Asian Affairs, Washington D.C. and a Member of the Foundation of Raja Rammohun Roy Library, Ministry of Culture. He regularly writes opinion and op-ed articles for various national/international journals and dailies. His latest books include *'The Great Game in the Buddhist Himalayas: India and China's Quest for Strategic Dominance'* and *'India and Central Asia: The Strategic Dimension'*

Lt General Vinod Bhatia, PVSM, AVSM, SM (retd) is a former Director General Military Operations of the Indian Army and Colonel of the PARACHUTE REGIMENT. After superannuation, he was the Director at Centre For Joint Warfare Studies, a New Delhi Based Think-Tank. He writes and speaks on Defence and security related topics both at national and international forums.

Soumya Chaturvedi is a security scholar and is currently with India Foundation as a Senior Research Fellow. A lawyer by education, she holds a postgraduate degree in International Relations and a specialization in Asia Pacific Security. She secured the first rank in the Dean's List and a distinction for her post-graduation thesis. Since August 2019, she has been steering the Jammu and Kashmir Security Tracker Project as part of her endeavours to contribute towards counter-terrorism studies in India. Her research interests include internal security, terrorism, peace and conflict studies. She regularly contributes on South Asian security through chapters, journal articles, newspaper and blog articles.

Dr. Sanchita Bhattacharya is Research Fellow in New Delhi based Institute for Conflict Management, India. Her core area of research is Madrasa Education in Pakistan, India and Bangladesh. She works on terrorism and socio-political issues of Pakistan. She also has an avid interest in the Af-Pak region. Her articles and commentaries have been published in East Asia Forum, The Kabul Times, The Outlook, The Pioneer, South Asia Monitor etc. She has written research papers in national and international journals and also contributed chapters in various edited volumes.

Lt Gen Syed Ata Hasnain, PVSM, UYSM, AVSM, SM, VSM** (Retd) served 40 years in the Army spending much of his command and field tenures at the LoC and LAC in Jammu and Kashmir. He commanded the Indian Army's elite 15 Corps at Srinagar. He continues to pursue the study of the dynamics of J&K and is currently the

Chancellor of the Central University of Kashmir. He is also a Member of the National Disaster Management Authority of India. He writes frequently for mainstream media and is a regular commentator on Afghanistan, Pakistan, China and issues connected with India's National Security.

Devyani Rao is a journalist and writer. She has worked as a correspondent for the leading Spanish news agency, Agencia EFE. Between 2006-2007, she lived and worked in Kabul as a correspondent for The Pioneer. Fluent in Hindi, English, Spanish and Portuguese, she has reported for various foreign media such as CNN enespañol and her articles have featured in numerous local and international publications, among them The Pioneer, The Indian Express, Business Standard, Tehelka, El País and El Mundo. She is an alumna of Modern School and Lady Shri Ram College. Devyani is an accomplished rider and dedicates much of her time to helping animals.

Sanghamitra Sarker is an Associate Professor in the Department of Political Science of Surendranath College for Women, Kolkata, under the University of Calcutta. She is also a member of the Board of Studies, Department of Political Science of the University of Calcutta. Her main areas of study include International Relations and Political Sociology. Apart from these, she also works on security issues in South Asia. She edited a book titled "21st century South Asia ". She is a media personality who has contributed several articles in journals and newspapers. She has directed an internationally acclaimed Docu-feature "Anwesha" on Indian classical music and dance and their women performers.

M. Ashraf Haidari is the Ambassador of Afghanistan to Sri Lanka, and concurrently served as the Director-General of the South Asia Cooperative Environment Program (SACEP) until recently. He was the Director-General of Policy and Strategy of the Ministry of the Foreign Affairs of Afghanistan until 2018, and previously served as Afghanistan's Deputy Chief of Mission to India. He was also Afghanistan's Deputy Assistant National Security Advisor, prior to which he served as Afghanistan's Chargé d'Affaires to the United States. In the 1990s, he was a humanitarian aid worker with stints at the UN World Food Program (WFP) and the UN High Commissioner for Refugees (UNHCR) in Afghanistan, Central Asia, and Switzerland. He is a visiting senior fellow at the INSSSL in Colombo, ORF in Delhi, and ASIS in Kabul.

Nadeem Shah is a journalist, counter terrorism researcher and author from Saraiki Region of Pakistan. He is Hubert H Humphrey Fellow and was awarded a fellowship at Philip Merrill College of Journalism, University of Maryland, by the US State Department in 2010, where he studied under cover investigative journalism and new media. His accomplishment certificates were signed by the then US President Barack Obama and Secretary of State Hillary Clinton. He has published "Saraiki Region: Roots of Radicalisation" based on his 18 month long research in 11 districts of the region.

1

Afghanistan: The New Great Game

Alok Bansal

On 15 August 2021, as India celebrated her 75th Independence Day, the Taliban entered Kabul, almost two decades after it had been ousted by the US-led offensive in the aftermath of 9/11. President Ashraf Ghani, who until then had been talking of resisting the Taliban, deserted his countrymen to escape to the United Arab Emirates, which granted him asylum. The Taliban's return to Kabul marks a historic low for global peace. The manner in which the Afghan government and its armed forces, which had until then exhibited exemplary fortitude and strength, capitulated, has raised many questions. Undue haste exhibited by the USA to pull out and more significantly announce it publicly, coupled with active military support from Pakistan's military and tactical advice received from the ISI, contributed in large measure to the collapse of the Afghan government. Despite an overwhelming majority of Afghans opposing the Taliban, it managed to capture power in a brisk move and the collapse of the resistance was sudden.

More significantly, unlike 1996, there was no significant resistance to the Taliban, as the forces opposing it had no axis to fall back upon to seek external assistance. For some time, the National Resistance

Front based at Panjshir Valley was seen as the solution to this gigantic problem, but even the Taliban's sponsor—the Inter-Services Intelligence (ISI) of Pakistan—saw the danger and Lieutenant General Faiz Hameed, the Director General (DG) of ISI personally camped in Kabul and supervised the operations to ensure that the last vestiges of resistance were eliminated. The manner in which the Taliban captured all the border posts and provinces in the periphery before closing in on Kabul shows that they were not only receiving a high level of military advice, but also some sort of active military support from some of its external sympathisers. The way in which the US military vacated some of its strategically important military bases, without informing the Afghan National Security Forces, and thereby facilitated their capture by the Taliban along with a large quantity of military hardware, raises serious questions about the American intent. These developments have created a wave of fear in the region. The images of desperate Afghan citizens running to board aircraft taxiing on the runway and their fall from the air will continue to haunt the conscience of the global community for a long time.

Like most of the international community, India, which had a strategic partnership agreement with Afghanistan, did not expect the government and the Afghan National Army to crumble so easily. More significantly, there was a feeling of betrayal in New Delhi, as it appeared that the US had cut a deal with the dreaded Taliban without taking Indian interests into account. There was also a considerable sense of loss as India had invested large sums in Afghanistan and had won the admiration and respect of the Afghan population cutting across, social, ethnic, and sectarian divisions. Indian soft power was clearly visible to any casual visitor to Afghanistan, where India was a popular destination for most Afghans for their education, medical treatment, as well as holidays. From heads of government to ordinary Afghans, all travelled to India and enjoyed Indian films and soap operas. India also helped in the establishment of infrastructure and from the parliament building, hospitals, and dams to educational institutions, roads and electric grids, Indian footprints were everywhere. Unfortunately, despite this overwhelming influence, it had no capacity to resist the brutal hard power of the Taliban.

Consequently, there was a deep sense of shock and awe, so much so that many 'analysts' as well as certain sections of the government in India, started speculating about reaching out to the Taliban. Some even began hallucinating that the Taliban had transformed into a benign moderate entity with a modern outlook with which India and the global community could do business. Consequently, Indian statements in the immediate aftermath of the catastrophe in Kabul were quite muted, as New Delhi was logically concerned about the presence of a large number of its citizens in Afghanistan and needed to ensure their repatriation. However, all hopes about a transformed Taliban evaporated with the passage of time as they started showing their true colours and returned to their primordial, beastly attitude. Not only that, they also reneged on most of the promises that their representatives had made while negotiating with the US representatives at Doha.

Even more dismal was the reaction of the international community, especially the big powers. The US role in the tragedy has always been under a cloud. Even the rest of the Western world shirked away from any moral responsibility for the fall of Kabul. At the other end of the geo-political spectrum, Russia and Iran, which had earlier opposed the Taliban from 1996 to 2001, were already hobnobbing with the Taliban to ensure the American withdraw from the region and continue to deal with them, even after they had moved in to Kabul. Beijing realised that the Taliban were the creation of Pakistan's ISI and visualised a huge window of opportunity for itself. It sought to enhance its influence in the region, both in order to build transport highways through Afghanistan, as well as to extract its huge mineral resources. Even the Central Asian Republics, which should have been concerned about the future of their ethnic compatriots in Afghanistan and worried about the presence of the Taliban and its radical ideology next door, were not on the same page. With the sole exception of Tajikistan, the other Central Asian Republics maintained an ambivalent attitude about the developments in Kabul. More significantly, Uzbekistan and Turkmenistan, the Turkic-speaking Central Asian neighbours of Afghanistan—have maintained the status quo and have even kept their borders open. They not only maintained communications with the Taliban, but are also actively trading with the Emirate of Afghanistan. Their actions are probably driven by the growing Turkish influence. Turkey under Erdogan probably wants to recreate the Ottoman Empire and now perceives an enhanced role for itself in the Islamic world. These are classic cases of how long term interests of the countries have often been sacrificed at the altar of perceived short term economic or geo-political gains.

With the passage of time, Afghanistan has become a chessboard, where numerous external powers are trying to influence events. Pakistan perceives that it has finally achieved the elusive strategic depth with respect to India that it has been seeking for decades. The US, having negotiated a pull-out from its longest war, still wants to retain its influence, without in any way committing the physical presence of its troops. The US is probably confident that the regime in Kabul will prevent the al-Qaeda or any other global *jihadi* outfit from targeting the US again. Its withdrawal from Afghanistan has severely dented its global standing, which is now perceived as an unreliable ally. Russia, which in the 1980s as part of the former Soviet Union had faced its Waterloo in Afghanistan, has managed to get back at the United States. It also believes that the Taliban can be used to control the threat from the Islamic State. It is, however, concerned about Taliban ideology percolating across the borders into the former Soviet Republics in Central Asia, as well as in the restive regions of the Russian Federation like Chechnya and Dagestan. The Central Asian Republics are themselves looking at the issue differently. Although, they are all concerned about radical Islamist ideology percolating into their territories and the Taliban's treatment of its Tajik, Uzbek and Turkoman minorities, most of them, with the notable exception of Tajikistan, see economic opportunities under the new regime. China perceives that the new regime will help Afghanistan become an integral part of its Belt and Road Initiative (BRI) and promote connectivity from China to West Asia through Afghanistan and Central Asia. It also eyes Afghanistan's resources and vast population, but is concerned about the impact of radical Islamist ideology affecting its own restive Uighur population in Xinjiang Uyghur Autonomous Region.

Various countries in the Islamic world are also looking to bring Afghanistan under their own sphere of influence. The neo-Ottoman regime in Turkey wants to use its influence in Central Asia, and its good relations with Pakistan and Qatar to bring Afghanistan under its sphere of influence so as to occupy the leadership position within the Islamic world. Saudi Arabia, which apart from the United Arab Emirates (UAE) and Pakistan, was the only regime to have recognized the previous Taliban government, is concerned about Turkey's attempts to regain leadership of the Islamic world and is concerned with the new developments. The UAE, by giving asylum to Ashraf Ghani, sees a role for itself in Afghanistan's future. Qatar, which housed the Taliban office until their arrival in Kabul and played a major role in facilitating negotiations between the USA and the Taliban, also sees an enhanced stature for itself. It has been one of the first countries to provide humanitarian aid to Afghanistan after Taliban captured power. Iran, on the other hand, had collaborated with the Taliban to see the back of the United States, but realizes that the obscurantist radical ideology of the Taliban will inevitably pit it against Shia Islam and Iran. It is therefore concerned about the Shia minority in Afghanistan and Taliban actions have done nothing to reassure it on this count. It is also concerned with the growing influence of Pakistan, Turkey and Saudi Arabia in Afghanistan.

Similarly, India also strives to regain its lost influence in Afghanistan, but does not know whether to engage with the Taliban or build a resistance to it. It is justifiably concerned about the women, children and minorities, both ethnic as well as sectarian, in a Talibanised Afghanistan. All the external powers today are trying to shape Afghanistan to further their geopolitical interests, not realizing the fact that an ideologically rigid outfit like the Taliban is unlikely to be malleable enough to follow externally-sponsored agendas and would eventually pursue its own path based on its own radical ideology. This book deals with the 'New Great Game' being played in Afghanistan by external powers. Unlike the previous 'Great Game', where only two powers were jostling for space, there are now numerous actors in this new great game. The irony is that this new Great Game is being played at a time when the Afghan population is facing a grave humanitarian crisis. Taliban rule has seen the vanishing of food grains, medicines and other essential commodities from Afghanistan. The international community is still trying to figure out how to help the Afghan population without in any manner legitimising or strengthening the Taliban.

This book is a potpourri of chapters written by experts from different nationalities on different aspects of Afghanistan. Some have described their personal experiences, whilst others have talked about the recent historical developments in Afghanistan, which had a bearing on contemporary issues. This book also looks at the emergence of Afghanistan as a modern state as well as the evolution of its ethnic and religious identities. It attempts to look at the impact of the recent developments in Afghanistan on the world at large, especially as far as the pre-eminence of America in global affairs is concerned. It obviously brings out Pakistan's linkages with the Taliban, its likely impact on terrorism and its linkages with terror-financing, radicalisation, and narco-terrorism. It analyses the long-term impact of the Taliban's presence in Afghanistan on the region in general and India in particular, especially the Union Territory of Jammu and Kashmir. It also looks at the whole process of bringing the Taliban back to power and how it has created a big humanitarian crisis and has endangered peace.

The chapter by Col Harjeet Singh deals with "Contemporary History of Afghanistan" and apprises the reader about the history of modern Afghanistan, spanning three centuries. The genesis of many problems of Afghanistan lies in the realms of history and it is essential to understand the historical evolution of Afghanistan to understand the factors that complicate the current scenario. The author, who is a defence and strategic analyst, has done it precisely by summarising the mammoth civilizational history and revisiting all the crucial moments that have had a significant bearing on present-day Afghanistan. He begins his exploration from the Durrani Empire of 1732 CE and moves on to cover the British interests, various rulers during the monarchy, the coups and the subsequent communist era with the Soviet involvement and the American-sponsored *jihad*. He has traced the *mujahideen* resistance and the emergence of the Taliban, post-Taliban governments and the Doha talks leading right up to the American withdrawal.

Dr. Omar Sharifi, an Afghan national, an Assistant Professor in the American University of Afghanistan and former Kabul-based Director of the American Institute of Afghanistan Studies, has authored the chapter "Imagining the Historical Nation: The Dialogical Project of Nation-Making, Religious and Ethnic identity in Afghanistan". The chapter highlights the fact that historical events alone do not mark the evolution of a nation. A nation is a product of its people, society, and the multiple identities that they subscribe to. The chapter traces the history of Afghanistan through the religious and ethnic identities that define the people and the nation of Afghanistan. He makes a case for distinguishing traditional or historical Islam as was practised by Afghan society from the *jihadist* political Islam propagated by the Talibani emirate. Arguing against the portrayal of the Taliban and *jihadist* groups as the only solution to ensure stability, he is in favour of seeking a solution through the shared understanding of cultural and religious traditions practised in Afghanistan.

The events in Afghanistan, apart from impacting its citizens, have also impacted the global standing of the United States of America. Professor Harsh V. Pant, Head of the Strategic Studies Programme at the Observer Research Foundation and Saaransh Mishra, his Research Associate, in their chapter "America's World after Afghanistan Withdrawal" analyse the contemporary developments in Afghanistan through the American lens. The authors explore how American domestic politics evolved due to its involvement in Afghanistan through the tenure of different American presidents. After analysing the domestic opinion, they explore the multiple reasons that led to the American withdrawal from Afghanistan. They also reflect on the effect on global geopolitics due to the hegemonic contestations with China and Russia and its likely implications for India.

The contest between the British Empire and the Russian Empire for control over Central Asia, including Afghanistan, was termed as the 'Great Game'. Col Ajay Singh, a defence analyst with interests in military history and geopolitics, in his chapter "Afghanistan and the Changing Geopolitical Order" explores the new facets of power contestations over Afghanistan. He explores the various stakeholders that are affected by the fall of Kabul and the Taliban takeover of Afghanistan. He discusses how the interests of China, Iran, the UAE, and Russia evolve, given the new dynamics after the American withdrawal. He also reflects on the impact of this changing geopolitical dynamics on India's interests.

The next chapter delves on "America, Pakistan and the Afghan Frankenstein—India must learn from past follies to draw own strategy". The author, P. Stobdan, is a renowned Indian academic from Ladakh, who has been India's Ambassador to a Central Asian Republic. He has unlatched the complex Afghanistan, Pakistan, and American trap. He argues that the current forces at power in Afghanistan are the creation of Pakistan and that America has repeatedly walked into Pakistan's artifice. He makes a case for the current American agenda vis-à-vis its national interests and suggests that India must devise a strategy on Afghanistan, independent of America; one that protects India's national interests and vision.

Former Director General Military Operations of the Indian Army, Lt Gen Vinod Bhatia, in his chapter, "Afghanistan: Pakistan Rides the Taliban Tiger" reflects on Pakistan's involvement in Afghanistan since the inception of the Taliban. He brings to light how Pakistan has manoeuvred the Taliban in Afghanistan and has used it to serve its own interests. Considering the state of politics and security within Pakistan, he explores the various nuances within Pakistan that will be influenced by the unravelling in Afghanistan. He also discusses the fallout of the Taliban's capture of Kabul and implications it may have on Pakistan's adversaries.

Taliban rule in Afghanistan in the past had resulted in the biggest terror attack in modern history. Consequently, it, as an organisation and its leaders, have been designated as global terrorists. However, with the fall of Kabul and capture of power in Afghanistan, the Taliban have been making repetitive claims of peace in the region and have been asserting that Afghan soil will not be allowed to be used for launching terror attacks against other states. Soumya Chaturvedi, a Senior Research Fellow at India Foundation, in her chapter, "Taliban and Terrorism: The Complex Security Dynamics", argues that the ideological underpinning and composition of the Taliban makes it inseparable from terrorism. She explores the complex security dynamics of the Taliban with terrorism, its implications for Afghanistan, and the neighbourhood and suggests international policy interventions that are necessary to establish and maintain regional peace and stability.

Dr. Sanchita Bhattacharya, a Research Fellow in the New Delhi-based Institute for Conflict Management, in her chapter, "Pakistan's Terror Machine and the Re-emergence of the Taliban", explores the relationship between Pakistan, the Taliban, and terrorism. In a detailed analysis, she has traced the terrorism-induced origins of the Taliban and the reasons that are responsible for Pakistan's constructive relationship with it over the years. She has also analysed religion, geography, funding, and logistical support that harnessed the Taliban-Pakistan relationship. The support provided by Pakistan's Intelligence Agency—the ISI—and Pakistan-based terrorist groups supporting the Taliban is explored in detail to establish the intrinsic link between the terrorism sponsored from Pakistan and the Taliban.

There have been several propositions that the terrorism-induced security scenario of Afghanistan resembles the situation of Jammu and Kashmir (J&K) in India, while the intensity of conflict may differ by great proportions. The Chancellor of the Central University of Kashmir and a former Corps Commander, Lt Gen Syed Ata Hasnain, in his chapter, "Effects of the Events in Afghanistan on the Situation in Jammu & Kashmir", argues that while unravelling of events in Afghanistan definitely has an effect on terrorism in J&K, its extent is quite limited. He has described the spectre of terrorism in J&K in the 1990s, which was the time-frame that coincided with the first Talibani Emirate in Afghanistan. He goes on to shed light on how the changed Indian approach to J&K will limit Pakistan's aspirations for the region and the influence that the second Talibani Emirate may have on it.

Devyani Rao, a journalist with varied experiences, who also worked in Kabul, explores the contemporary history of Afghan society in a highly personalised account in her chapter, "Thriving in the Graveyard of Empires". She goes on to describe as to how the society has evolved over the years. She presents a kaleidoscopic view of Afghanistan based on her personal interactions and experiences while visiting the country on journalistic assignments. She reflects on her own observations on how the complex violent reality of Afghanistan has shaped the perceptions of women, teenagers, and children. In this personal account, she shares a few instances and interactions with the local Afghani population and how they moulded her perception about Afghan society.

With the passage of time, Afghanistan's humanitarian crisis under an inexperienced regime has been worsening. Sanghamitra Sarker, an Associate Professor in the Department of Political Science at Surendranath College for Women, Kolkata, in her chapter, "Afghanistan: Confronting the Humanitarian Catastrophe", argues that while the nature of the Talibani government and its obscurantist ideology is restricting international aid and assistance, the hapless people of Afghanistan should not be the collateral victims of the actions of a government, they never chose. She emphasises that for the sake of the dignity of Afghan life, the international community should come forth not just in providing humanitarian aid but also ensuring that it reaches the targeted audience.

The humanitarian crisis of Afghanistan predates the conception of the Taliban. However, the situation has further deteriorated owing to the nature of politics unfolding in Afghanistan after the Taliban takeover. M. Ashraf Haidari, a seasoned Afghan diplomat and Afghanistan's Ambassador to Sri Lanka, in his chapter, "Pakistani Aggression Perpetuates Humanitarian Crisis in Afghanistan", reflects on the complexity of the causes that have contributed to the humanitarian crisis in Afghanistan for which he revisits the humanitarian situation in the pre-war era as well as during the periods of conflict in Afghanistan. He argues that only a sound understanding of the root causes of the crisis can lead to the emergence of a durable solution to Afghanistan's externally imposed humanitarian crisis.

Nadeem Shah, a Pakistani national and a journalist from Seraiki region, in his chapter "Endangered Peace", has proposed possible eventualities after the Taliban's capture of power in Afghanistan. He discusses the key challenges that the Taliban factions face and then details the possible scenarios that could play out owing to these challenges. He argues that the socio-political reality of Afghanistan has been exploited for years and the situation will further deteriorate due to the nature of politics practised by the Taliban.

The Taliban's perceived victory over the 'hegemon' or 'superpower' has already enthused various radical Islamist outfits across the world. It has also fulfilled an extremely significant theological prerquisite (control over a territory) of *jihad*. Consequently, in the days to come, recruitments to various jihadi outfits are quite likely to increase, both in India and its neighbourhood as well as in other parts of the world. The al-Qaeda has already given a clarion call for *jihad* in Kashmir after celebrating the Taliban's triumph in Afghanistan and the Taliban have never explicitly disassociated themselves from such calls of the al-Qaeda. Besides providing theological legitimacy and ideological support, the Taliban regime also has a history of providing safe haven to terror outfits from far and wide. Although, it has tried to reassure the global community that they will not be allowed to launch attacks from its territory, it has never ever publicly criticised them or expelled their members.

Currently, the Taliban is busy consolidating power and its position in Afghanistan. The opposition to its rule or the so-called "Panjshir Resistance" has been dealt a crushing blow, although the remnants are putting up a token fight under the likes of Amrullah Saleh, the Vice President of Afghanistan, who has assumed the mantle of Acting President after Ashraf Ghani deserted his countrymen. It needs to be appreciated that if this resistance is completely wiped out, the foot soldiers of the Taliban who have known no other profession will move out of Afghanistan to other parts of world, including India. Many argue that the new Taliban is moderate and accommodative. However, even if the Taliban leadership, in the wake of gaining international recognition, is compelled to step away from their theological beliefs, their radicalised foot soldiers may gravitate towards the Islamic State,

Taliban's arch nemesis. This will further complicate the security complex of the region, making it more volatile.

After reading this book, readers may like to form their opinions about the way this New Great Game will unfold. They may empathise with the hapless citizens of Afghanistan, who have been left to fend for themselves in front of a gang of terrorists. There may be differing solutions on how the global community in general, and India in particular, must engage with the Taliban. However, one thing is quite clear; that the citizens of Afghanistan face a long winter under the rule of this medieval outfit. While opinions may differ on short-term tactics to ameliorate the sufferings of Afghans and to enhance peace in the region, in the longer term, the only solution lies in either weaning the Taliban away from its obscurantist ideology, or strengthening the National Resistance Front to free Afghanistan from the Taliban.

2

Contemporary History of Afghanistan

Harjeet Singh

Afghanistan is often called the 'crossroads of Central Asia' and 'the graveyard of empires.' Its location has made it an ideal trade and invasion route for centuries. As a result, its history has been turbulent. Conquerors from the West passed through it to reach the Indian subcontinent and Indian empires extended their territories from the East through the same routes. The armies of Darius, Alexander the Great, Kanishka, Genghis Khan, the Shahi rulers of India, Muslim rulers, the British, the Russians, the USA and many others have left their footprints in the country.

Modern Afghanistan traces its roots to 1747 when Ahmad Shah Durrani founded an empire and a monarchy that lasted until 1973. During the 19th century, Afghanistan was the buffer between the British and Russian empires in their "Great Game." Successive Pakhtoon kings ruled until 1973, when a coup brought about a brief five-year period during which Afghanistan was officially a republic. It marked the beginning of the events occurring today.

The Durrani Empire

In 1732, Nadir Beg, who later became Nadir Shah of Persia, invaded Herat and then captured Kandahar and Kabul a few years later. By 1739, his empire extended into India, when he occupied Delhi and his troops pillaged Mughal palaces. His war trophies included the Koh-i-Noor diamond and the Peacock Throne. Nadir Shah was assassinated in 1747, triggering the collapse of his Safavid Empire.

Ahmad Khan, the commander of Nadir Shah's bodyguards, then emerged as the ruler. He proclaimed himself as Ahmad Shah Durrani and extended his control over a vast area from the Arabian Sea in the south to the Amu Darya in the north, and from Delhi and Kashmir in the east to easternmost Iran in the west. He is known as the founder of the Afghan nation and united the Pakhtoon tribes and by 1760 built an empire which fragmented after his death in 1772. He was from the Pakhtoon tribal confederation and the first in a long line of Afghan rulers from this tribal federation that lasted until the Marxist coup d'état in 1978. The ability of one tribal group to dominate other tribal groups enabled the federation to exist. The Durrani dynasty of indigenous Pakhtoons continued into the 19th century, by which time the British were looking to expand their territory beyond what they had acquired through the East India Company.

The Anglo-Afghan Wars

By the 19th century, the British Empire was expanding out of India toward the north and west looking to offset what they saw as the expansion of Russia into Central Asia. Russia was also concerned with British expansion into areas that they saw as their sphere of influence. The British would be involved in three Anglo-Afghan wars, the first two being extremely ferocious, with the Pakhtoons earning a reputation as among the bravest, and certainly the cruellest fighters.

The First Anglo-Afghan War

The First Anglo-Afghan War (1839–1842) was aimed to establish a pro-British government in Afghanistan through Shah Shuja, who ruled Afghanistan from 1803 until 1809, and had lost the throne during an internal tribal power struggle. His deposition from power came shortly after signing a treaty of friendship with the British, to prevent the Russians from encroaching on India. The British reinstalled Shah Shuja in power, but were soon under heavy attack from the Afghans. The war began with a massive British invasion, the toppling of ruler Dost Mohammad, and the occupation of Kabul and other cities. After the British political agent was assassinated, the remnants of the first British expeditionary force (16,000 soldiers, dependents, and camp followers) tried to retreat to the British fort at Jalalabad. They were all killed or dispersed, except for a lone regimental surgeon who returned home to tell the tale. The British consider the defeat in the First Anglo-Afghan War as one of the biggest in their history. The subsequent British punitive expedition killed thousands of Afghans and destroyed three cities, including Kabul. The British then withdrew. Dost Mohammad again became the ruler and spent the remainder of his reign consolidating power, usually with a British subsidy.

The Second Anglo-Afghan War

In 1879, the British initiated the Second Anglo-Afghan War in order to halt Russian encroachment in Afghanistan. To end the war, Yaqub Khan ceded control of Afghan foreign policy to the British. However, the hostility towards the British quickly ended the occupation. Yaqub Khan abdicated in 1880, ceding power to Abdur Rahman Khan who established a centralised government by persuading the tribes and ethnic groups to unite under his rule. At the conclusion of the second Anglo-Afghan War, Britain and Russia agreed to the establishment of borders that would become the present-day Afghanistan, and Britain retained effective control over Kabul's foreign policy. The latter served as a catalyst that would spark the third Anglo-Afghan war.

Abdur Rahman Khan is considered to be the founder of modern Afghanistan. In 1887, the Amu Darya River was established as the border between Afghanistan and Tsarist Russia. British India negotiated its border with Afghanistan six years later. Called the Durand Line, it was drawn by the British envoy, Sir Henry Mortimer Durand, to separate Afghanistan from India. It also divided the

Pakhtoons, leaving a third of them in Afghanistan and two-thirds in western India, which later became modern Pakistan. The results of the first two wars with Britain were long-standing Afghan-British tensions, an increase in Afghanistan's xenophobia, and an unresolved issue over the homeland of the Pakhtoons, which was split between two countries. The Durand Line is the current Pakistan-Afghanistan border, a porous boundary that divides Pakhtoon tribal areas along most of its length.

Later, Abdur Rahman Khan's son, Habibullah, became the ruler, continuing his father's project of modernising Afghanistan. He embraced Western influence in government and society. But he was murdered in Kabul in 1919 by anti-British groups.

The Third Anglo-Afghan War

Paradoxically, the Afghan leaders fought against British encroachment, but then after besting or severely vexing the British to establish that independence, often ended up taking subsidies from them. The British in return gained control over Afghan foreign policy. The subsidies were generally used to strengthen the Afghan army and further the internal power of the central government in Kabul. This rather stable situation continued until 1919, when the third Anglo-Afghan war won them the total independence. Interestingly, Afghan rulers were the strongest within their nation when they were supported by foreign subsidies. Low or no subsidies meant taxing the locals and, at times, harsh conscription. These measures were never popular. The people were eager to salute the national rulers but not willing to allow them to interfere with the local autonomy.

The Third Anglo-Afghan War followed World War I and established full independence. It began with the mysterious death of the old emir, Habibullah, who did not want another war with Britain because it had paid him a healthy subsidy. He had ruled peacefully for nearly two decades and kept Afghanistan neutral during the First World War. The new emir, Amanullah—the third son who seized power from those with stronger dynastic claims—was allegedly involved in his father's death as he wanted a showdown with the

British. The Third Anglo-Afghan War involved very few battles as the war-weary British gave in to Afghan demands for full independence. The war ended British subsidies—a key revenue source for Afghan leaders—and Britain's encroachment on Afghan sovereignty.

The Treaty of Rawalpindi, signed on 19 August 1919, granted Afghanistan full control of its foreign affairs and is celebrated as Afghan Independence Day. In 1921, the Afghan government signed a treaty of friendship with the newly-established Soviet Union (USSR), which became the first country to diplomatically recognise Afghanistan. The Soviet-Afghan relationship remained undisturbed until the Soviet invasion nearly 60 years later.

The Monarchy

From 1919 to 1933, there was an abdication and a series of assassinations caused by attempts at reform and modernisation, which alienated some conservative members of the clergy. The country remained an absolute monarchy until 1922, when a state assembly and legislature were established and ministers appointed to the cabinet. Amanullah's use of scarce resources for economic development and his push for Western-style social reforms rendered him vulnerable to revolt. His government disintegrated in January 1929 after a decade in power, when a rebel army led by Habibullah Kalakani, an ethnic Tajik, arrived at the gates of Kabul. Afghanistan was ruled by him for the next nine months, the only period between the mid-18th century and the fall of the monarchy in 1978 that Afghanistan had a non-Pakhtoon leader. Habibullah's tenacious but tenuous hold on power ended when Nadir Shah, a Pakhtoon leader from the Peshawar region, took control of Kabul. Nadir Shah introduced further changes in the political structure and, in 1931, crafted a new constitution. Under his leadership, the government reunified Afghanistan before opponents assassinated him in 1933.

Zahir Shah

In 1933, Amanullah's nephew, 19-year-old Mohammad Zahir Shah, the last king of Afghanistan, began a 40-year reign, by far the longest in Afghanistan's modern history. Zahir Shah introduced a democratic constitution that allowed the formation of political parties. During Zahir Shah's reign, the "Pakhtoon Question" became the centre of international focus. After India was granted independence and the state of Pakistan was created, tensions immediately flared. The Durand Line was always an issue, and from time to time the status of "Pakhtoonistan" was formally placed on the table by Afghan nationalists who demanded a plebiscite. Afghanistan even cast the only vote against Pakistan being admitted to the United Nations (UN) in 1947.

Zahir Shah's government insisted that because Pakistan was a new state and not a successor to colonial India, all border agreements drawn by the British (including the Durand Line) were nullified. Kabul wanted self-determination for the Pakhtoon tribal territories that spanned the existing border. Border skirmishes, supported by both Kabul and Islamabad, proliferated. Because Pakistan aligned with the United States (US), Afghanistan sought military training assistance from the Soviet Union. Nonetheless, Afghanistan maintained an official policy of non-alignment during the early decades of the Cold War.

The political climate became even more liberal during Zahir Shah's reign. From 1946 to 1952, the liberal-leaning parliament under Prime Minister Sardar Shah Mahmud Khan sanctioned greater political pluralism. As a result, in 1953, religious leaders and conservatives backed the successful efforts of Lieutenant General Mohammed Daoud Khan, Zahir Shah's cousin, to become the Prime Minister. In a surprising move, after becoming the Prime Minister, Daoud approached the Soviet Union for support. The Soviets, looking to extend their influence towards the southeast, became a major trading partner in the ensuing years. Social and educational changes were introduced, but the political climate remained rigid.

Further tensions developed along the Pakistani border in subsequent years, leading to Daoud's resignation in 1963. As a result, Zahir Shah was, for the first time, the true holder of power in

Afghanistan. The position of prime minister changed hands repeatedly over the next 10 years, reflecting an increasingly unstable political environment.

In 1964, a new constitution was drafted. Among other things, it specified free elections, female emancipation, and universal suffrage. It also prohibited members of the royal family from being appointed to ministerial positions—perhaps an attempt by Zahir Shah to keep his uncles and cousins from trying to regain power. Competitive multi-party elections were held and journalists were given a wide latitude to write about political developments. But the reforms put Zahir Shah at odds with religious leaders and conservatives. Towards the end of his reign, King Zahir Shah was accused of corruption and combined with poor economic conditions, a military coup led to his ouster in the summer of 1973.

The Afghan Republic

In 1973, Daoud Khan seized an opportunity to stage a bloodless coup and regain power from his cousin, King Zahir Shah. He dissolved the Afghanistan monarchy, declared Afghanistan a republic, and named himself President. However, Afghanistan's government leadership remained dynastic, with one cousin having simply replaced another. Daoud's once-close ties to the Soviets increasingly diminished during his five years in power. In 1977, Daoud's visit to Moscow ended abruptly after he told Soviet leader Leonid Brezhnev: *"...we will never allow you to dictate to us how to run our country and whom to employ in Afghanistan.... Afghanistan shall remain poor, if necessary, but free in its acts and decisions."*

Daoud's life and Afghanistan's independence did not last long after that. Afghan Communists, who had begun to emerge on the political stage 10 years earlier, were opposed to Daoud and his policies. In 1978, Daoud was assassinated and the People's Democratic Party of Afghanistan (PDPA) took control of the country, with the support of the Soviet Union. A relatively small band of leftist army officers, with some logistical help from Soviet advisors, attacked the palace, killing Daoud and his family. The urban coup d'état, called the *Saur*

(April) Revolution, marked the birth of the Democratic Republic of Afghanistan. However, the government was fractured from within and was greatly resisted by a large number of Afghans. It also became apparent that the PDPA would be unable to survive without increased assistance from the Soviet Union.

The Communist Era

The PDPA was a party with two very different factions. The *Khalq* (Masses) faction, with great strength in the security services, was led by Nur Mohammad Taraki and Hafizullah Amin. A more moderate and broad-based group, the *Parcham* (Banner) faction, was led by Babrak Karmal. The PDPA named Soviet-supported Nur Mohammed Taraki as President of the Revolutionary Council and Prime Minister of the new Democratic Republic of Afghanistan. From the beginning, infighting and bitter rivalries within the PDPA, which was ideologically split between its factions, created a tense internal political situation. In the Afghan countryside, the government faced increasing protests and rebellions against the PDPA's attempts to implement its secular and Marxist policies. In February 1979, US-Afghan relations nose-dived when radicals in Kabul kidnapped US Ambassador Adolph Dubs. Against American advice, a sloppy, Afghan-led, Soviet-advised rescue attempt ended up in the killing of the kidnappers and the Ambassador. US aid programmes ended and the US diplomatic profile was reduced in the country.

During the fall of 1979, Nur Mohammad Taraki was killed in a coup led by Hafizullah Amin, his rival within the *Khalq* faction. The leaders of the *Khalq* faction, Nur Mohammad Taraki and Hafizullah Amin were radical ideologues with a penchant for rapid modernisation. Their programme—formed over Soviet objections—seemed almost designed to bring about an insurrection. Its main features were land reform, usury reform, and equal rights for women. All of these were unpopular. As political unrest increased and Moscow began to believe that Hafizullah Amin was making initial moves to abandon his socialist ties; the Soviets invaded Afghanistan in December 1979.

Land reform was particularly destabilising. It was brutally applied and was most unpopular among peasants, who saw it as immoral and inconsistent with Islam. On top of all this, the PDPA changed the national flag's colour from Islamic green to socialist red. Caught somewhat by surprise, Moscow was publicly enthusiastic about the prospects for the new regime but concerned that the PDPA was alienating the people. They urged the PDPA to go slow. Soviet theorists were privately scornful of a socialist revolution in what they viewed as a feudal state.

The Soviet invasion in late December 1979 was a well-executed operation. Previously infiltrated commandos moved into the palace and killed Hafizullah Amin and his entourage. Paratroopers seized bases in and around the capital. The Soviet-supported PDPA *Parcham* leader Babrak Karmal became the head of Afghanistan's government. Two motorized rifle divisions of reservists from the Central Asia Republics brought the number of Soviet troops to 50,000 by the first week of January 1980. Over time, the reservists would be withdrawn and the Soviet force increased to 120,000.

Babrak Karmal was not successful in unifying the government. Afghan army forces that did not desert continued to perform poorly, just as the resistance—energized by the invasion moved into high gear. Soviet forces were not trained for counter insurgency and, lacking experience in mountain warfare, did not perform well in the Afghan environment. Later, the Soviets would move in large-scale formations to clear areas of strong *mujahideen* ('holy warriors') presence.[1] They rarely held areas in the country side and never tried to govern them systematically. They did not see their mission as protecting the population, nor did they exercise great care regarding civilian casualties and collateral damage. Afghan refugees increased, along with international outrage.

Pakistan, Saudi Arabia, and the USA, usually working through Pakistani intelligence, came to the aid of the *mujahideen*, who had sanctuaries in Pakistan. During the second Reagan Administration, the *mujahideen* were provided with shoulder-fired Stinger anti-aircraft missiles, which took a high toll of Soviet aircraft. At its height, US aid to the *mujahideen*, nearly all distributed by Pakistan's Inter-Services Intelligence (ISI) directorate, rose to $400 million per year.

Moscow grossly underestimated the domestic economic and political costs of the invasion and occupation of Afghanistan. The Babrak Karmal government never controlled much beyond Kabul, forcing the Soviets to shoulder the costs for security and administration. Moscow also met with strong opposition to the occupation from the West and the Islamic world. As a result of a common enemy, seven different groups in Afghanistan formed a loose alliance to fight the PDPA and Soviet forces. By 1987, the Afghan *mujahideen* had fought the Soviet forces to a stalemate. Moreover, the USSR had been unable to install a government in Kabul that could elicit strong support from the Afghan people. Those factors, coupled with Pakistani support for the US interests and the Afghan resistance, ultimately brought the Soviets to the negotiating table in Geneva to sign the Geneva Accords.[2] In accordance with the accord, the last Soviet soldier withdrew from Afghanistan on 15 February 1989. The Soviet exodus removed the common enemy (the country's key centripetal or unifying force), thus returning Afghanistan to its old tribal and factional rivalries. As a result, the fighting did not end with the Soviet Union's withdrawal in 1989.

The *Mujahideen* Resistance

The Islamic movement grew in strength and number during the Soviet occupation. The US and other governments, hoping to weaken Soviet influence, supported the movement's *mujahideen* rebel fighters. From Pakistan, the *mujahideen* recruited large numbers of young men from the refugee camps and acquired better weapons.

While many expected the departure of the Soviet army in February 1989, to mark the end of the war, it did not. Pakistan and western aid, including weaponry continued to flow to the *mujahideen*, despite the accord at Geneva. At the same time, the Soviet government continued to provide aid and assistance to the regime of Afghan President Mohammad Najibullah, who had been picked by Moscow to replace Babrak Karmal in 1986. Najibullah's government survived for two more years, largely because he leveraged Soviet-supplied money, arms, and other assistance to *mujahideen* militias in return for their loyalty to the government or at least their agreement to a cease-fire. With a 65,000-man army, an air force of nearly 200 planes and helicopters, and many well-paid militia units, Afghan government forces were able to hold off the *mujahideen*. This became clear in May 1989 when a number of *mujahideen* groups attacked, but failed to seize the city of Jalalabad in eastern Afghanistan. The army was simply a better and more cohesive force than the fractious insurgents. The disparate *mujahideen* groups—dubbed the Peshawar Seven—failed to cooperate and often fought viciously among themselves. Mohammad Najibullah was well supported by the Soviet Union and fought effectively for three years.

In March 1992, lacking foreign supporters after the demise of the Soviet Union, Najibullah stopped fighting, but was unable to leave the country and took refuge in the UN Compound where he remained until seized by the Taliban in September 1996. The Taliban took Najibullah and his brother, tortured and killed them, dragged their bodies behind vehicles, and then hung the pair on a lamp post near the Presidential Palace.

Further internal struggle, fighting, and a lawless state emerged in the aftermath of Mohammad Najibullah's fall in April 1992. Warlords and militia leaders, who profited from the sale of illegal drugs, took over the countryside and parts of the larger cities. Kabul, in particular, suffered greatly as it became a battlefield in a lengthy power struggle between Afghan President Burhanuddin Rabbani and rival political/militia leader Gulbuddin Hekmatyar and his allies for control of the central government. Afghanistan descended into a civil war that further ravaged the economy. In 1992, with UN help, a provisional government was formed to rule the country. It failed because of infighting amongst the *mujahideen*. The conflict was particularly bitter between the eastern Pakhtoon, *Hezb-i-Islami* followers of Gulbuddin Hekmatyar who received operational, financial and military support from Pakistan, and the Tajik fighters of Ahmed Shah Massoud's *Jamiat-i-Islami*, who came to control Kabul. Burhanuddin Rabbani, a Tajik and the political head of the *Jamiat-i-Islami* group, was ultimately named president; Gulbuddin Hekmatyar was designated prime minister of the interim government and Ahmed Shah Massoud was selected as the defence minister. Sadly, the government never met at the conference table, only on the urban battlefield. Despite several temporary alliances, struggles among the armed groups continued.

The civil war featured fierce fighting over Kabul—occupied by Massoud but desired by Hekmatyar, his arch-rival—and in some other major cities, which to that point had escaped most active combat. From April 1992 to April 1993, much of Kabul was destroyed and 30,000 inhabitants were killed, with another 100,000 wounded. Other cities were often more peaceful under the control of local warlords such as Ismail Khan in Herat and Abdul Rashid Dostum in Mazar-i-Sharif. In many other places, however, law and order disintegrated. Local or regional warlords were dominant and men with guns made the rules. In Kandahar and other locations, rape, armed robbery, kidnapping young boys, and other crimes of violence were all too common.

Emergence of the Taliban

Fearing the instability in Afghanistan, and disenchanted with the *mujahideen* groups it had assisted since 1980, the Pakistan government began to slowly withdraw its support from them in 1994 in favour of Afghan and Pakistani *madrassa*-Islamic schools—graduates called the Taliban, a group focused on *Sharia*-based law and order. The leaders of these students were radical Islamists, many of whom were self-educated holy men. While zealous and often devout, there were no great Koranic scholars or religious thinkers among them, nor were there many engineers, physicians, or experienced government bureaucrats. Taliban leaders often supplanted Pakhtoon tribal leaders. They were led by Mullah Mohammad Omar Akhund, a country cleric from Kandahar and a former anti-Soviet resistance commander who had lost an eye in battle. His deputies included many wounded veterans of the war with the Soviet Union.

The Taliban's basic ideology enforced a purist way of life, based on their fundamentalist interpretation of Islam. They received support from like-minded Islamist groups in the Middle East and Pakistan. After a few small-scale local successes in the Kandahar region, a Taliban field force with modern weaponry emerged from Pakistan, first operating around Kandahar and then nationwide. They drew on recruits from extremist *madrassas* in Pakistan, and those located from Ghazni to Kandahar in southern Afghanistan. In Spin Boldak, the Taliban seized some 18,000 Kalashnikov rifles, dozens of artillery pieces, large quantities of ammunition, and many vehicles that belonged to Pakistan's ISI and were being guarded by fighters from the Hezb-i-Islami group.

With Pakistani advice and armaments, the unified Taliban attacked the contending *mujahideen* groups with great alacrity. In 1994, they took Kandahar and then other major cities. In 1996, the disintegrating Burhanuddin Rabbani regime lost Kabul to the Taliban, aided by the defections of Gulbuddin Hekmatyar and Jalaluddin Haqqani, who ended up becoming allied with the Taliban. Ahmad Shah Massoud made an orderly retreat to the north, where he was later joined by Hazara fighters and Uzbeks under the Uzbek warlord, Rashid Dostum.

The Taliban pursued and took Mazar-i-Sharif, lost it, and seized it again. On the Taliban's second capture in 1998, seeking revenge for past massacres against its own cadres, its forces massacred Hazara defenders and also killed Iranian diplomats, causing an international crisis that drove a deep divide between the Sunni Taliban and the Shia regime in Tehran. In all, the new Northern Alliance of Tajik, Uzbek, and Hazara fighters never occupied more than 10 percent of the countryside. The Taliban, aided by *al-Qaeda*–trained Afghan and foreign cadres, kept up pressure on the Northern Alliance until 2001.

The Taliban set up its capital in Kabul and appointed ministers, but the command element remained in Kandahar with Mullah Omar. It often contradicted Kabul's repressive and at times ludicrous government. Clever with religious symbols, Mullah Omar literally put on the cloak of the Prophet Mohammad, which was kept in a Kandahar shrine, and proclaimed himself *Amir-ul-Mominin*,

Commander of the Faithful, raising his status amongst even the most radical extremists. *Al-Qaeda* seniors and the Pakistani Taliban accorded Mullah Omar great respect and acknowledged him by his self-awarded title. The Taliban regime was recognised as legitimate by only three nations—Pakistan, the United Arab Emirates, and Saudi Arabia—though the latter two maintained only a limited diplomatic presence in Kabul. The USA and the UN continued to give aid to the people, but Afghanistan's seat at the UN and most embassies abroad remained occupied by representatives of the previous regime led by Burhanuddin Rabbani. The only opposition to the Taliban within Afghanistan was the Northern Alliance, which fought hard to establish and expand control over territories, mainly in northern Afghanistan.

Al-Qaeda and the Taliban

Out of the Afghan resistance of the 1980s evolved an Islamic terrorist organisation that became known as *al-Qaeda* ("The Base"). Its founder was Osama bin Laden. He first came to Afghanistan shortly after the Soviet invasion in 1979 to assist in the *mujahideen*'s fight against the Soviets. Backed by his family's fortune, bin Laden subsequently founded the *Maktab-al-Khidmat* (MAK), or "Services Office," a resistance organisation with a Jordanian-Palestinian partner.

MAK helped to recruit and transport to Peshawar, in Pakistan, any would-be *mujahideen* from the Middle East and other Muslim countries; these fighters were colloquially called "Afghan Arabs." From Peshawar, some of these recruits subsequently received training at camps in Afghanistan that were financed by bin Laden.

Towards the end of the Soviet occupation, bin Laden formed *al-Qaeda* as an independent group, with the intent of expanding resistance operations from an anti-Soviet *jihad* to a global *jihad* targeting the USA and its allies, who were perceived to be supporters of "infidel" governments. *Al-Qaeda* soon strengthened its ties with other radical Islamic organisations—most notably, the Egyptian *al-Jihad* (Islamic *Jihad*) organisation headed by current *al-Qaeda* leader Ayman al-Zawahiri. Until 1991, *al-Qaeda* was based in Afghanistan and Peshawar. It then relocated to Sudan where it remained for about five years until bin Laden and other top leaders returned to Afghanistan.

In 1996, Osama bin Laden established ties with the Taliban, which shared his anti-Western views. To strengthen his influence in Afghanistan, bin Laden provided the Taliban with finances and some of *al-Qaeda's* most committed assault forces. In return, the Taliban provided shelter to *al-Qaeda* and refused subsequent US requests for bin Laden's extradition.

Osama bin Laden reportedly saw Afghanistan as the first state in a new Islamic caliphate. Although he did not know Mullah Omar earlier, bin Laden held him in high regard, and intermarriage took place between the inner circles of *al-Qaeda* and the Taliban. In return for sanctuary and freedom of action, bin Laden provided funds, advice, and, most important, trained cadres, Afghan or otherwise, for the Taliban war machine. Pakistan was also generous in support, which it saw as a sure bulwark against Indian influence. In 1998 alone, Pakistan provided $6 million to the Taliban.

In Afghanistan, bin Laden took over or set up training camps for *al-Qaeda* and Taliban recruits. As many as 20,000 Afghan and foreign recruits may have passed through the camps. Many of these trainees gained combat experience in fighting the Northern Alliance, raising *al-Qaeda*'s value in the eyes of the Taliban leadership. Afghanistan became a prime destination for international terrorists. In February 1998, bin Laden declared war on the USA from his safe haven in Afghanistan. Accusing the Americans of occupying Arabia, plundering its riches, humiliating its leaders, attacking Iraq, and more, bin Laden claimed that *de facto* the USA had declared war on Islam and its people. In an allegedly binding *fatwa*, or religious binding, bin Laden and his co-signers declared a defensive *jihad* against the West.

Map 1: Political Map of Afghanistan

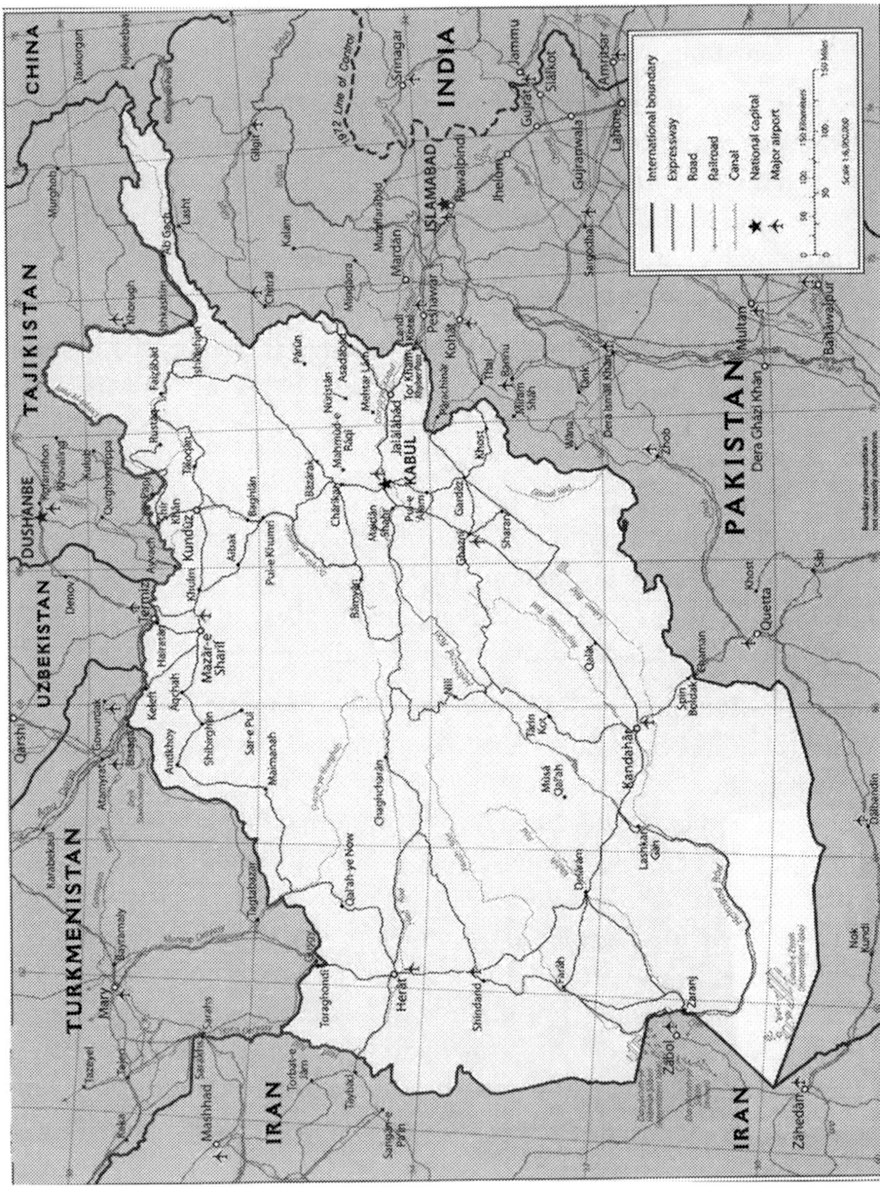

Ahmed Shah Massoud

Known as the 'Lion of Panjshir' for his success in resisting Soviet efforts to seize the strategic Panjshir Valley, Ahmed Shah Massoud was Minister of Defence in the first government formed after the fall of the Najibullah regime. He subsequently led the Northern Alliance, a group of anti-Taliban militias mostly fighting in the northern and western parts of the country. By September 2001, Massoud's forces held virtually all parts of Afghanistan that were not under Taliban control. He became a symbol of resistance against the Taliban. On 9 September 2001, two *al-Qaeda* members posing as Algerian journalists managed to get permission to meet Massoud face-to-face for an interview. The bomb that ended Massoud's life was hidden in their camera.

11 September 2001

By 2001, *al-Qaeda* had 5,000 trained militants and cells in 50 countries. The organisation functioned much like a corporation or a combination of strategic partnerships. On 7 August 1998, *al-Qaeda* carried out bombings on the US embassies in Kenya and Tanzania in East Africa. Both embassies were severely damaged. The casualties, mostly African, numbered over 220 killed, and nearly 4,200 wounded. Among other measures, US retaliatory Cruise missile strikes were aimed at *al-Qaeda* camps in Afghanistan, but had little effect. Among its terrorist actions, *al-Qaeda* claimed responsibility for the attack on USS Cole in Aden harbour (2000), and the attacks on the World Trade Centre and the Pentagon in the USA on 11 September 2001. It is believed that target selection, preparation, and planning was confined to bin Laden (the "contractor") and a handful of *al-Qaeda* leaders.

Perhaps *al-Qaeda* did not fully comprehend the passions that it would invoke, both in the USA as well as amongst its allies by the attacks on 9/11, which killed 3,000 people from 90 countries. Washington asked the Taliban to hand over bin Laden. Mullah Omar refused again, as he had in 1998. The US President, George W Bush, then went to Congress for support that authorised him in a Joint Resolution: *To use all necessary and appropriate force against those nations, organisations, or persons he determines planned, authorised, committed, or aided the terrorist attacks that occurred on September 11, 2001, or harboured such organisations or persons, in order to prevent any future acts of international terrorism against the US by such nations, organisations or persons.*

Operation 'Enduring Freedom'

The war in Afghanistan began on 7 October 2001 with the US and British warplanes targeting Taliban forces and *al-Qaeda*. Cruise missiles were fired from warships. On ground, the US, British and other Allied special forces troops worked with the Northern Alliance to launch a military offensive to overthrow the Taliban. Aided by the bombing and massive defections, they captured Mazar-i-Sharif on 9 November. This led to coordination between Allied air attacks and ground attacks by the Northern Alliance which led to the fall of Kabul on 13 November 2001, as the Taliban retreated from most of northern Afghanistan. As more Allied troops entered the war and the Northern Alliance forces fought their way southwards, the Taliban and *al-Qaeda* retreated toward the mountainous border region between Afghanistan and Pakistan. The Taliban were restricted to a smaller and smaller region, with Kunduz, the last Taliban-held city in the north, captured on 26 November. Most of the Taliban fled to Pakistan.

The war continued in the south of the country, where the Taliban retreated to Kandahar. Whilst in Kandahar, the Taliban agreed to surrender but the deal was rejected by US Secretary of Defence, Donald Rumsfeld as it would have provided amnesty to Taliban leader, Mullah Mohammed Omar. Meanwhile, in November 2001, the US military and its allied forces established their first ground base in Afghanistan to the south west of Kandahar, known as Forward Operating Base (FOB) Rhino or Camp Rhino. After Kandahar fell in December 2001, remnants of the Taliban and *al-Qaeda* continued to mount resistance.

The Battle of Tora Bora, involving the US, British and Northern Alliance forces took place in December 2001 to further destroy the Taliban and suspected *al-Qaeda* elements in Afghanistan. In early March 2002 the US military, along with allied Afghan military forces, conducted a large operation to destroy *al-Qaeda* in an operation code-named 'Anaconda'.

President Bush emphasised that Operation 'Enduring Freedom' was only the first phase in a broader war on terrorism. He outlined two strategic aims of the war on terrorism during his State of the Union Address on 29 January 2002. The first was the destruction of terrorist camps, the disruption of terrorist plans, and the judgment of terrorists in a court of law. The second was the prevention of terrorist and rogue regimes from threatening the USA and its allies with weapons of mass destruction.

Map 2: Afghanistan: Administrative Divisions

Bush's Light Footprint, 2001–2006

The Bonn Agreement was the initial series of agreements passed on 5 December 2001 to re-create the State of Afghanistan following the US invasion. Since no nationally agreed-upon government had existed in Afghanistan since 1979, it was felt necessary to have a transition period before a permanent government was established. The Taliban was, however, excluded from the discussions and it focused on survival and rebuilding its forces. After managing to evade US forces throughout the summer of 2002, the remnants of the Taliban gradually began to regain their confidence and renewed their insurgency.

On 9 October 2004, Afghanistan elected Hamid Karzai as president in its first direct elections. The following year, the Afghan parliamentary elections were conducted on 18 September 2005. An Afghan Constitution Commission was established to draft a new constitution in consultation with the public. A judicial commission was formed to rebuild the justice system in accordance with Islamic principles, international standards, the rule of law, and Afghan legal traditions. Hundreds of schools and mosques were constructed, millions of dollars in aid distributed, and the occurrence of violence reduced.

The Taliban Insurgency

From 2005 to 2007, the Taliban increased its attacks using suicide bombers and other tactics acquired from the Iraq War. The US-led coalition success in quelling the Taliban insurgency faltered. As the war dragged on, the Taliban demonstrated they could not be defeated, thanks to their sanctuary in neighbouring Pakistan.

While military forces interdicted insurgents and assured some form of security, Provincial Reconstruction Teams were formed and tasked with infrastructure building, such as constructing roads and bridges, assisting during floods, and providing food and water to refugees. Many warlords participated in an allegiance programme, formally recognising the legitimacy of the government of Afghanistan, and surrendering their soldiers and weapons, though subsequent actions led to questions about their true loyalties.

In January 2006, the NATO International Security Assistance Force (ISAF) began combat duties in southern Afghanistan. It was chiefly made up of the British, Canadian and Dutch forces (and some smaller contributions from Denmark, Romania, Estonia and Norway, as well as air and artillery support from the USA). The US military also conducted military operations separate from NATO in other parts of Afghanistan; in areas such as Kandahar, Bagram, and Kabul. The focus was the remote strongholds in the ungoverned and inaccessible areas of Afghanistan. Because of the difficulty of mounting coalition operations in the land-locked and foreboding environment of Afghanistan, the Taliban was able to operate without fear of interdiction as long as the remote strongholds existed. The critical vulnerability was the Taliban leadership, which enjoyed safe haven in Pakistan.

In the spring and summer of 2008, the violence in Afghanistan claimed more coalition (foreign) troops than those who died in the concurrent Iraq War. The Taliban displayed resurgence and showed that it could launch large, coordinated, and effective attacks on coalition and Afghan forces. Meanwhile, the Afghan National Army, Afghan National Police, and Afghan Border Police were raised and trained to assume the task of securing their nation.

Obama's Doubts and Withdrawal Deadlines

US President Barack Obama came into office in January 2009 promising to turn around what many of his advisers and supporters saw as "the good war" in Afghanistan. He opted to send reinforcements to Afghanistan: 21,000 troops in March and then, more reluctantly, another 30,000 in December, putting the total number of US troops in the country at close to 100,000.

Over the next three years, the surge stabilised the most important cities and districts, vitalized the Afghan army and police, and rallied support for the government. The threat from *al-Qaeda* receded after the death of bin Laden on 2 May 2011 at the hands of US special operations forces in Pakistan. Yet the costs of the surge outweighed the gains. Obama came to see the war effort as unsustainable. By 2013, more than 350,000 Afghan soldiers and police had been trained, armed, and deployed, but they depended on US advisers and air support to defeat the Taliban in battle. Their performance was mixed, marred by corruption and by "insider attacks" carried out on the US and allied advisers.

In May 2014, the US President Barack Obama announced that troop levels in Afghanistan would fall from 33,000 to 9,800 by 1 January 2015 with the US role focusing on advising Afghan security forces and conducting counter-terror operations. A year later, he stated that the number of troops in Afghanistan would halve to about 4,900 and then by the beginning of 2017, settle at an embassy presence of about 1,000.

Operation 'Freedom's Sentinel'

On 31 December 2014, Operation 'Enduring Freedom' concluded, and was succeeded by Operation 'Freedom's Sentinel'. It was part of the NATO-led Resolute Support Mission, which began on 1 January 2015 and had two components: counter-terrorism and working with allies as part of Resolute Support.

The new Afghan President, Ashraf Ghani, who won the 2014 election, actually had very little overall support among the people. Barely a third of eligible voters cast legitimate ballots in the two elections of 2014. In contrast, the Taliban had the support of approximately a third of the Afghan people. The Taliban recast its mission from one resisting foreign occupation to one confronting a government it considered a western pawn.

Talks/Negotiations with the Taliban

Donald Trump, when he took over as the US president in January 2017, inherited a war that he had campaigned against and had promised to end. He initially approved an increase of US forces in Afghanistan to roughly 14,000. However, he was looking for an exit and soon started negotiations with the Taliban in 2018. At the same time, he swore off nation building and did not invest in civilian reconstruction and stabilisation. In September 2020, peace talks between officials from the Afghan state and the Taliban started in Doha, Qatar, to limit the Taliban's options to a single undesirable path: ceasing *jihad* in return for integration into a system they abhorred.

The Taliban however viewed ousting the foreign troops from Afghan soil by force as the most realistic strategy. Only then could they negotiate with the government in Kabul and other Afghan groups.

Trump appointed Zalmay Khalilzad as special representative for Afghanistan reconciliation. The talks took place without any pre-conditions on the Taliban—e.g., to denounce *al-Qaeda*, accept a ceasefire, or recognise the new Afghan constitution. As part of the peace process, on 22 September 2016, a treaty was signed between the Afghan government and the *Hezb-e-Islami, a* militant group led by Gulbuddin Hekmatyar. A second peace treaty was signed between the USA and the Taliban on 29 February 2020, which called for the withdrawal of American troops from Afghanistan within 14 months if the Taliban upheld the terms of the agreement—a pledge by the Taliban that Afghanistan would not be used as a base for attacks against the USA or its allies—for which there were no enforcement mechanisms.

The US Withdrawal

When US President Joe Biden took office in January 2021, the Taliban were making some gains against the regime in Kabul, while *al-Qaeda* enjoyed safe haven in Pakistan. It was uncertain if the Afghan government could hold on without external support. Biden chose to follow through on the deal at Doha, claiming that the mission had already been accomplished when US forces killed Osama bin Laden and justified a withdrawal by saying, "It's up to Afghans to make the decision about the future of their country."

On 15 August 2021, Afghanistan was back in the hands of the Taliban, in a rapid consolidation of their hold on Afghanistan, with the US and allied forces in chaotic withdrawal from Kabul Airport. President Ashraf Ghani, who was unwilling to resign, fled the country in a helicopter. The Taliban vanquished the Afghan National Army that the USA and its allies had built over 20 years, in less than 10 days.

In the largest non-combatant evacuation operation ever conducted by the US military, which commenced on 14 August 2021, US military aircraft evacuated more than 79,000 civilians. They included 6,000 Americans and more than 73,500 third-country nationals and Afghan civilians, enabled by US military service members who were securing and operating the airfield. The last C-17 aircraft departed with Army Major General Chris Donahue, the commander of troops in Kabul, and US Ambassador to Afghanistan Ross Wilson aboard on 30 August.

More than 800,000 American service members and 25,000 civilians served in Afghanistan during its two decade long mission. The US spent more than $2 trillion on the war in Afghanistan (in direct war-fighting costs as well as in training more than 300,000 Afghan forces). Nearly 2,500 Americans died fighting on Afghan soil, along with almost 1,000 troops from allies like Britain and Canada. The toll for Afghans has been far higher: at least 240,000 Afghans died, many of them civilians.

Looking Ahead

The Taliban announced an interim government in Afghanistan led by Mullah Mohammad Hassan Akhund, one of the movement's founders, declaring the country an "Islamic Emirate". However, the legacy of its history weighs heavily on the country. Every possible divide—ethnic, gender, religious, class, and political—has been exacerbated; every family suffers from its burden of tragedy. The most important question, however, is the ultimate impact its history will have on Afghan national identity. By far the single greatest source of conflict in Afghan society is the millennium old animosity between the northern and southern ethnic groups. The political divide remains the largest obstacle to nation-building. It is this animus and chasm of trust that has driven the Afghans to war since 1973 and will determine Afghanistan's fate in the years ahead.

NOTES

1. *Mujahideen* is the plural of Mujahid, which means a warrior fighting a *jihad*, a holy was as mandated in Islamic theology.
2. The Geneva Accords were signed by Afghanistan and Pakistan, with the United States and the USSR as guarantors on 14 April 1988 at Geneva. Among various other provisions, it also contained the timetable for the withdrawal of the Soviet troops from Afghanistan.

3

Imagining the Historical Nation: The Dialogical Project of Nation-Making, Religious and Ethnic Identity in Afghanistan

Omar Sharifi

ABSTRACT

The Taliban occupation of Kabul in August 2021 is seen as the ultimate victory of *Jihadist* Islam in Afghanistan. However, a closer look in the Afghan conception of religious and ethnic identity and the historical evolution of state-building in Afghanistan shows that since its inception in 1747, Afghanistan was never ruled by a clerical regime (except between 1996-2001 or the first Taliban Emirate) nor did the various Afghan dynastic rulers sought to legitimize their rule by endorsing political Islam. After declaring independence in 1919 the Durrani monarchs felt the need to convert this dynastic legitimacy into a nationalist legitimacy in which they and the people of Afghanistan were declared to be bound together in some intrinsic fashion. But the project of constructing a common national identity in a country that was home to so many different ethnic and linguistic groups, and where regional identities had far deeper roots than an Afghan nation state, was no simple task. It remained a work in progress as the country reached its centenary. The paper attempts to discuss the complexities of historical evolution of the Afghan state and religious identity in the midst of a bloody ideological war between various Islamist/

> Jihadist groups collectively gathered under the umbrella of the Taliban Emirate on one side, and the Afghan government/s and the people on the other side. This paper is also an attempt to discuss the dialogical interactions between the "traditional/historical Islam" discourse and the *Jihadist* political Islam in order to explain why the Taliban as a government is an anomalous phenomenon in Afghan history.

The link between state formation, political stability, and governing legitimacy is well studied in political science and sociology. A number of scholars from various disciplines have wrestled with questions about the authority of the state in the Afghan context as well.[1]

Afghanistan has always been a mosaic of different ethnic and linguistic groups, the major ones being the Pakhtoons, Tajiks, Hazaras, and Uzbeks. Popular and scholarly concern about Afghanistan has long been characterised by how the actions of elite players, tribal politics, religious leaders, and state institutions jointly determine interethnic relations, communal relationships, and faith practices. The visibility of Islamic radicalism in Afghanistan, coupled with the overt ethnonationalism among many diaspora elite in the post-2001 government, have prompted some observers to portray the Taliban and *Jihadist* groups as the only solution in ensuring stability in the country.

In this chapter I am arguing that the answer lay not only (or even mostly) in the state's policies (whether the Taliban regime or other governments), in popular forms of political pragmatism or political Islam, but in the ways that various Afghan communities define themselves through shared understandings of their historical, cultural and religious traditions.

Historical versus Modern Islam

In addressing the above question, the common theme is the division between those who favor a "traditional" Afghan version of Islam and those who contend that "new" or "modern" practices should replace them. The traditionalists see themselves as the defenders of an indigenous and authentic Islam practiced for centuries by people renowned for their defense of that faith and attacked the practices, the modernists wish to force upon them as "foreign and misguided."

The "modernists" contend that they represent a purer and more universalistic Islam and that Afghans are out of step with the times.

This debate began in the aftermath of the Soviet invasion in 1979. The event sparked a call for a *jihad* against the Soviet occupation in the 1980s and mobilised millions of Afghans in support of *Jihadist* political parties that could supply them with arms and money. They promised to free the country from the communist infidels and establish a true Islamic government. Before the Soviet invasion, these parties had little political or religious influence in Afghanistan in part because they had adopted religious practices that (although they proclaimed them "modern" and "true") were the products of Middle Eastern and South Asian political Islamic movements. Before the war such practices held little popular appeal to Afghans, but because both the Pakistani government (channeling American aid) and Saudi Arabian donors restricted funding for the Afghan resistance only to Sunni parties that followed this line, they now had a much bigger voice. After the fall of the communist regime in 1992, the new *Mujahideen* government took power and was followed by the harsh Taliban *Jihadist* theocracy in 1996. The chaos of *Mujahideen* government and the brutal Taliban policies has led to a new founded appreciation for the time of peace that had existed before 1978. In people minds, the "traditional," "historically rooted" and "authentic" Afghan and Islamic practices of that time were pillars of stability that now needed to be defended. On many occasions, people who remembered the civil war and the Taliban rule condemned *Mujahideen* and Taliban for "beliefs and attitude that defamed Islam." Many Afghan Muslims across the country viewed the restoration of their "customary" practices after the fall of Taliban as a natural and necessary step after their experience of living under the Taliban's "new/modern" version of Islam. They never accepted the premise that their traditions were contrary to accepted Islamic principles. They argued that, on the contrary, their "traditional practices" were well rooted in their historical knowledge and understanding of religion.

Another aspect of the debate about Islam in Afghanistan that has not been examined is the view that many of the new varieties of Islam are suspect foreign imports. In the wars against the British and more particularly the Soviet Union, the concept of a *jihad* that pitted believers against unbelievers was used as a way to unite Muslims into a community of resistance where differences did not matter. Following the withdrawal of the Soviet Union and the collapse of the communist government in 1992, the civil war that followed was a battle for power within the Sunni Muslim community. In the turmoil that followed the explicitly *Jihadist* Taliban government sought to impose its radical variety of Islam on everyone in the country. Taliban leaders like Mullah Omar had been students at Deobandi madrassas in Pakistan where they were taught that the Islam of Afghanistan was backward and full of superstition. Muslims within Afghanistan took this as an insult against their own faith and history of independence. Pakistan's influence over the Taliban and boasts that Afghanistan would be now become its *de facto* "fifth province" looked a lot like a new attempt at colonisation. For example, when Mullah Omar issued a fatwa on the destruction of Afghanistan's pre-Islamic heritage, one of his reasons was the need to counter negative image of Afghans in the Muslim world. Rather than an effort to purify Islam, many Afghans saw Taliban leader's *fatwa* more as an effort by Taliban to appease their Islamist allies/patrons in Pakistan and funders in the Middle East who were backing their imposition of foreign ideologies at the expense of Afghan faith and culture. The perception that the Taliban and their ideology as foreign import helps explain the rapid demise of the regime in 2001 when it was attacked by the United States.

While the Taliban were driven from power in 2001, the question of what constituted "proper Islam" remained a live issue. The *jihadi* groups including the Taliban insisted that their was a "new Islam" or "modern Islam" that should replace what they viewed as an Afghan Islam infected by superstition and unjustified modifications to a purer faith. Yet to call that version "modern or new" was a bit of a misnomer. It was grounded in the proposition that pious Muslim believers must return to the practices of the faith's early decades of the seventh century and not seek to adapt itself to the contemporary world. It was modern or new only in the sense that the outsiders bringing it to Afghanistan in the 1980s and 1990s were deemed modern or new because they and their ideas had recently arrived. Before that, Afghans simply assumed that as pious Muslims their traditional practices must be in accord with a faith that was central to their own identity. During the decades of war, however, millions of refugees fled to Iran and Pakistan where they experienced different Islamic practices. A younger generation, particularly those educated in Pakistani *madrasas,* learned to condemn whatever practices and beliefs their teachers disapproved of. Far from being impressed with this new model of religious piety, most of those who lived and were educated in Afghanistan took such attacks on their customs and history as noxious religious zealotry that demanded a robust response.

In constructing a new binary distinction between the "modern" and "traditional" forms of Islam, represented by ordinary Afghans and the Taliban/*Jihadist* groups, the traditionalists have also turned the tables on their opponents. It is not their traditions that are backward, they say, because they seek peace, spiritual progress and social solidarity by means of a clear understanding of what they believe and why. In their opinion, it is "modernists" and proponents of a "new Islam" or the *Jihadists* who are the representatives of backwardness, chaos and social disruption—and that they demonstrated it when they were in power. The opposition to excessive politicisation of religion and the rejection of imposing of any one type of Muslim belief on people is one of the hallmarks of the traditionalists' point of view. In a country that has suffered decades of conflict, they believe that religion needs to withdraw itself from politics and ideological battles to ensure communal solidarity and safety.

The visibility of personal expressions of faith and opposition to the *Jihadist* narrative common in many spheres of life in Afghanistan (symbolised through many cultural traditions such as Nauroz New Year Festival in Mazar-e-Sharif) demonstrate the people's efforts to define themselves as components of a historical and correct Islam.

During the Taliban insurgency and their threats and brutal attacks on civilians, mosques, shrines, religious festivals, such discourses at personal level about the relationship between religious practices and cultural traditions have been a crucial component in constructing what it means to have true Afghan Islamic faith. This process always occurs in the context of community discourse and communication about what a religious practice entails and how to carry it out in an accepted manner. Such knowledge has multiple sources, often called "the Islamic cultural sphere" [*farhang-e Islami* or *saqafat-e Islami*]. This includes a notion of Islamic heritage [*meeras tarikhi Islami*] that is directly associated with the history of Islam in Afghanistan. *Meeras-e tarikhi Islami* encompasses more than just aspects of faith. It also includes many facets of social life that occur in homes, families, mosques, and shrines. This serves to confirm to oneself and to others that a religious action or belief is pure. For example, in 2012 on the eve of Nauroz, the Ulema Council of Balkh organised a gathering in the Shrine Ali to protest the proselytizing activities of Wahhabi and Deobandi groups commonly known as *Jama'at–e Tablighi* (Association of Proselytizers) who, according to some accounts, were based in Pakistan. When the Tablighis traveled to Mazar-e Sharif on the eve of Nauroz to condemn what they considered heretical practices, the Ulema of Balkh challenged them to an open debate on the issue. Perhaps unnerved, the Tablighis rejected the challenge and left the city. Many of the residents of Mazar-e Sharif at the time expressed appreciation for the city's clerical council stance with regard to "those who lost the true path" [*ashkhas-e gumrah*], i.e., the Deobandis and Wahhabi. These processes of validation and contestation have contributed to shifts in the atmosphere of Afghanistan since 2001. Despite decades of war and brutal Taliban rule and attacks, the traditional Islamic forms of worship have held their own and pushed back against the Islamists more than in other countries. In other words, importance and value is not placed on the strict adherence of textual based religious practices as an end in itself, but on the understanding and observance of religious issues within the larger cultural and historical context. In fact, it is the end result of "true" and "correct" religious understanding. Beyond fulfilling one's religious duties and obligations properly and correctly, it is also of crucial importance to have the knowledge necessary to ensure social harmony in a multi-ethnic and multi linguistic community, something the *Jihadist* groups including the Taliban have failed to deliver despite their promises.

The State-building Project and the Question of Nation-ness

As in many multiethnic and multilinguistic Central/South Asian contexts, the relationship between the state and society in Afghanistan has historically depended on a system of reciprocity that bound national leaders to the local elite, and the local elite to the government. Until the rise of Amir Abdur Rahman Khan (r. 1880–1901), Afghan monarchs made a point of respecting local traditions and cultivating ties with regional elites as a way of linking themselves with their subjects. Unlike the classical Persian model of absolute rule or the postcolonial, quasi-Westernised systems or military dictatorships in the rest of the region, Afghan leaders engaged in continuous negotiations as a way to build consensus between the central authorities and local elites.[2] Those that thought this unnecessary, such as King Amanullah in 1919–29, or the Khalqis (a faction within the People's Democratic Party of Afghanistan) in 1978–79, soon found themselves unable to rule and were ousted from power.

The pattern was based on a historic solution to an old problem: how does an elite minority reach beyond its own small group to buttress its authority? For 700 years that regional minority was composed of conquerors of Turko-Mongolian descent who created a dualistic system in which the ruler combined men of the sword (Turks) with men of the pen (literate Persian speakers).[3] The former provided the ruler with his coercive force, the latter with needed administrative capacity. When a Pakhtoon dynasty came to power in 1747, it adopted this model, with the Durrani Pakhtoons and Turkic groups such as the Qizilbash now dominating the military, and Persian speakers filling their traditional administrative role.[4]

In this system, the government was not expected to provide services to the population, but was expected to prevent the emergence of *fitna* or chaos. In return for his protection, subjects were required to obey the ruler, but any replacement who could maintain the bargain was deemed legitimate should the incumbent fail. One restriction on this process of replacement, however, was that among the Turko-Mongolian people, only those born from aristocratic descent had the right to compete for power. This was very unlike the egalitarian

Pakhtoon system in which a much wider range of notables could serve. Although Pakhtoon in origin, the Durrani dynasty that founded and ruled the Afghan state managed to graft this old Turkic aristocratic tradition onto their own royal house so that only members of certain Durrani clans were deemed eligible to compete for power. Different lines of descent within these Durrani groups regularly warred with one another: three different lines took power in the monarchy's 230-year history that lasted until 1978.

State Building under the Iron Amir

Amir Abdur Rahman Khan fundamentally changed the nature of the state that had existed earlier and created a new model of governance that redefined the relationship between the state and local populations by imposing direct control over the entire country for the first time since the formation of the Afghan state in 1747. Unlike his predecessors, Amir Abdur Rahman Khan deliberately destroyed local autonomous governance structures, such as the Amirs of Qataghan and Andkhoi,[5] often employing extreme violence, in every region and city across the country. He extinguished the autonomy of the Kohistani Tajik chiefs (1881–84), suppressed a Ghilzai revolt (1886–88) with a rapacity that was unprecedented in Afghan history, and then impoverished them through direct and extortionate taxation. After crushing these groups, which had played the most crucial role during the first and second Anglo–Afghan wars, he abolished the autonomy of Afghan Turkistan, defeating his cousin Ishaq Khan, the governor of Mazar-e Sharif, who had rejected his centralisation policies.

Abdur Rahman Khan's next campaign (1891–93) was against the Shia Hazara areas of central Afghanistan, where his regular army and tribal levies broke the resistance of Hazaras, killing many, enslaving thousands, and forcing many more to flee to Baluchistan and Iran. The Hazaras were impoverished through sheer destruction of their property, enslavement, and the distribution of their pasturelands to Pakhtoon nomads. His last campaign was against the Kafirs (1895) who lived in the eastern Hindu Kush mountain region. In a short military operation, the region was conquered, renamed Nuristan (the land of light), and incorporated into modern Afghanistan. Unlike the brutal destruction of Hazaras, the Amir treated the newly converted Kafirs with leniency and recruited thousands of them into the army and administration.[6]

By destroying all regional elites and power structures, Amir Abdur Rahman Khan brought the different polities that had previously defined the diverse regions of Afghanistan into a single national state. His standardised taxation system, laws, single currency, and unitary administrative structure made all Afghans his subjects to be ruled from Kabul. His policies were not limited to removing the local governance structures; they also targeted the religious establishment. Before his rule, the ulema functioned as a polity independent from the government. He abolished their independence by bringing all *waqf* (religious endowments) under direct central government control by forcing them to pass government examinations and making them dependent on the government for their livelihood.[7]

Abdur Rahman Khan created a model of unitary state institutions that successive Afghan governments keenly followed and adopted in modified forms, often justifying them as means to preserve the national unity of Afghanistan. As Thomas Barfield has noted, *"much as the establishment of the Durrani Empire by Ahmad Shah in 1747 is seen as the beginning of Afghan history, Amir Abdur Rahman's reign is seen as the beginning of Afghanistan as a nation-state."*[8] Afghanistan's history in the twentieth century was shaped significantly by such policies and processes. Even when the time came to forge a new government after the fall of the Taliban in 2001, Afghanistan remained captive to Abdur Rahman's legacy. Rather than reconfigure the structure of a political system that had collapsed twice in the preceding century in (1929 and 1992), the 2004 constitutional Loya Jirga (General Assembly) restored it by reinstituting a government with a rigid top-down decision-making process where the leader's power had few checks or balances, and where decisions made in Kabul were deemed non-negotiable. Abdur Rahman's centralisation had put so much power in the hands of the ruler that it left other government institutions weak and ineffective. His emphasis on making Kabul the only power center in the country also starved other regions of investment and human talent. And while the policy of sidelining regional elites increased Kabul's power, it did not follow that the center alone could achieve political legitimacy, maintain stability, or promote national identity without them.

With the Soviet invasion of Afghanistan in 1979, the trajectory of the state building project in the country entered a period of prolonged crisis. At this moment, the Afghan story departed from the Andersonian model; as Midgal would have it, the country's social forces took hold of the nation-making project. Many observers conflated the profound failure, if not collapse, of the Afghan state with the demise of the Afghan nation. Throughout most of the 1980s and 1990s the country was fragmented along regional lines, a fragmentation interpreted by many as the beginning of its disintegration into ethnic and tribal enclaves. Even after 2001, many political analysts and Western diplomats argued that the "breakup of the country along the ethnic lines [held] real dangers."[9]

With the collapse of the Afghan communist regime in 1992, various *Mujahideen* groups who fought the Russians, and later the Najibullah-led government, took control of the country. The *Mujahideen* Islamic State of Afghanistan [*Dawlat-e Islami Afghanistan*] that ruled Afghanistan from 1992–96 was divided into a number of competing factions. The Persian-speaking Tajiks dominated the *Jamiat-e Islami* party under the political leadership of Burhanuddin Rabbani, who served as the country's president, and also the military leadership of Commander Ahmad Shah Masoud. It was opposed by the *Hezb-i-Islami*, a predominantly Pakhtoon partly led by Gulbuddin Hekmatyar, a favorite of Pakistan, who shelled Kabul from his bases just south and southeast of the city. A former communist general based in Mazar-e Sharif, Abdul Rashid Dostum, led an Uzbek party, *Junbish-e-Milli*, while the Hazaras were organised into the *Hezb-e Wahdat-Islami* led by Ali Mazari until his murder in 1995.

Mujahideen disunity and infighting opened the way for the Taliban, a Salafist religious group from Kandahar led by the one-eyed Mullah Omar, to take power. Drawing heavily on a southern Pakhtoon base of recruitment, the Taliban displaced Hekmatyar's *Hezb-i-Islami* in 1995. In 1996, they captured Kabul and installed their new Islamic

Emirate of Afghanistan (1996–2001). Once the Taliban took Kabul in 1996, they abandoned the notion of the Afghan *dawlat* and declared themselves to be an Islamic emirate, *D'Afghanistan Islami Emirat*, under the personal leadership of Mullah Omar as Commander of the Faithful. The Taliban, acting within a network of regional and local Islamist groups, had developed their own conception of political legitimacy, one that relied purely on a Salafi/Jihadist interpretation of Islam and a corresponding opposition to nationalism in its secular forms.

This opposition was strongly rooted in the notion of a political Islam that had emerged in Pakistan and South Asia more generally during the 1980s. The Taliban's political Islam aspired to introduce a more inclusive national identity based on religion that would include all ethnic groups. They existed, ideologically, outside the bounds of a historically grounded understanding of Afghanistan and the Afghan state, remaining perpetually linked to a transnational network of Islamists. Such links made many Afghans view the Taliban as an anti-Afghan phenomenon.[10] As a religious movement led by Afghan Pakhtoons who were trained in Deobandi madrasas across the border in Pakistan, they sought to banish anything they deemed "un-Islamic."

Under these circumstances, it is easy to see why observers, Afghan and foreign alike, might have feared the demise not only of the state-based political order but also the plural, historically grounded, and expansive conception of the Afghan nation as it had existed heretofore. From 1996–2001, the civil war pitted the Pakhtoon-dominated Taliban emirate against the United Front alliance of the above mentioned Tajik, Uzbek, and Hazara parties (also called the Northern Alliance). The United Front insisted that it was still the legitimate government of the continuing Islamic State of Afghanistan, a case buttressed by the Taliban's failure to garner international recognition beyond that of Pakistan, Saudi Arabia, and the United Arab Emirates even after they held 80 percent of the country.

And yet, in spite of the United Front's hostility to the Taliban, it does not appear that any of their component groups used anti-Pakhtoon rhetoric to mobilise their own people, mostly located in the non-Pakhtoon areas of northern and central Afghanistan. They rejected all allegations of representing an anti-Pakhtoon block and continued to justify their war against Taliban as defending a legitimate Afghan government's sovereignty and independence from a usurping Taliban regime that was Pakistan's cat's paw. Similarly, the Taliban movement and its later emirate always asserted that it was a legitimate government that met and accepted Islamic standards of inclusiveness. While the Taliban drew most of its supporters from the Pakhtoon areas of Afghanistan and certainly had a strong Pakhtoon tribal base, it continued and still continues to portray itself as a government that transcends ethnicity and region. And similarly, nonetheless, their declaration of Pashto as the language of government was neither an innovation, nor particularly radical. Previous monarchical regimes going back to the mid-nineteenth century had done the same with little success in a bureaucracy that continued to be run on a Persianate model of administration that had persevered for a thousand years.

Similarly, ethnic preferences and exclusions in government positions were more a byproduct of a traditional spoils system that rewarded supporters, mostly Pakhtoons, and excluded perceived opponents, mostly non-Pakhtoons. The result was an ethnic bias, but not one rooted in ethnic nationalism. The strongest evidence that the Taliban was a *Jihadist* rather than an ethnonationalist movement could be seen in their policies that pitted a strict *Jihadist*/Salafist interpretation of Islamic sharia law against some of the core values embodied in the Pakhtoon code of honor, or Pakhtoonwali. For example, the Taliban outlawed the tradition of resolving blood feuds by the exchange of girls in marriage [*baad*] between the groups in conflict, although the effective enforcement of this law is still debated.[11] They also discouraged the use of traditional Pakhtoon tribal councils, jirgas, to solve disputes based on customary law in favor of the clerical (ulema) councils that employed *sharia* law. In this respect, ironically, the Taliban resembled the communist PDPA, as both sought to replace customary practices with their own universalistic laws enforced by the power of the state.

A closer examination of the civil war in the 1990s, and the current Taliban insurgency will show that no faction ever advocated secession from Afghanistan, even as a threat. Despite the active war between these factions, which led to many atrocities, no political group seemed to believe that breaking up a unitary Afghanistan would be beneficial to its cause. The narrow focus on the dangers of ethnic division as a recipe for state collapse became a kind of policy and academic "MacGuffin," a thesis that seemed of obvious and critical importance initially but one that proved less and less relevant when examined in the Afghan cultural context. In an era when many nation-states are being challenged by ethnic conflict and the fragmentation of previously unified multiethnic political communities, and others are undermined by transnational patterns of migration and wars, Afghanistan—despite its civil war, its political fragmentation in post-Soviet invasion, and a complete breakdown of the state system during the 1990s—never witnessed any separatist movement nor any secessionist tendencies. On the contrary, separatist tendencies were strongly rejected by all political and ethnic groups.

In fact, all Afghan factions in the 1990s sought to avoid the label of rebels, regional militias, or ethnically based movements. Each claimed to be a legitimate state (*dawlat*) that had the capacity to represent all ethnic groups and regions in the country and vehemently opposed any notion of ethnic exclusivity. It was always their enemies or political rivals who would label them otherwise. The United Front painted the Taliban as an exclusively Pakhtoon movement, while the Taliban denigrated their United Front rivals as a cabal of Tajik, Uzbek, or Hazara warlords. Each group's effort to claim a more plural constituency stood in stark contrast to an ethnonationalism that would consciously invoke a shared group history, language, and tradition to exclude non-members and unite its own. Such ethnonationalist movements saw the single ethnic polities as a necessity because otherwise they would not have a state to rule. While factions in Afghanistan during the 1990s derived their core supporters from one or another ethnic group, to define themselves that narrowly would undermine their claims as legitimate caretakers of the state.

The power of the state to define the nation remained limited and always in dialogue with the society as represented by elites, intellectuals, and ordinary Afghans. The historical conditions that characterised the development of the state and a sense of nation-ness in Afghanistan were in many ways unlike the ones Benedict Anderson described in his *Imagined Communities*. In particular, Afghan history unfolded under conditions in which state institutions served only sometimes as the key authors of the national narrative. Often, especially in recent history, they were either nonexistent or too weak to promote national ideas and values. And yet, despite competing ideologies, foreign infiltration, the destruction of infrastructure, the migration of millions of people, and the total absence of strong state institutions, ideas about the nation proved remarkably stable as Afghans continued to imagine themselves as a people located in a territorially and culturally determinate space.

The opening of Afghanistan to the world, the effects of international intrusions, and the return of millions of Afghan refugees not only gave people a renewed sense of national attachment to the country, but also gave them an opportunity to redefine "Afghan" more inclusively. This was reflected in the 2004 constitution where, besides naming Pashto and Persian Dari as the country's official languages, many other languages (Uzbeki, Turkmeni, and Baluchi, among others) were also recognised, meaning that education could be conducted in them in their native regions. Fourteen specific ethnic groups were also listed, and Sunni and Shia legal systems were both given equal status for use in their respective communities.

Less appreciated in the wrangling over the installation of the new government was the definitive end it represented to a quarter century of rule by ideological states in Afghanistan. The communist PDPA and the Islamist *Mujahideen* and their Taliban successors were all advocates of radical (if diametrically opposed) ideologies that they believed needed to be imposed on the Afghan people, by force if necessary. The new government had no overarching ideology that it sought to implement. However, while the post-2001 government did reflect many new aspects of unity and did not seek to impose a unitary ideology on a diverse country, there was a new political division between Afghans who had lived through the wars in the country or been refugees in Pakistan and Iran, and what many saw as a new ruling elite who had returned from the West after 2001. Because of their education, language skills, and familiarity with Western institutions, these people became the main partners of the international community in post-Taliban Afghanistan. Many were members of the old Kabuli elite, a predominantly Persianized group of elite Pakhtoons, or came from professional classes who settled in the West after the Soviet invasion. Some of them returned to Afghanistan after the fall of the Taliban regime to either reclaim their property, or join the newly formed government. Until the fall of Kabul to the Taliban in August 2021, they held the majority of key government positions and remained the most dominant group in the Afghan government.

As a matter of fact, the influence of these returnees from the West had been critical even before the new government came to power in Kabul. Themselves proponents of the ethnic "MacGuffin", it was this returning elite that convinced the international community, with support from Pakistan, that only a Pakhtoon could lead Afghanistan, and that the non-Pakhtoons who made up the United Front were too heavily represented in the government and had to be sidelined where possible.[12] For example, at the Bonn Conference in December 2001, the various Afghan political groups and parties had initially selected Abdul Satar Sirat, an Uzbek and close confidant of the former king Zahir Shah, as interim President. However, this Afghan selection was rejected by the international community, including its UN organiser Lakhdar Brahimi, on the grounds that the country had to be Pakhtoon-ruled. Thus, and instead of Satar, they pressed the Afghan delegation teams to install Hamid Karzai, who was not only a Pakhtoon but a Durrani Pakhtoon.

Despite efforts by top Afghan former government political figures to ethnicize politics, or the Taliban imposition of radical *Jihadist* interpretation of Islam, has not shaken the customary view of national attachment that takes pride in Afghanistan's long history as a unitary state. The Afghan example of national imagination makes clear that the sense of nation-ness does not necessarily proceed in a linear way, nor along a steady evolution based on previous conceptions of belonging or ideological policies. Instead, understandings of the nation find expression as they overlap with other solidarities. They are generated not only through state-led nation-building, but also through cultural practices and social and religious interactions that exist beyond the grip of government. Ultimately, differences and conflicts about specifically imagined worlds are addressed, discussed, and disputed, through the combined work of state initiatives and cultural practices defined by their practitioners, elite and ordinary alike.

NOTES

1. Astri Suhrke. "Statebuilding in Afghanistan: a contradictory engagement." *Central Asian Survey,* vol. 32, no. 3 (2013), pp. 271-286. Shahrani, Nazif M. "War, Factionalism, and the State in Afghanistan." *American Anthropologist,* vol. 104, no. 3 (2002), pp. 715-722.
   Barnett R. Rubin. *The fragmentation of Afghanistan: State formation and collapse in the international system*. Yale University Press, 2002. Mukhopadhyay, Dipali. *Warlords, strongman governors, and the state in Afghanistan*. Cambridge University Press, 2014. Maley, William. "Political Legitimation in Contemporary Afghanistan." *Asian Survey,* vol. 27, no. 6 (1987), pp. 705-725.
   Thomas Barfield. *Afghanistan: A Cultural and Political History* (Princeton University Press, 2010), Hasan Kawun Kakar. *Government and Society in Afghanistan: The Reign of Amir 'Abd al-Rahman Khan*. Vol. 5 (University of Texas Press, 2011). Nawid, Senzil K. "Tarzi and the Emergence of Afghan Nationalism: Formation of a Nationalist Ideology." *Boston University* (2009).
2. The Persian model had a *shahanshah* or "king of kings," but one who recognised the subsidiary solidarity despite the absolute rule of the shah. It allowed a top-down system to exert absolute sovereignty yet provide autonomy to the provinces where local elites could rule in their name as governors or even subsidiary kings (Barfield, *Afghanistan a Cultural and Political History, 74*).
3. Notable exceptions are the Ghurid Dynasty of Afghanistan and North India 1148-1215 and the Kartids of Herat 1219-1389 AD.)
4. Thomas Barfield. op. cit., pp. 67–77.
5. Jonathan L Lee. *Afghanistan: A History from 1260 to the Present* (Reaktion Books, 2018), pp. 198-204.
6. Hasan Kawun Kakar. op. cit., p. 42.
7. Hasan Kawun Kakar. op. cit., p. 45.
8. Thomas Barfield. op. cit., p. 160.
9. Glatzer, "Is Afghanistan on the brink of ethnic and tribal disintegration?"; see also Wilder and Lister, "State-building at the Subnational Level in Afghanistan: A Missed Opportunity; Rashid, *Descent into Chaos*.
10. Gopa and Strick van Linschoten, "Ideology in the Afghan Taliban."
11. M. Dols. "Traditional Practices in Afghan Marriage, Responding to Women's Health Needs." (2010).
12. Philip H. Gordon. "NATO after 11 September." *Survival,* vol. 43, no. 4 (2001), pp. 89-106.

REFERENCES

Abdul Hai Habibi. *Afghanistan during the Mughal Empire* (Kabul: Government Publishing House, 1963).

____. *Brief History of Afghanistan* (Kabul: Government Publishing House, 1968).

Ahmed Rashid. *Descent into Chaos: The US and the Failure of Nation Building in Pakistan, Afghanistan, and Central Asia* (Penguin, 2008).

Amin Saikal, A.G. Ravan Farhadi and Kirill Nourzhanov. *Modern Afghanistan: A History of Struggle and Survival* (London: I.B. Tauris, 2012).

Anand Gopal and Alex Strick van Linschoten. "Ideology in the Afghan Taliban," Kabul: Afghanistan Analysts Network, 2017. https://www.ecoi.net/en/file/local/1403761/1226_1499755260 _201705-agopal-asvlinschoten-tb-ideology.pdf

Anand Gopal. "Rents, Patronage, and Defection: State-building and Insurgency in Afghanistan" (PhD diss., Columbia University, 2016).

Andrew Wilder and Sarah Lister. "State-building at the Subnational Level in Afghanistan: A Missed Opportunity," *Building State and Security in Afghanistan* (Princeton: LISD & WWS, Princeton University, 2007), pp. 84-102.

Antonio Giustozzi. *War, Politics and Society in Afghanistan, 1978-1992* (Washington, DC: Georgetown University Press, 2000).

Ashraf Ghani and Clare Lockhart. *Fixing Failed States: A Framework for Rebuilding a Fractured World* (Oxford: Oxford University Press, 2009).

Benedict Anderson. *Imagined Communities: Reflections on the Origin and Spread of Nationalism* (London: Verso, 1991).

Brian Glyn Williams. *The Last Warlord: The Life and Legend of Dostum, The Afghan Warrior Who led US Special Forces to Topple The Taliban Regime* (Noida: Harper Collins, 2017).

Constitution of Afghanistan 1987 (Kabul: Government Publishing House, 1987), https://www.refworld.org/cgi-bin/texis/vtx/rwmain/opendocpdf.pdf?reldoc= y&docid=54783a5f4

Constitution of the Preeminent Government of Afghanistan, 1923 [*Niẓāmnāmah-ī asāsī-ī dawlat-i ʿillīyah-ī Afghānistān*],], https://www.wdl.org/en/item/15007/, https://www.constitution.org/cons/afghan/const1923.htm

Dipali Mukhopadhyay. *Warlords, Strongman Governors, and the State in Afghanistan* (Cambridge: Cambridge University Press, 2014).

Ernest Gellner and John Breuilly. *Nations and nationalism*, Vol. 1 (Ithaca, NY: Cornell University Press, 1983).

Faiz Muhammad Katib. *Siraj ul Tawarikh*, 3 vols. (Kabul: 1913-1915).

Fredrik Barth. *Ethnic Groups and Boundaries: The Social Organization of Culture Difference* (Illinois, Waveland Press, 1998).

G. Whitney Azoy. *Buzkashi: Game and Power in Afghanistan* [3rd edition] (Long Grove, IL: Waveland Press, 2012).

Hannah Arendt. *Between Past and Future* (New York: Penguin Books, 1993 [1954]).

Hassan Kawun Kakar. *Government and Society in Afghanistan: The Reign of Amir 'Abd Al-Rahman Khan* (Austin: University of Texas Press, 2011).

Joel S. Migdal. *State Power and Social Forces: Domination and Transformation in the Third World* (Cambridge: Cambridge University Press, 1994).

M. Nazif Shahrani. "Local Knowledge of Islam and Social Discourse in Afghanistan and Turkistan in the Modern Period." *Turko-Persia in Historical Perspective* (1991), p. 88.

____. "War, Factionalism, and the State in Afghanistan," *American Anthropologist*, vol. 104, no. 3 (2002), pp. 715–722.

Mohammad Seddique Farhang. *Afghanistan dar Panj Qarn-e-Akhir*. [Afghanistan in the last five centuries.] (Kabul, 1992).

Nancy Hopkins. *Afghanistan in 2012: A Survey of the Afghan People* (Kabul: Asia Foundation, 2012).

Nile Green. "From Persianate Pasts to Aryan Antiquity: Transnationalism and Transformation in Afghan Intellectual History, c. 1880–1940," *Afghanistan* vol. 1, no. 1 (2018), pp. 26–67.

Noah Coburn. *Bazaar Politics: Power and Pottery in an Afghan Market Town* (Stanford: Stanford University Press, 2011).

People's Democratic Party of Afghanistan. "Manifesto of the People's Democratic Party of Afghanistan," Kabul, 2006, http://www.payamewatan.com/hezbe_watan_nazaryat_ didgahha/menifesto _watan_party.htm. Accessed 2018.

Robert L. Canfield. *Faction and Conversion in a Plural Society: Religious Alignments in the Hindu Kush* (Ann Arbor Mich: University of Michigan, 1973).

Sayed Askar Mousavi. *The Hazaras of Afghanistan: An Historical, Cultural, Economic and Political Study* (New York: St. Martin's Press, 1997).

Senzil Nawid. "Language Policy in Afghanistan: Linguistic Diversity and National Unity." In *Language Policy and Language Conflict in Afghanistan and its Neighbors: The Changing Politics of Language Choice* (Leiden: Brill, 2012), pp. 31-52.

___. "Tarzi and the Emergence of Afghan Nationalism: Formation of a Nationalist Ideology," 2009, http://www.bu.edu/aias/nawid_article.pdf

Talal Asad. *Formations of the Secular: Christianity, Islam, Modernity* (Stanford: Stanford University Press, 2003).

Thomas J. Barfield. "Afghanistan's Ethnic Puzzle: Decentralizing Power Before the U.S. Withdrawal." *Foreign Affairs*, vol. 90, no. 5 (2011), pp. 54–65.

____. *Afghanistan: A Cultural and Political History* (Princeton: Princeton University Press, 2012).

V.V. Barthold. *Turkestan down to the Mongol Invasion* (London: Bibb Memorial Trust, 1977).

William A. Byrd. *Understanding Afghanistan 2014 Presidential Elections*. Report no. 370. (United States Institute of Peace, 2015).

____. *Understanding Afghanistan's 2014 Presidential Election: The Limits to Democracy in a Limited Access Order* (US Institute of Peace, 2015).

William Maley. "Is Afghanistan on the brink of ethnic and tribal disintegration?" In *Fundamentalism Reborn? Afghanistan and the Taliban* (New York: New York University Press, 2001), pp. 167-81.

Wolfgang F. Danspeckgruber, Robert P. Finn, and Woodrow Wilson School of Public International Affairs. *Building State and Security in Afghanistan* (Princeton, N.J.: Woodrow Wilson School of Public and International Affairs, Princeton University, 2007).

4

America's World after Afghanistan Withdrawal

Harsh V Pant and Saaransh Mishra

The departure of American soldier Major General Christopher T. Donahue on 31 August 2021 from Afghanistan marked the end of the longest and most expensive war in American history, spanning 20 years and costing over $2 trillion. The Taliban celebrated this moment as their official victory by firing guns in the air at Kabul airport. But, in reality, the signs of this inevitable victory had been glaring throughout as the militants continued flouting their end of the promise under the Peace Deal, and kept launching offensives and capturing territories across the country in recent months, which ultimately culminated in the fall of Kabul, something that President Joe Biden rather confidently assured would not happen for months after he announced the complete withdrawal of the 2,500 American troops remaining in Afghanistan.

In his Presidential announcement on 14 April 2021, Biden announced that the withdrawal would begin on May 1 and complete by September 11, the 20th anniversary of the most horrific terrorist attacks on American soil. He stated that after extensive consultations with various stakeholders and experts, it was evident that America's reasons for staying in Afghanistan had increasingly become unclear because it had achieved both of its primary objectives; to disrupt the *al-Qaeda* and capture the mastermind, Osama bin Laden. Hence, it was time for American troops to go home and resultantly, for the first time in 20 years, there would be no American troops on ground.

While the primary determinant behind America's war in Afghanistan was undoubtedly the presence of the *al-Qaeda* being harboured by the Taliban, the sudden manner in which this withdrawal came about despite no dearth of warning signs right from the signing of the Doha Agreement until the withdrawal; merits and has drawn tremendous criticism from all quarters. Under the agreement, the Taliban had an obligation to end their linkages with terrorism, take part in a negotiated settlement that would lead to a ceasefire among warring factions and reach an agreement over an inclusive future political roadmap for Afghanistan.

However, the Taliban blatantly failed to keep their end of the promise. It not only failed to reduce violence and move towards a comprehensive ceasefire, but also rather escalated violence to a great extent, carrying out targeted killings and bombings against Afghan government officials, human rights activists, journalists, and civilians across the country. Reportedly, 11 journalists and media workers were killed in Afghanistan in 2020, making it one of the most dangerous places for journalists and human rights defenders in the world. The United Nations Assistance Mission in Afghanistan's (UNAMA) Protection of Civilians in Armed Conflict Midyear Update 2021 also documented 5,183 casualties by July (1,659 killed and 3,524 injured), a 47 per cent increase compared with the same period in 2020. The Taliban also disrupted the peace negotiations mandated under the Doha agreement by boycotting the Istanbul Conference that was to be held between April 24 and May 4 to facilitate a just and durable political settlement in Afghanistan.

To compound concerns, the United Nations has warned that the *al-Qaeda* continues to remain in at least 15 provinces within Afghanistan, and warned of an expanding Islamic State presence within the country as well. In October 2020, Edmund Fritton-Brown, coordinator of the UN's Islamic State, *al-Qaeda* and Taliban monitoring team, had also warned that the relationship between the *al-Qaeda* and the Taliban had not substantively changed because of the Doha agreement, that the Taliban were talking regularly at a high-level with the *al-Qaeda* and assuring them that they would honour historic ties, a notion further validated by the *al-Qaeda*'s congratulatory message for the Taliban post the takeover of Kabul. Moreover, opposed to the disregard that they had shown for a military settlement earlier, the Taliban kept launching sweeping offensives across the country and capturing territories militarily. By the first week of July, the Taliban admittedly already controlled 85 per cent of Afghanistan.

In spite of clear warning signs indicating the militant outfit's malicious intentions, President Biden expressed no hesitation in moving forward with the withdrawal as he seemed to display unflinching faith in the 300,000 strong Afghan National Defence and Security Forces' (ANDSF) ability to shield the country from a Taliban takeover after years of extensive training and capacity-building by US and NATO forces. He conveniently ignored the well-known problems of desertion, incompetence, corruption, lack of motivation, etc., that the defence forces were plagued with. Biden also crucially assured that this was the end of America's military mission in the country but diplomatically the USA would not abandon Afghanistan, which holds heightened importance for the war-ravaged country heavily dependent on foreign aid.

Yet, unlike what the President had naively anticipated, the situation on the ground deteriorated at an unprecedentedly rapid scale. Disproving Western intelligence that said that it would take the Taliban at least a few months to take over, it took them less than 30 hours to reach the gates of the Presidential Palace in Kabul as the Afghan Defence Forces seemed relatively helpless, incompetent, and at times, surrendered even without a fight. Contrary to Biden's previous statements, one of the first things that America had to do was to close down its embassy in Kabul and frantically evacuate its entire diplomatic staff, essentially putting a temporary halt to

America's diplomatic engagement in Afghanistan, jeopardizing the lives of aid-dependent Afghan civilians. The USA also had to evacuate many American civilians who were stranded in Afghanistan but it is reported that there are still a few hundred Americans left in the country. Moreover, the USA also has a responsibility towards the thousands of former on-ground allies who helped the Americans carry on this 20-year war. Their lives remain at risk from the Taliban and the failure to protect them would impact the USA's diminishing reputation considerably more. Additional challenges in the form of preserving the social, economic and political gains of the last 20 years, especially the substantial progress regarding women's rights to educational and other freedoms, also loom large, but the current realities unfolding on the ground have made the bleak prospects of this preservation abundantly clear.

Despite promises of a moderate regime, the Taliban have shown their true colours by announcing regressive rules that segregate women and men from studying together in universities, ban women from taking part in sports, stop them from working until a system has been put in place for their safety, etc. The United Nations has also started to receive "harrowing and credible reports" of human rights abuses by the Taliban that include summary execution of civilians and combatants of the Afghan National Security Forces, arrests and brutal beating up of journalists by the Taliban for covering protests in Kabul. Forgetting their earlier promises of inclusion, the newly-formed Taliban interim government contains no women, minorities, or opposition members. The government is made up of hardliners and clerics who have pledged to implement a strict Islamic rule over the country, which would inevitably curtail women's rights to a concerning extent. Interestingly, Sirajuddin Haqqani, a designated global terrorist on the FBI's most wanted list, with known links to the *al-Qaeda*, has been appointed the Interior Minister, while at least 14 members of this Cabinet are on the UN Security Council's terrorism blacklist.

After having advocated for democracy and human rights for the last 20 years, all of these remain threatened in Afghanistan due to the

USA's sudden withdrawal in the face of alarming indications of what was to come. Under the Taliban's vision of an Islamic theocracy, with infamously radical personalities at the helm of affairs, democracy does not stand a chance and neither do rights for women and minorities, as is already evident. But to be sure, Biden was merely the President who pulled the plug on America's involvement in Afghanistan. There was consensus among the previous two presidents, Obama and Trump, to end this prolonged and expensive war.

Domestic Debates on Afghanistan through different US Presidencies

In the aftermath of 9/11, by the day's end President George W. Bush had already instructed his Secretary of Defence, Donald Rumsfeld, to develop a plan to attack the *al-Qaeda* forces in Afghanistan. Within a month of that, the President launched Operation Enduring Freedom, as a part of America's Global War on Terrorism. Bush's objectives in this operation were to topple the Taliban regime and to incapacitate the *al-Qaeda*.

Perhaps due to the indelible imprint and fear that the dastardly 9/11 attacks had left on the Americans, at that time there was an overwhelming domestic sentiment in favour of using military means abroad. A Pew Research Centre poll conducted a year after 9/11 found that more than 6 out of 10 Americans were worried about a new attack; 4 in 10 expected the terrorists to use chemical or biological weapons and more than half of the Americans believed that the perpetrators of the next attack were already inside the United States. Not surprisingly, Americans agreed, by a margin of 48 to 29 per cent, that enhancing military presence abroad rather than mitigating it was a more effective measure to combat terrorism. The decision to go to Afghanistan also enjoyed universal support among the political circles; legal authorisation to use military force in the country was approved by a whopping 98 to 0 in the Senate and 420 to 1 in the House.

Initially, the Afghan mission under Bush went extraordinarily well. The US was able to dislodge the Taliban regime from power and compel the *al-Qaeda* and Bin Laden to leave Afghanistan and flee to

Pakistan within a few months. The Bush Administration had hoped that after their mission was accomplished, they could safely hand power back to the Afghans but soon realised that unless they propped up an Afghan government with democratic ideals, they would simply be handing the country back to the Taliban. This resulted in the administration pivoting towards nation building and introduction of a Western-style democracy in the country.

This is where public support for the Afghan war started waning. Around 2002, at the height of the war, Gallup found that 93 per cent of Americans were willing to say that getting militarily involved in Afghanistan was not a mistake. But post the commencement of nation-building in Afghanistan, public support for the war initially fell to 70 per cent and then consequently to 60 per cent. This lack of support kept dwindling further over the years and could not be salvaged by the killing of Osama bin Laden (the mastermind behind the 9/11 attacks) or the irresponsible handling of the withdrawal by the Biden Administration that has plunged Afghanistan into chaos of gigantic proportions. Even though an overwhelming sentiment across all polls is that the withdrawal was handled rather badly, with roughly 44 per cent of the Americans saying that it went very badly and 30 per cent saying that it had gone somewhat badly, the latest survey by AP-NORC shows that 6 in 10 Americans think fighting in Afghanistan was not worth it and it was right for the troops to return home; a recent CBS News/YouGov Survey indicated that 63 per cent of Americans approved of the removal of US troops, while an NBC poll taken between August 14 and 17 showed that 61 per cent of Americans think that the war in Afghanistan was not worth it as well.

Policy decisions in democracies are more often than not largely impacted by public opinion. But, Afghanistan was different. Notwithstanding the growing sentiment against America's presence in Afghanistan over the years, the war got stretched over four presidencies, despite the last three presidents very clearly stating that they wanted to get out. But if leaving Afghanistan were easy, it would have been done a long time ago. It might be tough to precisely point out exactly why America kept fighting a war it did not want to fight.

Experts believe that the leaders realised all the options that America had for leaving would ultimately create an unstable Afghanistan, where no one could predict what was going to happen next and how it could make America less safe.

When President Bush left office in 2009, there were about 25,000 troops in Afghanistan. Following Bush's tenure, Obama reflected a larger scepticism of the war on terror in general and one of his most prominent campaign promises was to end the war in Afghanistan and Iraq. He did end the war in Iraq, but a resurgent Taliban around 2009 in Afghanistan forced him to preside over the largest troop presence in the country, touching 100,000 at one point in 2010. Obama's strategy was to ramp up forces in Afghanistan which would create conditions for the United States to transfer responsibility to the Afghans. One of the Obama Administration's most considerable victories during this period was the killing of Osama bin Laden, following which the President announced a troop withdrawal that intended to bring all American forces back home by 2014. Even though the troop levels started declining slowly and on 31 December 2014, Obama announced the end of major combat operations in Afghanistan, a year later, with his tenure nearing an end, he was compelled to leave 10,000 troops in Afghanistan, self admittedly to tackle the fragile security situation in the country that had made full withdrawal unfeasible.

Akin to Obama, his successor, Donald Trump, made the withdrawal of troops one of the centrepieces of his Presidential campaign. His views on Afghanistan had been well known over the years through his critical tweets on the US presence there. However, expectedly, it turned out to be tough for him to act on his rhetoric due to the Taliban's continued surge as well as the emergence of an Islamic State Affiliate in the country. In a 2017 speech outlining American strategy to resolve the then 16-year-old conflict in Afghanistan, Trump admitted that his original instinct was to pull out of the country but an exhaustive deliberation with his war cabinet had convinced him that a hasty withdrawal would create a vacuum for terrorists, including the *al-Qaeda* and ISIS. In the same speech, he criticized his predecessor's strategy of setting artificial timetables for ending American involvement in Afghanistan, and starkly contrasted this with his own strategy that he said would be comprehensive, condition-based, aiming for a political solution.

In pursuit of this political solution, the Trump Administration entered into full-fledged talks with the Taliban over 18 months and nine rounds, which led to the fruition of the February 2020 Doha agreement. Through this deal, he essentially did exactly what he criticized Obama for; set a timeline for the withdrawal of all US troops within 14 months of signing. In exchange, the Taliban had to basically sign a pledge stating that it would not harbour, recruit, train or raise funds for terrorist outfits that could pose a threat to America or its allies but nowhere in the deal did they have to denounce the *al-Qaeda*. Moreover, a gaping flaw in the deal was that there was no concrete enforcement mechanism in the deal for the Taliban to keep its word.

This deal, which has been termed a 'surrender agreement with the Taliban', H.R. McMaster (Trump's second National Security Adviser), has been largely blamed for the cataclysmic predicament of Afghanistan by current President Joe Biden. Biden has repeatedly said that the deal struck by his predecessor left him with two options; either to bring the troops back within the stipulated deadline under the agreement or to send in more American troops to deal with the wrath of the Taliban that would inevitably lead to escalation of the conflict.

Nevertheless, Biden's vocal scepticism regarding sending more troops into Afghanistan from his stint as Vice President under Obama would make it safe to assume his overwhelming proclivity towards the withdrawal even before he assumed the Presidency. Biden, the "in-house pessimist" on Afghanistan during the Obama Administration, had always argued the case for an overt counterterrorism approach to Afghanistan that sought ways to minimise involvement in the country by targeted killings of the Taliban and *al-Qaeda* leaders instead of relying on nation-building as a prelude to reduction in violence. He repeatedly clashed with Obama's Defence Secretary; Robert Gates, over the latter's preference for a 'surge' in troops in the country. While the current decision to go ahead with the 2020 Peace Deal-mandated complete withdrawal is different from his previous preference for limited involvement solely focused on counterterrorism, Biden's frustrations with the exorbitant war in Afghanistan are well-documented.

Reasons Behind Demand for Withdrawal

Initially, America ventured into Afghanistan to do away with the al-Qaeda that was being provided a safe haven by the Taliban regime. Notably, when the Taliban was pushed out of power and forced back to Kandahar, which was their last remaining stronghold in the country, it had offered to surrender under certain conditions, such as amnesty to its top members; the US did not quite accept it.

The Bush Administration's assessment was that simply leaving Afghanistan would be a recipe for disaster with a very strong probability of a Taliban revival, which ultimately resulted in a prolonged engagement ordeal in the country. Encouraged by experts, the US framed this problem as: Afghanistan lacked state institutions, a functioning security force, courts and knowledgeable bureaucrats, so the solution was to pour in resources and expertise in order to build a functioning state with all of these elements.

As the counter-terrorism mission morphed into nation-building, trying to create a democratic, cohesive and united Afghanistan with billions of dollars from American taxpayers' money and thousands of American and Afghan lives, the US seemingly forgot that this was something that had never happened in the aptly christened 'graveyard of empires'. Undoubtedly, a government was propped up in the country, but one that was filled with corruption, and lacked internal cohesion, incompetence among other issues, and could not prevent instability in the country which compelled the US to not only remain there but also keep pooling in a stratospheric sum of resources over the years that amounted to trillions of dollars. America's inability to attain results in the country despite the loss of American monetary resources and lives fanned the souring public sentiment among the general public and political circles as indicated by various surveys throughout the course of the war, became one of the primary reasons behind the demands for withdrawal only after a few years since the war had begun. This sentiment persisted until the actual withdrawal in 2021. Moreover, from Obama to Biden, every leader who presided over Afghanistan had an unfavourable opinion on nation-building in the country, which would appear to have strengthened these demands for withdrawal in general.

While President Obama did not completely disregard nation-building by cryptically calling on Americans to "heed Marshall's lesson" in 2008, which can roughly be translated as displaying willingness to reconstruct an Afghanistan in ruins by the end of his first tenure in 2012, he said that it was time to 'focus on nation-building at home', indicating frustration. Trump, in his televised Afghanistan strategy in 2017 clearly stated that America was not "nation-building again" and would rather focus on killing terrorists. Even Biden in his April 2021 address announcing the withdrawal, said that America did not go to Afghanistan to nation-build (something that he indicated as an unattainable goal) and that it is the right and responsibility of the Afghan people alone to decide their future and how they want to run their country.

Joe Biden, in his speech outlining the reasons defending his withdrawal decision, notably mentioned that terrorist threats had now expanded well beyond Afghanistan and existed in Africa, Europe, the Middle-East and elsewhere. Trying to strengthen the notion that America was going to keep a close eye on terrorist threats that might emanate from Afghanistan in the future, Biden added that as the Americans run counter-terrorism missions in all these terror-infested countries without a permanent military presence consuming billions of dollars, would do the same in Afghanistan as well. He reassured that the US had developed counter-terrorism over-the-horizon capabilities that would enable them to keep their eyes firmly fixed on the direct threats to the United States in the region and act quickly and defensively if needed.

However, an interesting explanation that the President provided was to do with power contestation to meet new challenges in the 21st century that required America to shore up its competitiveness so that it could do both; fight terrorism and take on new threats that are here now and will continue to be here in the future. With this, he seemed to be taking a clear dig at China and Russia who, he said, would want nothing more than the USA getting bogged down for another decade in Afghanistan. In fact, the U.S. National Security Strategy declares Russia and China as the two top threats to U.S. National Security.

Power Contestation with China and Russia

It is indisputable that the United States has been embroiled in a power competition with China for a while now. From the Obama Administration that adopted a multilateral approach to blunt China's moves towards becoming the dominant power within the Asia-Pacific, to the Trump Administration that entirely refocused US strategy towards competition and confrontation with China, the US arguably considers China as one of its primary concerns.

In the last few years, the US has clashed with China on various sensitive issues ranging from technology, human rights, diplomacy, trade, etc. These included Taiwan and Tibet, repression of Uighur Muslims in Xinjiang, suppression of democratic protests in Hong Kong by China, accusations by successive US administrations of Chinese firms stealing American technology, Chinese aggression in the South China Sea, accusations of China exploiting its trade relationship with the US by selling much more than buying which also resulted in punitive tariffs on Chinese goods and most recently regarding the origins of the deadly Corona virus in China, among other issues. The gravity of the friction between the two countries can be aptly gauged from the fact that despite Trump's well-known foreign policy preference to move away from multilateral institutions and alliances, his Administration advanced a strategy for a free and open Indo-Pacific, leading to the resurgence of the QUAD, an alliance comprising Japan, Australia, India and the US, which is widely perceived as a mechanism to counter a rising China.

To exacerbate concerns, the United States' relationship with Russia is also arguably the worst that has been in a few decades. Russia has been accused of interfering with the US presidential elections of 2016, combined with its supposed efforts to affect the 2020 elections as well and this has made Russia an important domestic issue within the US. The US has also collided with Russia on the annexation of Crimea, its support for Syrian President Bashar-al-Assad in perpetuating a gory civil war and also for Venezuelan President Nicolas Maduro who was de-recognised as the President of the country by the Trump Administration. While it is believed that Donald Trump came into office determined to improve ties with Russia, the rest of the US executive branch and the Congress have pursued punitive policies against Russia by imposing sanctions on individuals close to Russian President Putin and by impeding Russia's ability to access financial markets, hitting the Russian economy badly. Since 2014, the Russian economy has grown at an average of 0.3 per cent per year, while the global average was 2.3 per cent.

Individually, Russia and China continue to be strategically challenging the US and the two countries have also increasingly gravitated towards each other in the light of their slumping ties with the West. Turning towards China was a natural option for the economically-floundering Russia considering that the former is the world's second largest economy. China seems to have embraced its warming relations with Russia too, as its relations with the USA have been deteriorating in every aspect possible. Expectedly, economic cooperation has been at the centre of this relationship with bilateral trade crossing $100 billion in 2018, with a pre-set goal to double it by 2024. China and Russia have also deepened energy cooperation, including a $400 billion deal to transport natural gas from Russia and multiple joint nuclear power plant projects in China. Diplomatically, the two countries have also sided with each other in multilateral fora such as the United Nations Security Council on contentious issues such as the Syrian Civil War and in vehemently rejecting Western criticism over human rights violations. Ideologically, the two countries are also united on their preference for a multi-polar world order, unlike what their current assessment is, which is an overwhelming domination by the United States.

Essentially, it is undeniable that Russia and China currently are and can be expected to continue being a menace to the US and its allies in the foreseeable future. However, considering the substantial costs of this withdrawal in terms of human rights and quality of lives of Afghan women, minorities and civilians, the herculean security threats anticipated to rise due to extremism across the whole region of South Asia, Central Asia and possibly to the US, and the loss of US credibility amongst its allies, it must be examined how practically beneficial this withdrawal could be for the US in terms of countering China and also Russia.

As could be construed from Biden's speech, one of the strategic rationales behind withdrawal from Afghanistan is to re-focus US assets, systems, brainpower, and other US National Security resources deployed in Afghanistan elsewhere, in this case on impeding the rise of China primarily. It would appear from Biden's rhetoric that Afghanistan was acting as a distraction to the same. An unending pool of resources have undoubtedly been dedicated to Afghanistan in the last 20 years; however, a closer look would suggest that the current US presence in Afghanistan was not draining the force structure, nor was it hurting recruitment and retention—the US military has not suffered a single casualty in Afghanistan in the last year and a half and reportedly had less than 100 deaths in the last eight years. This is not to say that these lives do not matter, but given the scale of the war and the deep involvement of American forces in a highly insecure and unstable country like Afghanistan, these many casualties would proportionately seem relatively less alarming.

In the last few years, the US had arguably shifted its focus more towards the Indo-Pacific region and Afghanistan has stayed as a peripheral element of American foreign policy. But, it would be naïve to believe that every single strategic asset deployed currently in Afghanistan required diversion towards the Indo-Pacific to quell China. This is especially relevant considering that other influential and resourceful countries such as India, Japan, Australia and France, among others, share similar concerns about China's domineering demeanour in the region and have displayed willingness to cooperate amongst each other, including with the United States, to disrupt the same. Therefore, maintaining a limited presence in the country that could have at least acted as a buffer against the violent takeover of Afghanistan by Islamist militants, would not have consumed American resources to a debilitating extent, with respect to China.

America's humiliating abandonment of Afghanistan has caused serious credibility issues for the US, which is being used by China to further an anti-US narrative that is centred around the untrustworthiness of the US. It has given China a chance to gloat as highlighted by Chinese Foreign Ministry spokesperson Hua Chinying who attacked the US by stating that "The role of the US lies in destruction, not construction." She spewed more vitriol at the US by also saying phrases like "American myth down" and "more and more people are awakening".

While this critical rhetoric is unsurprising, given China is the USA's prime adversary, certain developments definitively point towards the loss of credibility that America has suffered among its allies post the Afghan debacle, especially among its British and European ones. When America's European allies pushed Biden to extend the 31 August deadline at a virtual G7 summit so that they could get more time to evacuate all their citizens, he disagreed stating that the risk of terror attacks was too large. But even before the deadline, various European officials were questioning America's credibility. Norbert Röttgen, Chairman for the German Foreign Policy Committee, Armin Laschet, the candidate running to replace German Chancellor Angela Merkel as well as Josep Borep Fontelles, a Spanish politician serving as High Representative of the European Union on Affairs and Security Policy have questioned American credibility in different terms in the last few weeks. The European Council President, Charles Michell, called for 'European Strategic Autonomy' by urging the bloc to invest more in its security capabilities after American withdrawal, and the rhetoric to reduce dependence on the US and become relatively autonomous has gained popularity. A similar call that points towards America's waning credibility has come from Taiwan, one of the US's critical strategic allies. In a recent address,

Taiwanese President Tsai Ing-wen said, "Taiwan's only option is to make itself stronger, more united, and more determined to defend itself" in the face of escalating Chinese aggression towards the country that has historically been at odds with China.

Moreover, instead of strengthening its own position to tackle China and the budding China-Russia friendship, the withdrawal has arguably fortified China's strategic importance. The US departure from Afghanistan, which China sees somewhat as its backyard, has left a vacuum that China seems to be eager to fill, not in terms of intervening militarily, but utilising it to enhance its influence in the whole region. At least, China's actions would suggest so.

To begin with, right after Trump said that the US would withdraw, China extended its Belt and Road Initiative to Afghanistan. Both China and Russia had regularly been engaging in talks with the Taliban and after the takeover, the Taliban have said that they hope to develop good relations with China and would never allow any forces to use Afghanistan's territory to harm China. At the 2021 SCO summit, Russian President Vladimir Putin said that Russia needs to work with the Taliban, while both China and Russia have also kept their embassies open in the region unlike other countries like India and the United States. In order to increase its leverage in a foreign-aid dependent country like Afghanistan, China has already provided humanitarian assistance of $31 million dollars, and has called on the international community to help Afghanistan at the SCO summit, making it an important actor for the Taliban as they look for economic assistance to run the dilapidated Afghan economy. China's efforts at forging strong relations with the Taliban primarily stems from their apprehensions about any instability in the country spilling over to China, especially to the Xinjiang region. Similarly, Russia is concerned about spillage of extremism and drugs towards Russia. But it is not just these two countries that are concerned about the security situation in the region. Countries around Afghanistan, namely, Central Asian Republics, Pakistan, India and Iran continue to be concerned about the same as well. Therefore, China's increasing influence with the Taliban and within Afghanistan could amplify its strategic importance to all the countries in the region.

Implications for India

As the United States withdrew from Afghanistan, experts have displayed mixed responses regarding the implications of this for India. While some believe that the chaotic withdrawal of the US is a clear sign of unreliability, others believe that this may "accelerate current trends in India's relationship with the United States", in terms of dealing together with China. Even though the Indian foreign minister insists that the United States is still the "premier power" that retains a very unique sort of standing for India, the US has undoubtedly acted in a manner that has hampered Indian interests on multiple fronts.

The sudden withdrawal that has created conditions extremely conducive for instability has serious implications for India, especially on the northern frontier. India is concerned about exacerbated security threats in the state of Jammu & Kashmir, perpetrated by militant outfits such as Lashkar-e-Taiba and Jaish-e-Mohammad that ostensibly have close relations with India's regional adversary, Pakistan. Historically, India has never engaged with the Taliban and has no leverage in Afghanistan any more, despite various efforts over the years through significant humanitarian and development assistance, which puts India in a disadvantageous position to protect its interests. The departure of the US has created a power vacuum that is seemingly being filled up by one of India's fiercest rivals, China. Even though Russia still continues to have good relations with India, the former has been sidelined on most discussions pertaining to Afghanistan through forums such as the Troika and Troika plus that India is not a part of, mostly due to the presence of China and Pakistan in these forums because of their more influence in Afghanistan. The withdrawal would also affect India's long-standing goal of gaining access to Central Asia by building a port and railway line through Iran and Afghanistan.

It would also certainly affect India's standing within the QUAD and its trust of the United States. As pointed out by Ashley Tellis, the anticipated security situation intensifies India's old dilemma between continental commitment and maritime commitment. He argues that if the continental challenge is attenuated, it frees India to play in the maritime space. In effect, the US has unintentionally weakened India's ability to be of assistance in the maritime space because of the additional security threats that India will have to pay close attention to. Additionally, considering that the US in Afghanistan has acted in a manner detrimental to Indian interests in various ways, the question would arise about how much trust should India bestow on the US in dealing with the China challenge. The QUAD is fast emerging as the most important instrument for India to manage China. For many in New Delhi, Washington's credibility in the Indo-Pacific has weakened as a result of its precipitous withdrawal from Afghanistan. Yet the real game of the 21st century will be played in the Indo-Pacific and it is imperative for both the US and India to work closely together. If the unfolding events in Afghanistan once again push New Delhi to become obsessed with the 'Af-Pak' theatre, then it would be a loss not only for Indian strategic ambitions but also for American interests.

5

Afghanistan and the Changing Geopolitical Order

Ajay Singh

The Great Game

On 11 September 2001, the twin towers came crashing down. Three weeks later, the first US troops landed in Panjshir province for the start of the 'War against Terror' that would go on for twenty years, cost over $2 trillion, claim 3,500 US and allied lives and over 250,000 Afghan security forces and civilians.

Almost exactly twenty years later, the war has ended with a chaotic US withdrawal from Kabul. With the withdrawal, the USA has ended its longest war. But the war has ended with the same Taliban that the USA had set out to oust, back in power and stronger than before; with the *al-Qaeda* and other Islamist groups still finding sanctuary there; with Afghanistan returning to the Islamic Emirate of Afghanistan, and with democracy and women's rights overturned—in other words, it is back to where it all began.

In the interim period, the world has changed. The USA is no longer the undisputed superpower it was 20 years ago (though it still has the world's largest economy and military might). Its position is being increasingly challenged by China. Russia is resurgent and seeking to adopt the mantle of the erstwhile Soviet Union in Europe and elsewhere. International alliances are fraying, institutions are decaying and new power centres are emerging. For centuries, the world powers played a 'Great Game' for influence in Afghanistan. The New Great Game continues even now, and the events unfolding there will find an echo in the New World Order itself.

The Global War Against Terror

Islamic fundamentalism, the scourge that led to the fall of the twin towers in the first place, will be the major victor in the emerging order. It is pointless to think that Taliban 2.0 will be a benign version of Taliban 1.0. The packing of the Afghan cabinet with hardliners is an indicator of the direction the new government is to take. Fourteen of the 33 ministers are on the UNSC terrorism blacklist, including acting Prime Minister Mullah Mohammed Akhund and both his deputies. The Interior Minister, Sirajuddin Haqqani, is a designated global terrorist with a bounty of $10 million on his head. There is already an alphabet soup of terrorist organisations operating in Afghanistan—the ISIS-K, LeT, JeM, Lashkar-e-Jhangvi, Shura-i-Etehad Mujahidin, TTP, Islamic *Jihad* Movement and a host of others. Emboldened by this victory, they will definitely seek to replicate the Taliban model elsewhere.

When a new President of the USA takes over, leaders from across the world vie to be the first to offer congratulations. When the Taliban took over Afghanistan, leaders of terrorist organisations across the world raced to offer similar felicitations. The Taliban success will now stand as a symbol of victory over elected governments and find an echo in groups as diverse as Hamas and Hezbollah in Israel and Lebanon, al-Shabab in Somalia, *al-Qaeda* affiliates in South East Asia, Islamic Maghreb in North Africa and many others. Just as the victory of the Mujahedeen over the Soviet Union in 1989 spawned a wave of Islamic fundamentalism the world over, the defeat of another world power by a new generation of the same actors (albeit in another avatar) could signal a resurgence of Islamic fundamentalism. The 'War against Terror', which the world tried to fight for the past 20 years, has just entered a newer and deadlier phase.

The effect would be most pronounced in the immediate neighbourhood. Pakistan is gloating over its 'victory' in Afghanistan and feels that it has achieved its long-standing goal of attaining strategic depth there. In the short term, it has attained its objectives, but it is Pakistan that faces the greatest threat in the long term. In trying to shape Afghanistan in its own image, it may find itself going the Afghanistan way—of becoming the Islamic Emirate of Pakistan. Pakistan is fertile ground for the radical brand of Islam that the Taliban and its affiliates—such as the Tehrik-e-Taliban Pakistan—follow, and that could spawn a resurgence of Islamic fundamentalism there.

The influx of Afghan refugees could also create its own chaos. Over 2.4 million Afghan refugees had moved into Pakistan following the US invasion, and there is a sizeable Afghan presence in the border areas of Waziristan. They have never accepted the Durand Line (a legacy of the Great Game of Britain and Russia) and when the fiercely independent Taliban shrug off their dependence on Pakistan, perhaps the demand for Pakhtoonistan will resurface with its attendant repercussions in Waziristan and the NWFP.

India too will face the fallout. It is a *quid pro quo* that the Pakistan will expect a return favour from the Taliban in Kashmir. The Taliban have so far made the right noises about non-interference in Kashmir, but murmurs from splinter groups are already rising. An estimated seven to nine thousand fighters from the JeM and LeT have fought with the Taliban and are likely to be funnelled back into the Valley along with other foreign fighters. They could also home on to perceived minority grievances and engineer strikes in the Indian hinterland. India will be able to stave off the threat, but the sheer persistence could create an environment of fear and uncertainty, hamper our economic growth and also affect our image and stature in the region.

Should the Taliban or the many splinter groups operating in

Afghanistan decide to take up cudgels for the Islamic cause, the same spectre could resurface in the Gaza Strip and the West bank in Israel, Chechnya in Russia and Xinjiang in China, and also in the Central Asian states of Turkmenistan, Uzbekistan, and Kazakhstan which have a sizeable Muslim population. That would also cause concern for moderate Islamic states like Saudi Arabia and the UAE, who could see their position threatened by an upsurge in Islamic fundamentalism in the years to come.

The Impact of the Fall of Kabul

One of the reasons given by Joe Biden for the US withdrawal from Afghanistan was to focus on emerging threats elsewhere, i.e., China and Russia in the Indo-Pacific and Europe. But by doing so, it has created a power vacuum in the region that these very powers will try to fill. And the shift in the power structure in Afghanistan and Central Asia will reflect in the Indo-Pacific.

The chaos of the US withdrawal has left the impression of a defeated superpower. The scenes of desperate Afghans clinging to giant US aircraft and falling from the sky was reminiscent of an earlier defeat—the fall of Saigon, when people clung desperately to US helicopters as they evacuated the embassy. The bomb blasts that killed hundreds of Afghans, (including 13 US Marines, its largest single loss of life in recent times) at Kabul Airport was a parting shot that symbolised the completeness of US defeat. The manner in which Afghanistan was abandoned has painted the USA as an unreliable ally—especially when the chips are down. The USA entered into talks with the Taliban without even keeping the Afghan government in the loop and signed a deal that virtually handed Afghanistan on a platter to the Taliban in return for a few vague promises. They engineered the withdrawal without consulting their NATO allies (which also had troops on ground in Afghanistan). It will now be difficult for the USA to win over allies, even as it looks for new alliances to counter China. Their own resolve is now suspect in places like Japan, South Korea or Taiwan. That itself could embolden China to try to take over Taiwan by military force—something they have refrained for decades because of the US commitment to it. Should they succeed, the entire balance of power in the Indo-Pacific will shift to China—just as it seems to be doing in Afghanistan.

The unlikely gainer of the Afghan situation is now China. The loss of US prestige has bolstered its own, and it now provides an ideological and economic alternative to the USA. Its proximity to Afghanistan and the fact that it has Pakistan to act as its front, will enable it to extend its influence there. Using chequebook diplomacy, it can make a slow creep into the strategically vital piece of turf. It maintains a diplomatic presence there—along with Russia and Pakistan—and the Taliban have repeatedly stated that they see China as an ally. It has stepped up with $300 million aid (coming at a time when the world has suspended aid and the US has frozen $9 billion of Afghan funds) and can provide the economic clout to enable the Taliban to have some modicum of governance. Should it enable the Taliban to stay afloat (which it can do with Pakistan as its proxy) its long-term strategy will be to extend the BRI and CPEC into Afghanistan, and use its surplus manufacturing to develop infrastructure projects. That will then enable it to take over critical areas in the region. Bagram base is already on China's radar and should it obtain control over it (in much the same manner in which it took over Hambantota and Gwadar) it will have a springboard into all of Central Asia.

In return for 'redevelopment', it could also gain access to around $3 trillion of mineral wealth—especially lithium, which powers the world's batteries—that lies beneath Afghanistan's mountains. Its proximity and vast infrastructural capabilities make it well positioned to exploit it. That could give it control over semiconductors and the electric car segment; and over much of the world's manufacturing in this critical field.

Yet, it too has its own apprehensions of the effect on the Uighurs of Xinjiang province—which shares an 80-kilometre border with Afghanistan. Islamic fundamentalism could rear its head there, but China seems to have already hedged its bets by getting assurances from the Taliban that they would not support the East Turkmenistan

Islamic Front—the militant wing of the Uighurs—or allow it to operate from their soil. Using Pakistan as a buffer, it can keep that threat at bay—for the time being at least.

Russia is still in the Great Game after 180 years and there is a smug sense of satisfaction at the USA's inglorious withdrawal—in much the same manner that was forced upon the Soviet Union forty years ago. It too sees the power vacuum as an opportunity to reassert its strategic imprint there—as it has done in Syria. And it too sees the weakening of US prestige and resolve as an opportunity to test the waters in Europe and beyond.

Other neighbouring countries will also enter the fray for influence in Afghanistan. Iran has been initially supportive of the Taliban but it is wary of its hardline Sunni-ism. During their earlier rule, the Taliban had murdered Iranian diplomats and slaughtered Shia Hazaras by the thousands. Yet, Iran may make common cause with them, (perhaps prompted by China with which it has signed a 25 year-economic and strategic partnership) largely to keep US influence away from the region. Its own position in the region has now been strengthened by the US withdrawal and it too professes an Islamic theocracy that the Taliban propagate. Saudi Arabia, the UAE and other moderate Islamic states have kept a wary watch on events and would like to distance themselves from the radicalism that is resurfacing in the region. The resurgence of Islamic fundamentalism in the West Bank, Gaza, Syria and Lebanon is on the cards, and the events of Afghanistan could lead to a fresh eruption in the Middle East, and derail the Arab-Israel rapprochement taking place there.

We are seeing a regional bloc of China, Russia, Iran and Pakistan converging around Afghanistan. Turkey too, could join. Each of them will seek to establish their economic and strategic presence there and use the very chaos of Afghanistan to further their interests. The strategic stranglehold they establish in this vital region will create an arc of influence that extends towards Central Asia, Europe and beyond.

India's Diminished Clout

Over the past twenty years, India has been able to consolidate a presence in Afghanistan with a favourably inclined democratic government and US security in place for our $3 billion worth of investments there. The flow of events has upended all that.

With a Taliban regime under the influence of the ISI, Indian clout will be gradually eased out to the benefit of Pakistan and China. Strategically vital infrastructure projects—such as the Chabahar port in Iran and the Zaranj-Delaram road which would have helped provide connectivity to Central Asia will also be affected.

This could have a long-term effect on India's strategic influence in the region. The loss of our presence in Afghanistan is damaging our image and can embolden our adversaries. A resurgence of terrorist activity in the hinterland will also consume precious resources and put Kashmir back on the boil—creating an unstable security and economic environment.

The US defeat in Afghanistan will thus have an effect which will extend across much of the world. It could be the defining event when the USA slipped into terminal decline and handed over the mantle of global leadership to China and its allies. It could well precipitate a China-Pakistan-Russia-Iran power bloc in the region. And though the USA seems to be focused on the Indo-Pacific—which it seems to be doing by its renewed emphasis on Quad and AUKUS—it may actually find its clout weakened even there. Twenty years of engagement in Afghanistan—plus a totally needless war in Iraq from 2003 to 2010—has left it war-weary and more inward looking. That could embolden both Russia and an increasingly triumphant China to expand the envelope and perhaps hasten a confrontation. The US defeat in Afghanistan could set the stage for its defeat for the mantle of being the world's dominant superpower.

The travails of Afghanistan are not over. It is slipping into economic chaos and a humanitarian catastrophe of unimaginable proportions is unfolding. The Taliban will find it increasingly difficult to run the country and will have to stave off challenges from the ISIS-K, rebel groups and splinter organisations seeking to carve out their own fiefdoms. The turmoil and instability provide fertile ground for external forces to play out their New Great Game in that strategically vital piece of turf—something that has been going on for centuries. India, like most of the world, can wait and watch. Unfortunately, the events that have unfolded in Afghanistan do not portend well for India or much of the world. It heralds a shift in the power structure and the games being played out in Afghanistan will find resonance, not only in the region, but in the world arena at large.

6

America, Pakistan and the Afghan Frankenstein: India must Learn from Past Follies to Draw Own Strategy

P. Stobdan

It was General Zia-ul-Haq and his ISI protégé, Hamid Gul, who first conceived and sold the "Afghan *Jihad*" idea in the late 1980s to the Americans and the Saudis as a recipe to bring down their Cold War arch-enemy, the Soviet Union.

In an interview, Zia told Selig Harrison, "We have earned the right to have a very friendly regime in Kabul. We won't permit it to be like it was before, with Indian and Soviet influence there and claim on our territory. It will be a real Islamic state, part of a Pan-Islam revival that will one day win over the Moslems in the Soviet Union, you will see."[1]

The USA and Saudi Arabia spent over $8 billion on the Afghan war, but Zia used the upshot of the *Mujahideen* triumph to create an illusionary "strategic depth" to realise the twin goal of (a) undermine the 'Afghan nationalism' that threatened to exacerbate the

Pakhtoonistan demand, and (b) draw Kashmir into the spectre of the Cold War. The project was launched under the patronage of the conservative Jamaat-i-Islami (JU). The ISI spent 50 per cent of the Western aid on its pointsman, Gulbuddin Hekmatyar of the Hizb-i-Islami, and the rest on the moderate "Peshawar Seven."

As Zia envisaged, the project helped Pakistan radicalize Afghanistan as well as divert the *Mujahideen*'s attention to Kashmir when it sent hordes of "Afghanis" to the Valley after the post-Soviet withdrawal.

However, the Afghan project soon boomeranged and to the American disbelief their protégé, Gulbuddin Hekmatyar, gradually turned Afghanistan into a breeding ground for international terrorists. By 1992-93 over 120 camps had sprung up in the Pak-Af frontier that trained 30,000 *jihadis* drawn from international Sunni terrorist networks. Shockingly, the US-supplied weapons, including Stinger anti-aircraft missiles, turned up in the hands of terrorists aiming to hit Western targets.

The blowback started in the early 1990s with the abduction of 6 Israelis in Kashmir, followed by the killing of two CIA officials in Langley in 1993. This was followed by the November 1995 bombings of the US base in Saudi Arabia *et al*. The incidents had sent shock waves in the Western world when it was discovered that the terrorists implicated in all the incidents turned out to be the *jihadis* trained with US aid to Pakistan.[2]

Throughout the Afghan war, Pakistan took the USA for a ride when it managed to replace the Soviet puppets with an assortment of its own and Saudi puppets in Afghanistan.

Ted Galen Carpenter aptly wrote, "If that outcome is a US policy triumph, one shudders to contemplate what a policy failure would look like...the United States was not merely a relatively passive accomplice in the destructive agendas pursued by Islamabad and Riyadh—it was an active collaborator in foisting an oppressive political system on the people of Afghanistan, the result of that policy is a damning enough indictment of American action."[3]

Washington's acquiescence led inexorably to developments that served the interest of Pakistan's growing elite while creating a long-term tragedy for the people of Afghanistan along with other adverse security implications for the region.

USA Once Again Walked into a Pakistani Trap

The G7 Paris Summit in 1996 finally called for tracking down the Afghan *jihadi* networks including locating the hideouts of the *al-Qaeda* run by Osama bin Laden. However, while rectifying its past follies, Washington once again walked into a Pakistani trap. It blindly relied on the ISI's prepared Afghan blueprint for placing yet another monster, the Taliban militia, with the promise to disarm the Afghan *jihadists*, curb the growing of opium, reunite the country and drive out all foreign terrorists sheltered in Afghanistan.

The Taliban was created in 1992 by the ISI after its old protégés, the *Mujahideens*, whom the ISI scrupulously nurtured, turned their back and refused to kowtow before Islamabad, and instead turned to Delhi for support once they formed their government in Kabul in 1992. This forms a separate story but by this time Benazir Bhutto and her Interior Minister, Naseerullah Babar (Gul's arch-rival), who came to power in Pakistan sought to revamp the entire Afghan project by abandoning the Zia-run Afghan *Mujahideen* network in favour of creating a fresh militia—the Taliban. This time, the project was launched under the patronage of the Jamiat-ul-Ulema-Islam (JUI) led by Maulana Fazlur Rahman.

Bhutto and her ISI officials also managed to hoodwink the Western world that found nothing wrong in supporting the newly-created monster, the Taliban, so long as it brought peace to Afghanistan. The USA was also convinced that the Afghan militia would help curtail Iran's strategic advantage; oil and geopolitics after the Soviet collapse.

The US anxiety had particularly grown after the Rabbani regime in Kabul went close to Tehran after the killing of the Shia leader of the Hizb-i-Wahdat by the Taliban in 1995. Tehran's help to bring about a patch up between Rabbani and Hekmatyar in June 1996 added to Washington's suspicions about the CIA's debacles in the Gulf.

Some of these momentous events in Afghanistan led to US Senator Hank Brown and Assistant Secretary Robin Raphel rushing to meet the Taliban leaders in 1995. The ISI chief, Naseerullah Khan Babar, also escorted the US Ambassador in Islamabad on a tour of the Taliban bases in Afghanistan. Eventually, a clear-cut American incentive in 1995 finally enabled the Taliban's surge of taking over one-third of Afghan territory within a few months.

The push for the Taliban also came against the Indian and Iranian financing of a strategic railway project to connect Central Asia for the first time with the Persian Gulf through Sarakh (Turkmenistan) with Tajan (Iran) that was completed in 1994.[4] The move quickly prompted the USA to support a Pakistani deal with the Union Oil Company of California (Unocal) and Saudi Delta to build a gas pipeline from Turkmenistan to Pakistan via Afghanistan as against Kabul's decision to sign a deal with the Argentinean Company, Bridas. Zalmay Khalilzad then negotiated with the Taliban for Unocal.

The USA and Pakistan were also perturbed by India's response to a power-sharing deal between the Rabbani regime and Hekmatyar in 1996. Not only did Indian Prime Minister Deve Gowda send a congratulatory message to Hekmatyar on his assuming the post of Prime Minister, he also invited him to the Independence Day reception at the Embassy of India in Kabul on August 15, 1996, hosted by India's Charge d'Affairs.

However, following a visit by Saudi Intelligence head Prince Turki al-Faisal Saud to Pakistan, it took only 50 days for the Taliban to capture Kabul on September 27, 1996.

The Taliban Victory

The USA welcomed the first flush of the Taliban's victory on September 27, 1996 and called in the militia "quickly to restore order and form an interim government that can begin the process of reconciliation nationwide."[5] Interestingly, Washington expressed only "regret" over the summary execution of former President Mohammad Najibullah by the Taliban on the same day.

The US spokesman, Nicholas Burns, admitted to Washington having contacts with the Taliban.[6] The *New York Times* described the Taliban as a moderate force that had brought a measure of stability to the country for the first time in years. Zalmay Khalilzad actively advocated US assistance to the Taliban as he argued that it was a fundamentalist force but does not practise an Iranian-style anti-US policy.[7] The Americans believed that the Afghan militia pursued 'anti-modernism' rather than 'anti-Western'. They were reviving 'traditional Afghan society' rather than 'exporting Islam'.[8]

But within a month of the Taliban victory, Washington had to withhold its decision to recognise the Taliban regime amidst mounting international criticism against the militia's appalling medieval-style savage rule that put off the world community, including the orthodox Iranian clergy. Washington's denouncement also came against the backdrop of the 1996 US Presidential election–supporting a medieval regime would have negatively affected Clinton's prospects.

In a u-turn, the US Assistant Secretary, Robin Raphel, soon declared that the "US supports none of the warring factions, and had no plan for bringing the conflict to an end."[9] Instead, it called for establishing a broad coalition government. But once the election was over, the USA again softened its stance while suggesting that "isolating the Taliban is not in Afghanistan's interests and instead the effort should be to moderate their policies by engaging them."[10]

But the damage had already been done. The Taliban's brutality against women had already caused huge embarrassment for the USA. US officials were rattled by the ISI's ill-conceived plan and horrified at the Taliban's defiance. Obviously, the Americans were made to look naïve as they were deluded by Pakistan into believing that the Taliban would be a good ally of the USA.[11] The USA repeated the same mistake despite the bitter experience of the past of patronizing the ISI's favourite, Hekmatyar, who proved, much to American disgust, to be a source of terrorist threats later.

More seriously, the USA was also worried about the Taliban's action prompting the Central Asian states to return to Moscow's camp. At the October 4, 1996 Almaty Summit, Central Asian leaders strongly condemned the Taliban movement that decisively altered its future prospects. With that, the high-pitched tone of the State Department and euphoria among Unocal and Delta Oil Company officials about the Taliban's success gradually died down.

Washington was misled by Pakistan that suggested that the Taliban's puritanical pronouncements would help stamp out the narcotics trafficking that funded terrorist camps in Afghanistan only to discover later that the Taliban were funding their own operations with drug profits. Instead, the Taliban also used opium production as a bargaining chip for gaining recognition. The desperate ISI made the Taliban indulge in narcotics blackmail. A British Minister noted that most of the heroin that reached the UK came largely from Afghanistan.

Despite the Taliban pledge to drive out foreign terrorists, including Osama bin Laden and his cohorts, from Afghanistan, Mullah Amir Kahn Mutaqi announced, "We don't want subversive actions to be launched from here against any other countries and promise not to shelter terrorists in Taliban-controlled areas.[12] Even Mullah Omar is believed to have told Osama bin Laden initially not to use Afghan soil to carry out political activities.[13]

However, as time passed by, Bin Laden was declared as a fellow 'Islamic brother in-arms' pursuing the cause of Islam. Mullah Omar cited the Afghan tradition of giving shelter to an enemy if asked for. Mullah Mohammad Sadiq, a senior Taliban leader, told *Time* magazine that "until we are sure that he committed crimes, how can we proceed against him? All we know is that Bin Laden is a good Muslim and has taken part in the Afghan *jihad* (holy war) against the Soviets."[14]

Omar even refused to hand over Osama bin Laden after the 9/11 attack when the Bush Administration asked Afghanistan to do so. Omar had justified in his interview with Voice of America, "We cannot do that. If we were afraid of attack, we could have surrendered him the last time we were threatened."[15] Omar rebuffed every US attempt to get Bin Laden out of Afghanistan for a trial even at the risk of being bombed out of power. Instead, Bin Laden was allowed to reopen some of the old terrorist training camps at Khost (Al Badr 1 and Al Badr 2) earlier run by Hekmatyar.[16] The Taliban's continued sheltering of al-Qaeda terrorists thoroughly exposed the Afghanistan fiasco long pursued by the USA.

Similarly, Washington was also misled by Pakistan that suggested that the Taliban's puritanical pronouncements would help stamp out narcotics trafficking that funded terrorist camps in Afghanistan.[17] However, the Americans soon found out that the Taliban were funding their own operations with the drug profits. In 1996, the Taliban-controlled areas produced 95 per cent of Afghanistan's opium crop of an estimated 2,248 tonnes that accounted for $75–80 billion in profits in the international market.[18]

The Taliban initially destroyed over 30,000 hectares of fields cultivated with hemp (hashish) but turned a blind eye towards poppy cultivation, which yields opium. It justified the production and export of opium for its consumption by non-Muslims.

The profit motives apart, poppy cultivation becomes necessary to maintain a hold over the territories the militia-controlled, especially for the fear of losing the sympathy of the rural population. Ahmed Rashid wrote, "Poppy farmers are benefiting from the relative peace and security that the Taliban militia had brought."[19]

The Taliban also used opium production as a bargaining chip for gaining recognition. A Taliban official once remarked, "We can stop the poppy cultivation if the West supports the Taliban government." The desperate ISI made the Taliban indulge in narcotics blackmail.

The Clinton Administration's flirtation with the Taliban gradually ended following differences over the latter's failure to curb terrorism, drug trafficking, and human rights violations. In January 1997, US Secretary of State Madeleine Albright deplored the Taliban's "despicable" treatment of women and children. It was none other than Hillary Clinton, supported by the American Feminist Majority (AFM) and the National Organisation for Women, who championed the cause against the Taliban's barbaric treatment of women.

But regardless of the Taliban's promises, the top Pakistani military commanders continued to shelter foreign terrorists who selectively targeted Western assets. Among them was Aimal Kansi who had killed two CIA officials in 1994. General Hamid Gul, who had nurtured Kansi in the Hekmatyar-run training camps, had challenged the Pakistani government's decision to hand him over to FBI agents. Kansi was eventually handed over to the FBI only on June 15, 1997; that too after the Taliban faced a military setback from the Northern Alliance. Seeing the Americans' cold response to the militia's takeover of Mazar-i-Sharif, Pakistan was compelled to oblige the USA or at least sought to fulfil some of their commitments of protecting American strategic interests.

By turning in an FBI fugitive for whose search the USA had spent \$3.5 million, and had offered a \$2 million bounty for information on him, Islamabad succeeded in deflecting some of the American anger and suspicions. In addition, and to win American sympathy, the Taliban decided to close down the Afghan Embassy in Tehran on June 2, 1997.

The USA's cold response was nevertheless viewed in the context of the Iranian Presidential election, which was due in June that year. Washington's strong action against Afghanistan would have spoiled the prospect of moderate leader Khatami's victory. Obviously, the Central Asian states too would not have welcomed such action by Washington.

No country except Pakistan recognised the Taliban government. Saudi Arabia and the UAE recognised it when it scored a victory over Dostum on May 24, 1997.

Washington, however, stayed away as the State Department official, John Dinger, said, "The issue of recognition is not actually germane since the US only recognises states and not governments."[20] Instead, the USA noted that there simply cannot be a military solution to the problem.

Obviously, Pakistan scrupulously worked on its own agenda. Like in the past when the ISI had withheld a substantial portion of weapons supplied for the *Mujahideen*, a good portion of an estimated \$2.5 billion sponsored for the Taliban operation was pocketed by ISI commanders.

To cut a long story short, the Reagan Administration in the 1980s gave a clear-cut incentive for the birth of Islamic extremism in Afghanistan only to face the blowback that came in the form of the *al-Qaeda*. In the 1990s, the Clinton Administration went along with the ISI's advice to support the Taliban as a vehicle for guaranteeing American interests including prospects of oil pipelines across Central and South Asia but only to face the 9/11 consequences.

One has to read *The Wars of Afghanistan: Messianic Terrorism, Tribal Conflicts, and the Failures of Great Powers* authored by Peter Tomsen, former US Ambassador to Afghanistan (1989-1992), to know why the American over-reliance on Pakistan not only backfired badly but led its policy to go astray in the region. He wrote that the USA by outsourcing its war efforts to Pakistan, practically accepted the Pakistani Army's aim to make Afghanistan a bastion for Islamic fundamentalism—a strategy that remained tenaciously in place until the September 11, 2001 attacks on the Twin Towers.

Tomsen's book exposed the duplicitous role played by the Pakistanis in duping the Western world into believing that Pakistan was inclined towards a negotiated settlement, but in practice, they wanted to install their clients in Kabul.

The USA reduced its dependency on Pakistan since 9/11, but the American naivety to gauge Pakistani motivation in Afghanistan continues to create a mess there.

An important underlining point was that the US-Pakistan-Taliban misadventure, though it ruined the Afghan peace prospects, the European countries led by Britain and Germany viewed Afghanistan as their own backyard and maintained commercial ties with the Rabbani government.

The Current US Game

So, what is the American latest deal with the Taliban and the urgency to withdraw troops from Afghanistan all about? It all started with Donald Trump's "America First" fixation combined with the US strategic shift of focus from counterterrorism to containing China.

President Joe Biden now vows to "fight the battles of the next 20 years, not the last 20."[21] This means that the USA's current Afghan game is all about China—to use the assortment of Islamic forces as potent weapons to liberate the Uyghur area of Xinjiang. Even the deeply worried Central Asians sense that the Taliban's surge will not be confined to Afghanistan.

But be watchful, Pakistan this time is running with the hare and hunting with the hounds while simultaneously trying to play the American, Chinese and Russian game with the sole aim of seizing a fresh opportunity to foment trouble in Kashmir.

If the world wants to see genuine peace and stability in Afghanistan, the major powers (America, Russia, China, and India) need to call the Pakistani bluff this time. For that to happen, India, Russia, and China need to separately arrive at a modicum of common understanding on Afghanistan, at least to protect their interests in Kashmir, Central Asia, and Xinjiang.

India Needs to Draw its Own Afghan Strategy

India needs to note that the Taliban was raised in the year when the Durand Line Treaty (12 November 1893) was set to expire its 100-year validity in 1993. The Treaty envisaged the return of Khyber Pakhtunkhwa to Afghanistan on the lines of Hong Kong's return to China in 1997. Delhi strangely kept mum on it that time!

India needs to remember Abdul Ghaffar Khan or Bacha Khan and other Khudai Khidmatgars steered the Bannu Revolution in June 1947 to seek an independent Pakhtoonistan and rejected joining Pakistan. For the Afghans, Pakistan represented a hegemon. Bacha Khan had felt betrayed by the Partition of India as he wrote to Gandhi with a sense of despair, 'You have thrown us to the wolves.'[22] For India to play its own long-term game, it needs to work on the Taliban to press for de-recognising the Durand Line. There is no other strategic option that India is left with on Afghanistan at this stage. And this cannot be realised unless India resets its geo-strategic calculus with Russia. The other considerations will just remain delusional thinking.

NOTES

1. M. Ehsan Ahrari, "Jihadi Groups, Nuclear Pakistan and the New great Game" (August 2001), https://www.files.ethz.ch/isn/47562/Jihad_Groups_ Nuclear.pdf
2. Wright, Lawrence. *Looming Tower*, (Knopf, 2006), p. 178, Chapter 9.
3. Ted Galen Carpenter, "The Unintended Consequence of Afghanistan," *World Policy Journal*, Spring 1994, pp. 76-87. Also read Chalmers Johnson, *Blowback: The Costs and Consequences of American Empire* (New York: Henry Holt, 2000).
4. P. Stobdan, "India and Central Asia: The Strategic Dimension" (2020), https://idsa.in/system/files/book/book-india-and-central-asia.pdf.
5. U.S. Department of State, *Daily Press Briefing*, September 27, 1996.
6. *The Hindustan Times*, October 10, 1996.
7. As quoted in *Times of India*, October 12, 1996.
8. As cited in *World Press Review*, January 1997, p. 23.
9. The *Washington Post*, November 4, 1996.
10. Robin Raphel said this at the UN meeting on Afghanistan.
11. "US Claims It Was Misled on Taliban", as reported by IANS, *Pioneer*, November 23, 1996.
12. *Time*, December 16, 1996, p. 12.
13. Robert Marwuand, "The reclusive ruler who runs the Taliban", *The Christian Science Monitor*, October 10, 2010.
14. *Time*, December 16, 1996, p. 12.
15. Peter Bergen. "The man who wouldn't hand over bin Laden to the U.S," *CNN*, August 21, 2015.
16. ANI, PTI quoted *London Daily* of November 20, 1996, "Guerrilla Training Camps Reopened in Afghanistan," *The Hindustan Times*, November 22, 1997.
17. P. Stobdan, "The Afghan Conflict and India", Delhi Papers 6, IDSA, 1998, New Delhi.
18. "Opium Poppy Production in Afghanistan: High But Stabilised, New UN Survey Finds", UN Information Service, Vienna, September 1996.
19. Ahmed Rashid, "Drug the Infidels", FEER, May 1, 1997, pp. 25-26; also see Robert Fisk, "Afghan Farmers Reap Lethal Crop", *The Independent*, London, as reproduced by *The Hindustan Times*, New Delhi, July 21, 1997.
20. "US Treading Warily on Afghanistan", *The Hindu*, May 29, 1997.
21. Remarks by President Biden on the Drawdown of U.S. Forces in Afghanistan, https://www.whitehouse.gov/briefing-room/speeches-remarks/2021/07/08/remarks-by-president-biden-on-the-drawdown-of-u-s-forces-in-afghanistan/ (Accessed July 8, 2021).
22. Khan Abdul Ghaffar Khan (Penguin Books India, 2010), p. x.

7

Afghanistan: Pakistan Rides the Taliban Tiger

Vinod Bhatia

"He who rides a tiger is afraid to dismount"

—Chinese Proverb

Lt Gen Hamid Gul, a former Director General of Pakistan's Inter Services Intelligence (ISI) agency, participating in a Pakistani television talk show said that in 'Afghanistan, Pakistan defeated the Soviet

Union with the help of the US and thereafter defeated the US with help of the US', much to the glee and laughter of the audience. Profound words these—however, what he left unsaid is a postscript that Pakistan with the help of the Taliban will defeat Pakistan in the future.

For two decades, Pakistan took full advantage of her geo-strategic location and 'ran with the hares and hunted with the hounds'. Following the sixteenth-century Machiavelli's political treatise, *The Prince*, Pakistan, specifically the ISI, partnered with the United States led Global War on Terror (GWOT) and at the same time sponsored and supported the Taliban of Afghanistan in their *jihad* against the USA. The USA, having burned its bridges with Iran, needed Pakistan to destroy Osama bin Laden and the *al-Qaeda* operating from a Taliban-ruled Afghanistan after 9/11 to mitigate the terrorist threat to the homeland. Operation ENDURING FREEDOM launched by the USA in October 2001 could only be sustained through Pakistan, which under an astute General Pervez Musharaff, the Chief Martial Law Administrator and President was more than willing to provide full and unstinted support to the USA. Seeing and seeking an opportunity of regaining strategic prominence on account of changing security threats with the attack on the Twin Towers, Pakistan was only too willing to be a part of the GWOT. Though opposed by a few of the then corps commanders, the *de facto* decision makers in Pakistan, Musharaff overruled all stating that Pakistan did not have a choice. Having nurtured, trained, supported, and armed the *Mujahideen*/ Taliban alongside after the Soviet invasion of Afghanistan in 1979, the USA would have assumed unstinted support from Pakistan especially in terms of intelligence and logistics, for which they were willing to bear all the costs and more. This was not to be, as the ISI continued to support the *Mujahideen*. The 20-year conflict has left about 69,000 Afghan security forces and at least 51,000 Afghan civilians dead, according to research by Brown University. About 2,500 members of the US military and 1,144 members of allied-NATO militaries died during the fighting at a cost of $300 million per day. The total cost of the lost war is nearly $2.26 trillion,[1] though some estimates put the financial cost as close to $3 trillion.

Irrespective of the ruling dispensation in Pakistan, it is the Army that drives all policy, be it domestic, foreign or economic. The political, domestic, and economic relevance of the Pakistan army is based on a perceived and propagated existential threat to its very existence from India. The liberation of Bangladesh and a comprehensive military defeat in 1971 are constant reminders to the people by the army, of the perceived Indian intent and her need for the so-called 'Strategic Depth' in Afghanistan. Hence, it served Pakistan's interests to be an integral part of the GWOT in Afghanistan and ensure that this war prolongs for as long as possible. As long as the GWOT continued, Pakistan appreciated that it could keep waging the 'Proxy War' against India with impunity, perpetuating terror not only in Jammu and Kashmir but across the entire country targeting metros and economic centres in high profile high visibility terror attacks, safe in the knowledge that the world and the USA in particular will have to ignore the very spread of terror to facilitate their own aims of destroying al-Qaeda and Osama. For the Pakistan army, the advantages were many; the army benefitted by providing the logistics at exorbitant costs, received grants in aid from the USA, traded intelligence, controlled Taliban leadership and was the dominant US partner outside NATO. The USA, with its vast and effective intelligence network, would have certainly been fully aware of Pakistan's covert support and involvement with the Taliban; however, a stoic silence served their purpose, despite the main target Osama bin Laden having been given sanctuary in Abbottabad just a few hundred metres from the prestigious Pakistan Military Academy. For Pakistan, it was always a win-win situation. The success of Op Enduring Freedom would have been a win for her as the USA could not have succeeded without its support. On the other hand, a victory for the Taliban again is a victory for Pakistan. The Taliban owes this victory to Pakistan.

Though scheduled, the sudden and surprise departure of the USA is an unprecedented victory for the Taliban and Pakistan. The abrupt withdrawal of forces from the Bagram air base in the early hours of 5 July abandoning state-of-the-art military hardware reportedly worth $86 billion led to the expected and eventual fall of the Afghanistan government to the Taliban on 15 August. The aspirations of the Afghan people of a much-sought-after, 'Afghan led, Afghan owned and Afghan controlled' peace process was set in motion; however, the very presence of ISI chief, Lieutenant General Faiz Hameed, who flew down to Kabul to ensure a Pakistan-friendly regime in Kabul has ensured a Pakistan-controlled regime, populated by proscribed terrorists. The much-reported gunfight and fisticuffs between the Taliban and the Haqqani faction during the government formation, injuring and sidelining the more moderate Mullah Baradar does not bode well for peace in Afghanistan. The AF-Pak region hence will be the epicentre of global terrorism and *jihad*, impacting not only the neighbourhood but also the world. The ISI-nurtured terror groups emerge as major victors having actively supported the Taliban takeover. The Hafiz Muhammad Saeed-led Lashkar-e-Taiba, which executed the 26/11 Mumbai attacks in 2008, with ISI support and training, has a close association with the Taliban with hundreds of terrorists embedded in the Taliban. Another beneficiary of the collapse of the Afghan government will be the Tehreek-e-Taliban Pakistan (TTP) that is ideologically aligned with the Taliban and has been targeting the Pakistan army for many years as also Chinese assets of late. The Afghan Taliban has sympathy and support for the TTP and is in touch with their fellow believers, as they will offer safe havens, giving the Taliban certain leverages over the ISI. The costs for Pakistan, specially so in the Pakhtoon-dominated areas, will be high. It is reported that Pakistan after the reiteration of the November 2003 ceasefire along the Line of Control (LoC) with India in February this year has moved one of its reserve Divisions from the East to the Western borders along the Durand Line, anticipating an increase in violence levels and influx of refugees from Afghanistan who come along with attendant security issues.

The emerging volatile situation in the world was blatantly and proudly propounded by none other than the Pakistan National Security Advisor, Moeed Yusuf, who in an interview to the Sky News correspondent on 29 August 2021 just prior to the formation of the Afghan Government, detailed the emerging security situation, which is more of a warning to the Western world and the USA. Yusuf is quoted as saying, "Mark my words.... If the mistakes of the Nineties are made again and Afghanistan abandoned, the outcome will absolutely be the same—a security vacuum filled by undesirable elements who will threaten everyone, Pakistan and the West." The Sky News interview, titled 'The West could face another 9/11' quoted him as saying: "Migrants will flow, terrorism will flow and none of us want that, so let's not make that mistake again. The dangers of abandonment, which came about in the 1990s, there was a breakdown of law and order, there was a breakdown of security, there were international terrorists who took root, there was an economic crisis, there was a governance problem and at the end of the day there was 9/11."[2] Moeed Yusuf went on to issue a warning alluding to a clear and present danger adding, "If there is no money in Afghanistan, if there is no administration there, if ISIS and *al-Qaeda* and other groups establish their roots, then what do you think can happen?" I want to tell you that it will not be confined to this area only. I read somewhere that this refugee crisis will not be confined to this region alone.[3] In essence, though Pakistan does consider the present situation a major victory, as most roads to Kabul go via Rawalpindi, the fact is that the strategic relevance and value of Pakistan to the comity of nations is on the rise, as most nations aim to protect and project their interests. Surprisingly, many, including the, British Chief of the Defence Staff General Sir Nick Carter described the Taliban as "country boys" who "happen to live by a code of honour." His comments provoked an outrage and led to him being accused of being a "Taliban apologist". He also told Sky News that people should "be very careful using the word 'enemy,' for them and added, "I do think that they have changed."[4] The 'Please Taliban' statement of the British CDS is indicative of the impending threat of global terrorism and *jihad* and the helplessness of nations to find ways to protect their interests and assets. The present situation is definitely sensitive and portends major security challenges in the region and the world. Historically, the many tribes of Afghanistan unite to fight a foreign invader or power and thereafter are known to revert to tribal loyalties and infighting. Given the many divided factions commanded by warlords it is only a question of time that tribal loyalties will lead to a civil war. With the number of small arms estimated to be over a million with around

650,000 fully loaded, state-of-the-art weapons left behind by the USA, a very violent situation is imminent. The violence, backed by a radicalised ruling dispensation in Afghanistan, will spill over to the region and in the near to midterm future, the most adversely impacted nation will be Pakistan. It is imperative to analyse and assess Pakistan's interests and the impact on India and the region in the near to midterm of an impending volatile security situation post the takeover by the Taliban perpetuated by Pakistan.

The Taliban takeover scripted by Pakistan is the result of the inherent insecurity within the Pakistan army establishment, seeking 'Strategic Depth' in Afghanistan. Pakistan learnt many lessons post 1971 and the liberation of Bangladesh. One of the major takeaways for Pakistan was that a nation like it that was carved out of India with multiple languages and culture cannot remain integrated if not bound by a common ideology. Gen Zia-ul-Haq, the then Army chief, declared martial law taking over as the President. Zia is responsible for vigorously starting the process of radicalisation within the Pakistan Army, society and people, with the aim of integrating the many divisions by propagating an extreme Islamic ideology. The radicalisation was not confined to Pakistan alone but also exported to a moderate modern Afghanistan. The rise of radicalisation took root in Afghanistan much faster and stronger than in Pakistan, where the Punjabis practised a more moderate Islam. The radicalisation also coincided with similar movements in West Asia and the Arab world. Though the established caliphate in Iraq/Syria may have been stillborn, it did show a glimpse of the appeal for *jihad*. More significantly, it exposed the resolve and response of the West and big powers to a Machiavellian Pakistani deep state with an existing fully equipped theological laboratory in the vicinity that could be activated with a furtive push in order to accomplish multiple goals. It is necessary to analyse the motivation of Pakistan to nurture a venomous snake in its backyard with the potential to spread not only across the Durand Line, but also in the Afro-Asian region.[5]

The accepted Westphalian sovereign international order of state responsibility and westernized societal behaviour stands threatened by the rise of revisionist states exploiting so-called sponsored and non-state entities to create political disorder in a fragile region, ravaged by war for over four decades. The resultant volatile global situation is further accentuated by transnational radicalism supporting anarchist groups occupying large geographical areas. While examples of the phenomena are peppered in history, it is only in the last four decades that coherent results, though in various forms and degree, have been achieved by the perpetrators. Be it Iraq, Syria, Egypt, Crimea or recently Afghanistan, anarchist ideological groups with an amorphous structure have captured geographical entities, which become a petridish for ideological and social experiments.[6] The Taliban has been nurtured and supported by Pakistan for over two decades now, providing safe havens, training infrastructure and instructors, safe homes for the Taliban leadership and their families, and extending medical treatment to injured terrorists including in military hospitals. This has directly contributed to the present explosive situation in Afghanistan, ensuring a culture of gun violence becoming a way of life. The Afghan people hold Pakistan responsible for the radicalisation and the ongoing violence. The common Afghan is unable to comprehend why Pakistan interferes, arming and encouraging the Taliban. Pakistan as usual is in denial mode. As Afghan President Ashraf Ghani argued in 2015 remarks in Washington, DC, "The problem fundamentally is not about peace with the Taliban, the problem is fundamentally about peace between Pakistan and Afghanistan. For 13 years, we have been in [an] undeclared state of hostilities and this is the definition that we offered to our Pakistani counterparts; they have accepted this definition of the problem. That is the breakthrough".[7] Despite the agreement reached in Murree between the then governments, Pakistan continued its unstinted support to the Taliban and the Haqqani Network.

Afghanistan and Pakistan have a long history of tense relations defined by five recurring drivers: sovereignty concerns, security interests, geopolitical dynamics, cross-border ties, and connectivity and trade.[8] Given the various conflicts within the Af-Pak region, violence and terrorism is likely to intensify. The numerous terrorist organisations like the ISIS-K, *al-Qaeda*, Haqqani Group, Jaish and

Lashkar may have intra organisation fights for dominance, prominence and power, but convergence and congruence of ideological objectives of global *jihad* will create certain synergies which will impact the security situation starting with the neighbourhood, specially Pakistan, before it spreads to take root in other neighbouring countries, the region and the rest of the world.

The Afghanistan-Pakistan relationship is likely to further deteriorate, and vitriol on both sides could foreclose any remaining opportunities to reach a negotiated settlement. Bilateral ties will likewise influence security, political, and economic dynamics. Given the present circumstances, and the deeply held grievances on both sides, compounded by the ongoing conflict, the outcome will be detrimental to a cordial and constructive relationship.

Reverting to the present situation in the volatile Af-Pak region. A Taliban-led Afghanistan and Pakistan are conjoined enhancing the geographical space as the epicentre of terrorism and global *jihad*. Major terrorist organisations such as, the Haqqani network, Lashkar-e-Taiba, Jaish-e-Mohammed (JeM), Tehreek-e-Labbaik, *al-Qaeda*, or the Afghan Taliban's *Quetta Shura*, Tehreek-e-Taliban Pakistan (TTP) will now grow in strength, operating with impunity in the region. The fact that 14 of the 34 ministers in the newly-formed Afghan government are proscribed terrorists and the Haqqani network's Sirajuddin Haqqani controls the all-critical Ministry of Interior Affairs. What does the immediate future portend? Either one or a combination of three scenarios is likely in Afghanistan. The Taliban rule continues under the fear of the gun, pushing Afghan people and the country back by a couple of hundred years; a second scenario is a negotiated settlement between various tribes and factions, which does not seem probable having witnessed the Taliban/Haqqani/Pakhtoon government formulation despite the call by certain moderate leaders for an inclusive government. The third and the worst-case scenario which is most probable is that of a civil war with the warlords fighting for supremacy in the provinces and the Taliban holding on to Kabul and some other key centres. The Taliban with active support from the Pakistan Air Force and the elite SSG may have defeated the National

Resistance Front led by Ahmad Massoud in the Panjshir for the present, however, the warlords still hold sway over their own loyal supporters and areas. The Taliban will need to suppress all dissent by force to implement the extreme ideology being propagated by them, which will lead to mass migration to neighbouring countries, specially Pakistan, as it already is home to nearly three million Pakhtoons. The Taliban will find the going tough as you can rule with the gun but cannot govern with the gun. Taliban 2.0 seems no different from the earlier avatar, with young Taliban fighters revelling in the power of the gun. The Taliban government desperately seeks an elusive legitimacy and a legal recognition from the comity of nations, with most nations still playing the 'wait and watch' game. Equally important is the infusion of funds as the economic situation is near collapse with banks closed and people selling their belongings on the streets of Kabul to survive and feed their families.

The Taliban takeover has created an uncertain volatile environment changing the security dynamics and dimensions. The hardliners within Af-Pak are emboldened with the takeover of Kabul and an embarrassed abandoning by the US forces, seen as a cowardly act by many within Afghanistan and elsewhere. This will further embolden the extreme elements giving the much-needed oxygen to global *jihad*. The resultant security threats are a challenge to Iran, the Central Asian Republics, West Asia, China, India and Pakistan. China in an unprecedented high-visibility visit hosted the so-called moderate Mullah Baradar even prior to the Taliban takeover and the imminent US withdrawal. The Chinese extracted a promise that the Taliban will not support the Turkistan Islamic Party or the Turkistan Islamic Movement, formerly known as the East Turkestan Islamic Movement (ETIM), an Uyghur Islamic extremist organisation founded in Western China, with its stated goal to establish an independent state called East Turkestan, replacing Xinjiang, promise that the Taliban claims to have fulfilled but the Chinese are unhappy with the limited action undertaken. Xinjiang region and people are a Chinese strategic concern, which China would like to be addressed. The Taliban Government too needs Chinese money and economic aid, and a strategic corridor and linking Afghanistan to the CPEC are attractive proposals for Afghanistan. China's interests in the rare earth metals in Afghanistan are well documented, as Afghanistan sits on the mother lode of lithium estimated to be worth $1 trillion. Pakistan would prefer that China invest more and more in Afghanistan so that China becomes more dependent on Pakistan. Increase of Chinese footprints in Afghanistan with China filling the strategic void left behind after the withdrawal of the US military is likely. China is already in talks with the Taliban government to take over the massive Bagram air base as reported in some quarters; however, China will only be too aware of the risks of a 'Boots on the Ground' policy. China will need to balance the economic and security considerations in the Af-Pak region and the impact or advantages of the China dream of the Belt and Road Initiative (BRI) and the CPEC. The increased terrorist attacks on Chinese nationals working on CPEC projects are a pointer to an increased threat to a seemingly unviable CPEC.

An unstable Pakistan with intra-regional conflicts on its western borders with calls for *jihad* and imposition of an Afghan-like Sharia is the next logical space for extreme violence. Pakistan was formed as a by-product of the 'Two Nation Theory' and to this day vies for validation of the same. The promise of a superior political, economic and social nation for Muslims of the subcontinent is still to be realised, specially vis-a-vis India, thereby calling into question the very raison d'etre for the creation of Pakistan. The establishment, having failed to provide social welfare for the citizens, seeks to position itself as a protector of "Islamic Ideology" to justify its rule. Promoting the Taliban internally as well as in international fora reinforces the Islamic credentials of the Pakistan and the Army.[9] It is often stated that most countries have an army but the Pakistan Army has a country. The army drives the foreign policy, economy and politics in Pakistan, with the so-called democratically elected government known as a "puppet government". Though all powerful, the authority of the Pakistan Army is likely to be challenged by out-of-control terrorist organisations like the TTP, Balochistan National Army, Sindhudesh National Army in addition to the ISI-sponsored and supported groups like the LeT, JeM, ISIS-K among others. Among the radicalised elements, the Pakistan Army is perceived by many as pro USA and hence anti-Islam. The calls for *jihad* and a more vigorous imposition of the Taliban version of the Sharia will find appeal and favour among the poor and impoverished masses. An imploding Pakistan may not seem a possibility just yet, but the world, region and particularly India will have to plan for such an eventuality, as it has direct security and economic implications. A reasonably stable Pakistan is in the interest of India and the world.

While India and the world at large is capable and geared to meet and mitigate the threat of terrorism perpetuating from Pakistan's deep state, it is now the nuclear threat by terrorists, either by design or default, that is a strategic concern and challenge. There are no easy answers and the many signals emanating from the Pakistan hierarchy, including their NSA Moeed Yussuf, are a clear pointer to future security threats and terrorism as a tool moving to a new and dangerous level. A nuclear armed terrorist dominated Pakistan poses major and insurmountable challenges to global peace, stability and development. The USA may have gone wrong in Iraq and not come across any of the much-touted 'Weapons of Mass Destruction', but Pakistan is a different story being one among the nine declared nuclear armed weapon states. Pakistan currently possesses a growing nuclear arsenal estimated at 165 weapons, and remains outside both the Treaty on the Non-Proliferation of Nuclear Weapons (NPT) and the Comprehensive Nuclear Test Ban Treaty (CTBT). It is also the sole country blocking negotiations of the Fissile Material Cut-Off Treaty (FMCT).[10] The fear and fact of these nuclear weapons now falling into the hands of radicalised elements within Pakistan and the possibility of these being passed on to the Taliban or the very 'threat in being' is a clear and present danger. The very threat of use of these nuclear weapons in whatever form can disrupt the world and the world order. Marvin Kalb, writing for Brookings on 29 September 2021, says, "Pakistani *jihadis* come in many different shapes and sizes, but no matter: the possibility of a nuclear-armed terrorist regime in Pakistan has now grown from a fear into a strategic challenge that no American president can afford to ignore. The nation that has both nuclear weapons and a dangerous mix of terrorists was—and remains—Pakistan."[11] Warning enough if one is required on the consequences of a victorious Pakistan. President Joe Biden declared, when justifying his pullout from Afghanistan and explaining his Administration's war on global terrorism in an August 31 speech, "that it is a 'new world' which will go "well beyond Afghanistan," alerted the world to focus on "the threats of 2021 and tomorrow". He will not have to look too far, for bordering Afghanistan, now again under Taliban rule, is Pakistan, one of America's oddest "allies." Governed by a shaky coalition of ineffective politicians and trained military leaders trying desperately to contain the challenge of domestic terrorism, Pakistan may be the best definition yet of a highly combustible threat that, if left unchecked, might lead to the nightmare of nightmares: *jihadis* taking control of a nuclear weapons arsenal of something in the neighbourhood of 200 warheads.[12] Former President Barack Obama had translated this challenge in carefully chosen words: "The single biggest threat to U.S. security, both short term, medium term and long term," he asserted, "would be the possibility of a terrorist organisation obtaining a nuclear weapon."[13] The strategic challenge is not for the USA alone or the West, it is for the world at large and India in particular. Pakistan, while waging a proxy war against India now for over four decades following Zia's philosophy of ' Bleeding India with a thousand cuts' under the rhetoric of a nuclear armed state, willing to employ these weapons of mass destruction, will now seek an opportunity of denial in the nuclear domain. A Pakistan-backed covert war in the nuclear domain is now a much greater probability and threat. Bruce Riedel argues that Pakistan is a looming problem with no satisfactory solutions. For Biden, no matter what policies he pursues, it remains a recurring nightmare, the stuff of a paperback thriller: a scary mix of terrorists who may one day be able to seize power and, with it, control the nation's stockpile of nuclear warheads—all of this happening in a shaky, strategically-located country that was once an ally.[14] Pakistan may have been once an ally of the USA, but as a mischievous neighbour, has been a continuous and constant threat to India, having waged four wars starting with a hybrid war immediately post its birth in 1947.

Marvin Kalb paints a rather dim view of Pakistan's nukes being taken over by extreme elements. As the world's oldest democracy, the USA and India, the largest, are the two most potential targets; he alludes to US military and physical intervention with Pakistan seeking China's active support. He argues that "since the American withdrawal from Afghanistan, geostrategic relationships on the Asian subcontinent have been undergoing important changes. Pakistan has tilted its future towards a closer relationship with China, while its principal adversary, India, has tightened its ties with the United States, both of them sharing an already deep distrust of China. In this increasingly uneasy atmosphere, the USA remains concerned about Pakistan's nuclear stockpile falling into terrorist hands. If this seemed to be happening, the USA would feel the need to intervene militarily to stop it. Pakistan would likely turn to China for help, setting the stage for the USA and China, because of Pakistan's nukes, to head towards a direct and possibly deadly confrontation which neither superpower wants or needs.[15] Hence the security challenges and fallout of the Pakistan-controlled Taliban takeover of Afghanistan poses a full spectrum threat to the world and India from the upping of the ante of the ongoing 'Low Intensity Conflict' or the Grey Zone war to nuclear war.

It is important to analyse the emerging threats and security challenges to India as a fallout of the blowback of the Taliban victory. However, that is a chapter in itself. The Taliban has been sending out mixed signals, possibly at the behest of the ISI. Earlier, in May this year, the Taliban clarified that it would not intervene in Kashmir as "The policy of the Islamic Emirate is clear that it does not interfere in the internal affairs of other countries." However, after coming to power, it made a clever variation by invoking the religious angle and saying that being Muslims, it is the Taliban's right to speak out for Muslims living in Kashmir and any other country. When taken in isolation, there is nothing disconcerting about this; but when related to *al-Qaeda*'s congratulatory message to the Taliban on its victory, Taliban's new approach acquires a more menacing connotation.[16] The *al-Qaeda* congratulating Taliban, has also given a call to liberate "The

Levant, Somalia, Yemen, Kashmir and the rest of the Islamic lands from the clutches of the enemies of Islam."[17] Given its congenital proximity with Pakistan, the Taliban's so-called "right to speak for Muslims" portends big trouble; however, at the behest of Pakistan and seeking Chinese money, there is no mention of East Turkestan or religious persecution of Uighur Muslims of Xinjiang in China. Along the LoC, India has an effective 'Counter Infiltration' grid backed by an equally effective counter terrorism grid in the Union Territory of Jammu and Kashmir. More importantly, the foreign terrorists (Taliban) are not only not welcome by the Kashmiri people but are hated for having perpetuated atrocities in the early Nineties. The call for global *jihad* may unfortunately have a few takers given that we live in an interconnected, networked world and some will be prone to radicalisation. The internal security agencies and the administration will need to monitor these activities, and aim to curb them in the initial stages. As the primary security challenge is from the Pakistan-sponsored proxy war, it is imperative to review and strengthen the Pakistan strategy. A 'Three P' strategy with Pakistan will be an effective deterrent and ensure that Pakistan does not cross India's 'Red Line' much like the surgical strikes post Uri and the precision air strikes on the Jaish terrorist training camp at Jabba Top. The 'Three P' strategy of 'Proactive, Pre-emptive and Punitive Operations' against the Pakistan army will raise the cost of its 'Low cost, High effect war'. This is a language that Pakistan understands. Suffice it to say, an effective military strategy, diplomatic isolation, economic sanctions and a demonstrated political will is required to deter Pakistan from exploiting the present fragile security environment post the Taliban takeover.

The Taliban victory in Afghanistan is quintessentially a victory for Pakistan and a reaffirmation for the call of 'Global Jihad', as propagated by the *al-Qaeda*, ISIS and similar extremist elements the world over. Pakistan's ISI has long sponsored and supported the Taliban, but the militant group's victory in Afghanistan could end up creating a serious blowback for Pakistan leading to civil war in Afghanistan spilling over to Pakistan. The various terrorist organisations and certain radicalised elements within the ISI and the Pakistan Army, emboldened by a false sense of victory having defeated two superpowers, may give a call for global *jihad*, thus disrupting peace and stability. The nation that has both nuclear weapons and a dangerous mix of terrorists was—and remains—Pakistan, and these weapons or even the threat of use of these weapons is a clear and present danger. In the immediate to near term, Pakistan will marvel at her strategic smartness in having fought the GWOT along the USA and at the same time supported the Taliban to defeat the USA enhancing Pakistan's strategic relevance and value. The military in Pakistan has benefited immensely from the US largesse and contacts. What appears to be a win-win situation in all likelihood will turn into a strategic blunder in the mid to long term, threatening to destroy the very identity that Pakistan seeks.

NOTES

1. https://www.aljazeera.com/news/2021/9/6/timeline-how-september-11-2001-led-to-uss-longest-war, (Accessed September 15, 2021).
2. Alex Rosi. August 29, 2021, https://news.sky.com/story/afghanistan-the-west-could-face-another-9-11-and-mass-refugee-crisis-if-it-abandons-country-says-pakistan-security-adviser-12394203, (Accessed September 28, 2021).
3. Ibid.
4. Kevin Hurley. https://www.khmertimeskh.com/50922518/the-taliban-are-country-boys-with-a-code-of-honour-is-this-really-an-apt-way-to-describe-these-cold-eyed-killers-of-women,/ (Accessed September 23, 2021).
5. Vinod Bhatia. (September 4, 2021), https://chanakyaforum.com/pakistan-riding-the-taliban-tiger/ , (Accessed September 12, 2021).
6. Vinod Bhatia. (September 4, 2021), https://chanakyaforum.com/pakistan-riding-the-taliban-tiger/, (Accessed September 12, 2021).
7. Jayant Prasad. "Afghanistan President Ashraf Ghani's Pakistan Gambit Was Based on 3 Promises and None Were Kept," (August 21, 2021), https://www.news18.com/news/opinion/ashraf-ghanis-pakistan-gambit-was-based-on-3-promises-and-none-were-kept-4081850.html, (Accessed September 27, 2021).
8. Elizabeth Threlkeld and Grace Easterly. *Making Peace Possible Peaceworks, Afghanistan-Pakistan Ties and Future Stability in Afghanistan* (August 2021).
9. Lt Gen Vinod Bhatia. (September 4, 2021)) https://chanakyaforum.com/pakistan-riding-the-taliban-tiger/ , (Accessed September 12, 2021).
10. https://www.nti.org/learn/countries/pakistan/nuclear/.
11. Marvin Kalb. The Agonizing Problem of Pakistan's Nukes (September 28 2021), https://docs.google.com/document/d/1lVyppWcluPVoq-m4dVlsR4MXSsjn8JSWzGrTtL652aA/edit#, (Accessed September 29, 2021).

12. Ibid.
13. Bruce Riedal. "Pakistan's Problematic Victory in Afghanistan" (August 24 2021), https://www.brookings.edu/blog/order-from-chaos/2021/08/24/pakistans-problematic-victory-in-afghanistan/
14. Ibid.
15. Marvin Kalb. "The Agonizing Problem of Pakistan's Nukes" (September 28, 2021), https://docs.google.com/document/d/1lVyppWcluPVoq-m4dVlsR4MXSsjn8JSWzGrTtL652aA/edit#, (Accessed September 29, 2021).
16. Nilesh Kunwar. "Why the World Can't Win the War on Terror", IDR Blog (September 6, 2021), http://www.indiandefencereview.com/why-the-world-cant-win-the-war-on-terror/
17. Ibid.

8

Taliban and Terrorism: The Complex Security Dynamics

Soumya Chaturvedi

Since its inception in 1994, the Taliban movement within Afghanistan has undergone tremendous changes. These changes are not limited to their tactical operations; they also include their strategic and ideological alignments. It is widely accepted that the Taliban is a part of an international *jihadi* terror network. The wider misconstrued and misinformed opinion suggests that the American 'War on Terror' brought the Taliban-Terrorism nexus to the forefront in 2001 after the 9/11 attacks. However, the 1998 twin bombings on US embassies in Kenya and Tanzania had brought the Taliban to the centre stage. On 7 August 1998, the American embassies situated in Nairobi (Kenya) and Dar es Salaam (Tanzania) were attacked by truck bombings, which resulted in a cumulative 224 people being killed. According to the declassified summary of the Federal Bureau of Investigation (FBI), these were coordinated attacks orchestrated by Osama bin Laden's terror organisation—the *al-Qaeda*, and the attacks were spaced out within the time difference of four minutes.[1]

Afghanistan had already succumbed to Taliban rule two years prior to the East African bombings, for reasons that have been elaborated in-depth in the previous chapters. The FBI's investigation trail led them to confirm Osama bin Laden's presence in Afghanistan. Using the standard diplomatic tools, America demanded that the Taliban surrender Laden and his associates. It was the Taliban's refusal that led to the United Nations Security Council (UNSC) Resolution designating the Taliban and its associated entities as terrorist groups and individuals as terrorists in 1999.[2] Thus, two years prior to the appalling 9/11 attacks on American soil, the Taliban-terrorism nexus was well established and acknowledged by the global fraternity. However, due to several reasons, including lack of American political will and international political cohesion, no severe actions were undertaken against the Taliban, although some sanctions against financial assets and a travel and an arms embargo did exist.

America's 'War on Terror' was followed by the fall of the Taliban, which was followed by a democratic exercise for more than fifteen years. However, with the Taliban's capture of Kabul on 15 August 2021, it has once again come to the forefront of political affairs in Afghanistan. Of the thirty-three ministers and heads of departments announced by the Taliban on 8 September 2021,[3] at least twenty are designated terrorists according to the UNSC.[4] Likewise, in the list that was announced on 21 September 2021,[5] at least three of the seventeen names announced are a part of the UNSC-designated list of terrorists.[6] This would entail that at least half the men holding an office of power in the Taliban government of Afghanistan are acknowledged and accepted as terrorists by the global fraternity. Not only do they have multiple sanctions and embargos against them, some also have huge bounties announced for their capture. It includes Mullah Mohammad Hassan Akhund, the Prime Minister; both deputies to the Prime Minister—Mullah Abdul Ghani Baradar and Moulavi Abdul Salam Hanafi—al-Qaeda; Moulavi Muhammad Yaqoob Mujahid, the Minister of Defence; Moulavi Sirajuddin Haqqani, the Minister of Interior; Moulavi Amir Khan Muttaqi, the Foreign Affairs Minister and Mullah Hidayatullah Badri, the Minister of Finance.

Scholars are divided between referring to the Taliban as what it was in their previous stint between 1996 and 2002 and a new 'Taliban

2.0'. While there may be convergences and disagreements on this, some facts remain uncontested. In this political run-up, the Taliban is diplomatically and technologically savvier than it was between 1996 and 2002. They have returned with a more potent military might and have significantly crushed military resistance against them. They also claim to have changed their approach and outlook towards governance and conduct of the country, making it in line with international standards. It is in this regard that the Taliban-terrorism nexus needs to be revisited. Owing to their ideological convergences and use of tactical support to recapture power in Afghanistan, there exists very little reason to believe that the Taliban has, in fact, changed this time. Even if they have, due to the nature of conflict prevalent in Afghanistan and beyond, there will be severe ramifications for not just Afghanistan but for the region as a whole. This chapter will explore the complex security dynamics between the Taliban and terrorism, detail the implications for Afghanistan and international interventions necessary to ensure peace and human security.

Ideological Underpinning

The American-Soviet rivalry, for the large part, was termed as an ideological war between capitalism and communism. The Soviet disintegration of 1991 was celebrated as capitalism emerging victor in the ideological war. However, when the development trajectory of *jihadi* terrorism or the most radical and extreme interpretation of Islam is considered, the end of ideological war appears far from the truth. In modern contemporary world history, *jihadi* terrorism is generally traced to the origins of the Muslim Brotherhood in 1928. Since then, several terrorist groups have emerged, assimilated, disintegrated, and disappeared with a single cause—to establish a puritan Islamic world order. However, it is primarily believed that the varied interpretations of 'puritan Islam', apart from other political factors, have influenced the assimilation and disintegration of these groups. One may argue that several nation-states have adopted Islam as the state religion with varying degrees of modernisation, and therefore, the Taliban's actions in Afghanistan should not be seen any differently with preconceived notions that are politically clouded. It is, however, the theological details of the Taliban's campaign that highlights its intrinsic connections with terrorism.

After the fall of the Soviets and following the events leading up to the Peshawar Accord, the 'Islamic State of Afghanistan' was established in 1992. However, the Taliban, as a distinct identity, emerged only in 1994, two years after a Soviet-free state and a recognised Islamic country was established. It implies that the need to create a separate identity of the Taliban was not necessarily a response to the Soviet invasion, but the need for a much more puritan Islamic society distinct from the Islamic nation-state envisioned in the 1992 Peshawar Accord. Thus, after the Taliban overthrew the local forces in power, they established the 'Islamic Emirate of Afghanistan' in 1996 as opposed to the 'Islamic State of Afghanistan' established by their predecessors. They called a gathering of sympathetic and supportive Muslim scholars or *ulema* and declared the head of the Taliban movement, Mullah Mohammad Omar, as the *amir ul momineen*, the commander of the faithful or the supreme commander. Every individual or force present in the territory under their control was to submit themselves to the authority of the *amir ul momineen*. Any resistance against this was considered defying Islam's divinely sanctioned authority and was hence, dealt with accordingly. The focus of the Taliban at the moment was on corrupt *mujahideen*, the behaviour of whom was not at par with the Islamic understanding of the Taliban. The American invasion of Afghanistan in 2001 made the Taliban alter their rhetoric. A similar gathering of sympathetic and supportive *ulema* was orchestrated, and a declaration was obtained calling for a *jihad* against foreign invaders (America, in the first instance, and later other countries that supported them) and the local Afghans supporting them (the likes of Northern Alliance).

The position of *amir ul momineen* was not necessarily given to the most supreme military or strategic commander of the Taliban. Instead, he was a religious scholar with a deep understanding of Islamic texts and religion. Every order, announcement, proclamation, or decree is in the name of the *amir ul momineen*.[7] Mullah Omar died of tuberculosis in 2013; however, this information was made public only in 2015. Thus, for two years, the position of *amir ul momineen* de facto lay vacant. In

2015, Mullah Akhtar Mohammad Mansoor became the second supreme commander, but could never command the loyalty of all factions, consequently, there were internal conflicts. *Al-Qaeda* eventually formally acknowledged him as the *amir ul momineen*. In less than one year of his becoming the leader, Mullah Mansoor was killed in an American drone strike when he was crossing over from Iran into Pakistan. Shortly after his death, in 2016, Mullah Hibatullah Akhundzada, a former Islamic judge of the Sharia court, was elected as the third leader and was immediately proclaimed as *amir ul momineen* by *al-Qaeda*. Since then, Mullah Akhundzada has continued to be the head of the Taliban. With Kabul's capture, he is now regarded as the head of the Islamic Emirate of Afghanistan, and every announcement or decree in the Islamic Emirate of Afghanistan is made under his name and authority. Thus, the centrality and primacy of the position of *amir ul momineen* has continued even in the present stint of the Taliban.

This alone does not suffice to explain the inherent connection of the Taliban with terrorism. The title of *amir ul momineen* is also used by the Moroccan king and is explicitly mentioned in their constitution.[8] One may argue that the mere use of a nomenclature by the head of a state does not necessitate such a critical analysis. In order to understand the need for this critical analysis further, it is important to briefly reflect on the origin and sustenance of the *al-Qaeda*. Of the many *mujahideen* who answered the call for *jihad* against the Soviet invasion, one was a millionaire by the name of Osama bin Laden. He, along with an Islamic scholar, Abdullah Azzam, formed the *al-Qaeda* in 1989 to take on the holy war to establish an Islamic rule. This grouping came after the Soviets had already withdrawn from Afghanistan, and hence, their agenda was clear from the beginning—*jihad* for a global Islamic rule and particularly against the Americans. If it was not clear already, Osama's intentions were made clear even in his letter addressed to American citizens in 2002.[9] In the years following the creation of the *al-Qaeda*, several terrorist attacks globally were attributed to them. The responsibility of attacks such as the 1992 bombings of Yemen Hotel and the 9/11 attacks on the Twin Towers was claimed by Osama, while some others such as the East African bombings in 1998, USS *Cole* bombing of 2000, Richard Reid's shoe-bombing attempt of 2001, etc., were traced to the *al-Qaeda*.

It is interesting to note that until 1996, the headquarters of *al-Qaeda* was situated in Sudan. After the Taliban took over Afghanistan in 1996, the *al-Qaeda*, along with Osama, relocated to Afghanistan. Osama and Mullah Omar had forged an extraordinarily strong bond over the years. Since then, not only did they enjoy sanctuary in Afghanistan, but they were also given the freedom to run terrorist training camps and host other terrorists in guesthouses. In return, Osama would provide financial and logistical assistance from the Arab sympathisers for the Taliban, who were still struggling to garner international recognition. Osama would also help in local recruitment of foot fighters for the Taliban while supporting their movement by supplying necessary arms and ammunition. The bonhomie between Osama and Mullah Omar was also strengthened when the *al-Qaeda* assassinated the leader of the resistance movement against the Taliban, Ahmad Shah Masoud of the Northern Alliance. As illustrated earlier, Mullah Omar refused to hand over the custody of bin Laden to the Americans despite their multiple demands and knowing fully well that the fear of American invasion was real since 1998 when the East African bombing was traced to his outfit, the *al-Qaeda*. It is widely believed that the destruction of the Bamiyan Buddha statues, which were of remarkably high historical and cultural relevance, was done by the Taliban at the suggestion of bin Laden.

The relationship between the *al-Qaeda* and the Taliban is not a materialistic symbiotic one; the depth of their relationship transcends it and is rooted in the very genesis of their existence. When the *al-Qaeda* calls for *jihad*, it is to establish an Islamic emirate that surrenders itself to the authority of the *amir ul momineen*. From the very beginning, Osama had offered *bay'ah* or a pledge of allegiance to Mullah Omar. This pledge has been renewed multiple times. After bin Laden was killed by American forces in Operation Neptune Spear, Ayman al-Zawahiri assumed the position of chief of the *al-Qaeda*. He also reaffirmed his and the outfit's allegiance to Mullah Mansoor. Although he has not made any remark on the Taliban takeover, the *al-Qaeda* released a two-page statement congratulating and celebrating the Taliban victory and implying the reaffirmation of their pledge of allegiance.

From a bird's-eye view of the situation, it appears that the *al-Qaeda*'s main agenda is to have a pan-global Islamic rule that will be headed by a religious leader. By aligning themselves with the Taliban and distinctly disassociating with the different iterations of Islamic State (ISIS, ISIL, ISK, etc., the details of which will be discussed subsequently), it is implied that the Taliban victory in Afghanistan is the culmination of their goals—Afghanistan under Islamic rule and the *amir ul momineen* as the head to whose authority everyone submits. As opposed to the case of Morocco, it is the convergence of interests between the Taliban and the *al-Qaeda* that brings the terrorism nexus to the forefront. This would also mean that their clarion call for *jihad* backed by theological arguments and directions will now stand illegitimate as their goal is achieved.

Expecting the *al-Qaeda* to forgo terrorism and reintegrate into society with normalcy would be wishful thinking. It has already reaffirmed the call for *jihad* for the 'liberation' of Kashmir while congratulating the Taliban on taking over Afghanistan.[10] Having achieved favourable outcomes in Afghanistan will only function as an impetus for the *al-Qaeda*'s expansionist agenda. Knowing this fully well and not disassociating themselves with the *al-Qaeda* and continuing to harbour them, the Taliban is complicit in the *al-Qaeda*'s end goal. The repercussions of this are already being felt and will be seen in even greater magnitude in the neighbouring countries of Pakistan, Iran, India, and central Asia in times to come.

Tactical Underpinnings

Security scholars and practitioners are often divided on the importance given to ideology while analysing different militant and terrorist groups. It is often argued that ideology is a cloak or façade used to hide political motives and thus, the real understanding comes when the cloak is removed. It is true that the nature of events unfolding in Afghanistan make it impossible to research on the current ideology driving the Taliban. However, this does not invalidate the nexus that it shares with terrorism and this can be validated rather more conveniently. The Taliban is not a homogenous grouping of individuals. It comprises several groups and one such group is the Haqqani Network, which has played the most significant role in the Taliban's survival, ascendance, and victory.

The Haqqani Network was formed in the 1970s by a renowned *mujahideen,* Jalaluddin Haqqani, to fight the anti-Soviet *jihad*. He was a close aide of Osama bin Laden, the founder of the *al-Qaeda* and was also a valued asset of the American CIA in the Eighties. He joined forces with the Taliban in 1995 and served as the Minister for Tribal and Border Affairs in its previous stint from 1996 to 2001. After the American invasion of Afghanistan, the Haqqanis shifted their bases to Miram Shah in North Waziristan, Pakistan, where they ran a parallel administration.[11] Sirajuddin Haqqani succeeded his father as the head of the Haqqani Network. When Mullah Mansoor was the *amir ul momineen* of the Taliban, one of his two deputies, Sirajuddin, was the *de facto* military chief of the Taliban. Thus, of the three most powerful Taliban leaders at the time, Sirajuddin Haqqani was responsible for the Taliban's military strength as the other two lacked the experience in the battlefield and military strategy planning. When Akhundzada, the second deputy, succeeded as the next *amir ul momineen,* Sirajuddin was formally given the charge to oversee the Taliban's activities in twenty provinces of Afghanistan. His contemporary, the other deputy of Akhundzada, Mullah Mohammad Yaqoob, who is the eldest son of Mullah Omar, was given only fourteen of the Afghan provinces.[12] The Haqqani Network under Sirajuddin continues to hold a distinct identity of its own, albeit owing its allegiance to the Supreme Council of Taliban and the *amir ul momineen.*

Following the regrouping after the 2003 invasion, the Haqqani Network emerged as the most powerful of all the groups fighting within the umbrella identity of Taliban. According to a United Nations Report, *"The Haqqani Network remains the Taliban's most combat-ready force"* and *"is reported to have a highly skilled core of members who specialise in complex attacks and provide technical skills, such as improvised explosive device and rocket construction"*.[13] Thus, it can be conveniently said that the Haqqani Network has been integral to Taliban's capture of Afghanistan. It is for this reason that Sirajuddin Haqqani's appointment as the Minister for Interior, one of the most powerful offices within the Taliban regime does not come as a surprise. However, what does raise a red flag is the basic concern such as the Haqqani Network being designated as a global terrorist organisation, Sirajuddin being designated as a global terrorist since 2007 and the American FBI's $10 million reward for his arrest.

Sympathisers may argue that the designation of Sirajuddin Haqqani and the Haqqani Network as terrorists was a part of the American agenda to criminalise the Taliban militants and is in essence devoid of any merit. However, what cannot be overruled is the conduct of the Network over the years. It is known to have contacts with the *al-Qaeda* and other terrorist groups such as Lashkar-e-Taiba (LeT), Jaish-e-Mohammed (JeM), Tehreek-e-Taliban Pakistan (TTP), Islamic Movement of Uzbekistan (IMU), etc. It has provided them safe havens and logistical and financial support.[14] The Haqqani Network is responsible for the bombing of the Indian Embassy in Kabul in 2008 in which a senior Indian diplomat and military official was killed along with a dozen other civilians. They were also behind the attacks on Indian labourers in Afghanistan between 2009 and 2012. Allegedly, it is the Haqqani Network that introduced suicide attacks to the Taliban after being inspired by the *al-Qaeda*. Disassociating itself from the Haqqani Network and Sirajuddin will be a death blow to the Taliban's ambitions and control over Afghanistan. Its association, albeit, only strengthens the Taliban's connection with terrorism.

Implications for Afghanistan and its Neighbourhood

Although there are four basic schools of jurisprudence in Islam, namely, Hanafi, Maliki, Shafi'I and Hanbali, off late newer schools of thoughts have emerged within these schools of jurisprudence. Some of these are fairly radical and these include Salafism, Wahabism and Deobandi. Each school regards itself as the purest interpretation of Islam and differs in accepting modernity in their interpretations. The earliest terror outfits propagating radical Islam, like the Muslim Brotherhood, brought Wahabism and Salafism to the forefront, whereas the Deobandi school of thought was brought to light by the Taliban. This difference in schools of thought has also nudged the possibility of cohesion between different terrorist outfits and, therefore, has significant tactical implications. While the Deobandi School of Islamic thought originated in India, post the 1947 partition, it was taken to Pakistan by Islamic scholars. Leaders of the Taliban were educated and trained in Pakistan, and therefore, they identified themselves to be followers of Deobandi Islam. On the other hand, the *al-Qaeda* was a brainchild of a Saudi businessperson—bin Laden—and therefore, they were believers of Wahabism. During the anti-Soviet resistance, religious education took centre stage as per a planned strategy of the Americans and Pakistanis. Financial support poured in from Saudi Arabia, and with money came the Wahabi influence to the Deobandi madrassas in Pakistan. Hence, Taliban's interpretation of Islam was an amalgamation of the Deobandi and Wahabi schools of thought. It is also for this reason that the Taliban and *al-Qaeda* forge ideological convergences.

The Islamic State, on the other hand, believes in Salafism, which is regarded as the purest form of Islam by its believers. The Salafis condemn the Wahabis and Deobandis for making modern concessions to the religion. Initially, when they were formed in 1999, they pledged allegiance to *al-Qaeda*. However, when the Islamic State declared a caliphate in Iraq and Syria, it came in stark opposition to the *al-Qaeda*. Abu Bakr-al Baghdadi of the Islamic State refused to surrender to the authority of Ayman-al Zawahiri, the *al-Qaeda* chief. In 2005, Baghdadi assumed the title of *amir-ul momineen*, even when the Islamic State had no territory under their control. After gaining control of territory in 2014 and following internal fallout between the *al-Qaeda* and the Islamic State, Baghdadi declared an Islamic caliphate in parts of Syria and Iraq. Thus, for all practical purposes, there were now two individuals claiming to be the supreme leader of Islamic territory, and the *al-Qaeda* continued to support the Taliban's narrative. This brought the Taliban at crossroads with the Islamic State. Now that the Taliban is in control of a territory and the Islamic State is not, a security threat will constantly loom over Afghanistan, and attacks have already begun in this direction. It is therefore expected that the cycle of violence will continue within Afghanistan as these outfits continue the theological war claiming themselves to be the purest representative of Islam. While the Taliban's resurgence reinforces their vision of an expansionist Islamic Empire, it poses a direct challenge to the Islamic State's vision of creating a global Islamic caliphate in the world. During the last decade, the world witnessed the rise of the Islamic State (IS) and its taking over a large territory in Iraq and Syria. The stark ideological divide between the Taliban and the IS will invariably cause severe friction between the entities as they aim for global supremacy. The conundrum has been on evident display as a faction of the Taliban fighters have reportedly moved on to join the Islamic State of Khurasan (ISKP). This divide will only intensify in the coming years, causing further instability in the region and the broader Islamic world.

Another implication of this would be the moving of foot fighters from one outfit to the other. A very significant fraction of the Taliban comprises fighters who have been constantly in a 'war mode' for over four decades. Over the years, the 'holy war' of these fighters, *jihad* has morphed from the fight against the Soviets to the fight against the USA and its allies. This phenomenon has created several profound and long-lasting changes in the socio-cultural milieu of Afghanistan. A major consequence has been the creation of a community of war-hardened fighters who are constantly in search of avenues where they can continue fighting their holy war. The Taliban is constantly making efforts to build their legitimacy around the world. An example has been the manner in which the Taliban tried to make its case for being represented at the United Nations during the United Nations General Assembly (UNGA) 2021. As the Taliban strengthens its efforts to develop a 'benevolent' image to gain acceptance at global forums, it might lead to a situation where it might, intended or intentionally, create a prima facie disassociation with the more extreme elements within its fold. The only activity or profession that these fighters have been engaged in for a major part of their lives has been war activities. Furthermore, the Taliban is not a grouping of homogenous identities.

It comprises several sub-groups that differ in their adherence to Islam and the political concessions that they seek from the Taliban leaders. Hence, this disassociation will necessitate these fighters to look out for more violent pastures as they may feel that by moderating their stance, the Taliban is indulging in corrupt interpretations of Islam. The Islamic State, which claims to follow the most strict and pure Islam, will definitely turn out to be one of the major benefactors as they can provide a conducive platform wherein these fighters can continue fighting for their stated objectives. Furthermore, the Haqqani Network and its allies have had a strong domination over the area along the eastern region of the Afghanistan-Pakistan border. Over the past few years several Taliban loyalists defected and joined the cadres of the Islamic State-Khorasan. For instance, Saad Emirati was a prominent commander within the Haqqani Network and was also in charge of his group within the Tahreek-e Taliban. Eventually, he defected and joined the Islamic State-Khorasan as a senior member. It is not to argue that the Islamic State has connects with the Haqqani Network. It only signifies that if the Haqqani Network is not accommodated as per their will by the Taliban, they can make easier inroads into the Islamic State, an arch rival of the Taliban.

Ever since the Western nations led by the USA initiated their fight against the Soviet Union in Afghanistan, *Mujahideen* fighters from across the world arrived there. In August 2021, as the Taliban came to the fore in Afghanistan yet again, many of these fighters will move back to their respective native nations. These fighters hold extensive experience in using weaponry laced with the latest technology. Apart from the fact that these fighters possess considerable experience of undertaking violent activities against the state apparatus, they also have exposure to the network of terrorist organisations that undertake terror activities in different parts of the world. As technology became ubiquitous in the 21st century, the spread of terrorism is not linked with a physical congregation of terror-minded individuals anymore. Digital penetration across the globe will ensure the smooth transition of these fighters from Afghanistan into the terrorist networks in their regions. As the localisation of *jihad* rises, it will cause a major security implication for various nations in South Asia and various parts of the world. Nations in the immediate vicinity, such as India and various European and African nations, would want to ensure that this critical externality of the re-emergence of Taliban in Afghanistan does not reach their doorstep.

The Taliban holds an absolutely puritanical vision of its Islamic rule. The narrow and obstinate view of the religion that the Taliban upholds and staunchly propagates shall not only create an immense threat for the minorities of other religions in Afghanistan but also develop extreme danger for the sects of the Islamic world that do not fall under the 'Real Islam' worldview of the Taliban. The example of the Ahmadiyya community's extreme sufferings in the Af-Pak region is a case in point wherein a minority sect within the Islamic fold witnesses immense suffering at the hands of its fellow Muslim brethren. The return of power in Afghanistan shall intensify the Taliban's efforts to impose its worldview within the country, creating an imminent threat to the lives and property of the Islamic minority communities living in Afghanistan.

Necessary Interventions

It is now well established that unless the Taliban publicly distances itself from the *al-Qaeda* and its affiliates and takes credible actions against them, there will always be a perception that the worldview of both the Taliban and the terrorist outfits converge. These outfits term their fight as *jihad* or the 'holy war'. Their interpretation of Islam ostracises foreigners and the various sub-sects within Islam such as the Shias, Ahmadiyyas, Bohras, etc. They incessantly rely on religious texts and doctrines to justify their war and actions and continue to draw the support of both foot fighters and financers. However, several Islamic scholars contest the theological interpretation of Islam propagated by the Taliban, its terrorist affiliates, and supporters, but their voices are marginalised. It must be acknowledged that religious identity plays an inextricable part in the lives of the people in most societies. When a few influential and powerful ones exploit this identity, the larger naïve masses are blindly led to the path of violence and destruction. There is an increasing need to promote research in the theological justification for violence that such organisations propound. Only when these are questioned and critically analysed will the more moderate interpretations of the religion find public space and credibility. For far too long, the evolving dynamics of Afghanistan and the region are being analysed through a political lens. The theological underpinnings of the Taliban and its affiliates must be explored, and their contentions delegitimized in the minds of their supporters. It is equally important to engage with religious scholars and give them institutional support to counter the extremist propaganda and rhetoric forwarded by such organisations and their charismatic leaders.

Identity plays a significant role in an individual's societal life. It, however, plays an extremely crucial role in conflict and war-like situations.[15] It mobilises individuals and assists in delineating or organising them in different fragments. In a conflict like that in Afghanistan, multiple attempts are being made to homogenise the country while systematically destroying ethnic and any other identity that does not fit in harmony with the Taliban's interpretation of Islam. Thus, in this regard, stronger measures and efforts should be taken by the international community to protect the multiple identities in the region and provide them with institutional support and thrust to promote their identities. If strategically planned, the strength and cohesiveness of heterogeneous identities can stand up against the forceful alienation propagated by the Taliban and its affiliates.

Although the Taliban have emerged victorious in Afghanistan on account of the financial support of their sympathisers and more importantly through the illegal trade in narcotics and arms; these means are not sufficient to run a country. The Taliban is desperate to revive Afghanistan's economy. Understandably, the Taliban will use all the tricks in the diplomatic book to seek international cooperation, aid, grant, and support. The responsible international community must unite and leverage its bargaining power. They must coerce the Taliban to disassociate themselves from the *al-Qaeda*, its affiliates and all the terrorist activities currently flourishing in Afghanistan. This should be made a precondition for extending any kind of financial support to Afghanistan. It must also be backed with an independent auditing mechanism that can ensure the Taliban keeps up their end of the promise. Such measures will warrant that all the support extended is flowing towards the targeted audience, in this case, the miserable population of Afghanistan, and is not directed towards the ill-deeds of terrorist masterminds and intellectuals.

The Afghanistan conundrum is not new. The population has been in a civil war-like situation for nearly five decades. Even during the experimental democracy phase, there were episodic stints of the Taliban and its affiliates. This implies that a significant portion of the population that acted as the foot fighters of *jihad* have known no other profession than to use arms and indulge in violence for decades. Now that the Taliban is making statements about bringing about normalcy, accommodating these foot fighters in the society is one of the most pertinent challenges. It is of utmost importance that avenues for absorbing these fighters are created through skill development, rehabilitation, or similar programs.

Terrorism does not operate in a vacuum, and it is supported and encouraged through an institutional mechanism of supporting state and non-state actors, including individuals, corporate houses, and non-governmental organisations. In order to break the nexus of the Taliban and its terrorist affiliates, the financial sources that sustain this propaganda must be targeted. It is not to argue or suggest that no action is being taken to prevent terrorism financing. The Financial Action Task Force has taken commendable steps in this regard. However, the very revival of the Taliban and the continuing use of Afghanistan as a sanctuary for terrorism is evidence enough that more stringent measures are necessary to nip the nexus in the bud. Only through a comprehensive approach can human security for all be ensured within Afghanistan and beyond.

Conclusion

The situation that has unfolded in Afghanistan presents a very grim situation. The ideological belief packed with theology and the practice makes disassociation of the Taliban from terrorism near impossible.

Even if the Taliban succumbs to international pressure and is forced to act against the terrorist groups that are thriving within Afghanistan's territorial borders, there will be massive remobilisation and regrouping of fighters towards joining the Islamic State. The nature of the conflict in Afghanistan has increasingly made the security dynamic highly complex and exceptionally challenging to resolve. Nonetheless, this nexus must be broken while also ensuring that terrorism in itself does not find breeding grounds. When an ideology is used to ensure violence, then it is the ideology itself that needs to counter such efforts. There is a pressing need for scholars to understand the nitty-gritty of the interpretations of Islam that are being exploited to brainwash the minds of the innocent while also developing a thesis within the religion to counter such narratives. Without a comprehensive approach and determination of the international community to break the nexus of terrorism, it is the security of the people of Afghanistan and global humanity that is at stake.

NOTES

1. FBI Executive Summary. "Hunting Bin Laden," *Frontline* (November 18, 1998), https://www.pbs.org/wgbh/pages/frontline/shows/binladen/bombings/summary.html.
2. UN Security Council, *Security Council Resolution 1267 (1999) [Afghanistan]*, 15 October 1999, S/RES/1267 (1999), http://unscr.com/en/resolutions/doc/1267.
3. Announcement made public by Suhail Shaheen, former spokesperson (September 8, 2021), https://twitter.com/suhailshaheen1/status/1435436428138356736?s=20.
4. United Nations Security Council Consolidated List, https://scsanctions.un.org/9jkvzen-all.html.
5. Announcement made public by Suhail Shaheen, former spokesperson (September 21, 2021), https://twitter.com/suhailshaheen1/status/1440322226922799116?s=20.
6. Op. cit., Note 4.
7. Op. cit., Note 5.
8. Richard Pennell. "What is the significance of the title 'Amir al-mu'minin'?, "*The Journal of North African Studies*, vol. 21, no. 4 (2016), pp. 623-644.
9. For the original text of the letter written by Osama bin Laden, please see 'Full text: bin Laden's 'letter to America', *The Guardian* (November 24 2002), https://www.theguardian.com/world/2002/nov/24/theobserver.
10. "Al-Qaeda congratulates Taliban, calls for Kashmir liberation," *Hindustan Times*

(September 1, 2021), https://www.hindustantimes.com/india-news/alqaeda-congratulates-taliban-calls-for-kashmir-liberation-101630435074168.html.

11. Institute of the Study of War, *The Haqqani Network*, http://www.understandingwar.org.
12. Abdul Sayed and Colin P. Clarke. "With Haqqanis at the Helm, the Taliban Will Grow Even More Extreme," *Foreign Policy* (November 4, 2021), https://foreignpolicy.com/2021/11/04/haqqani-network-taliban-relationship-afghanistan-pakistan-terrorism/
13. United Nations. *Twelfth Report of the Analytical Support and Sanctions Monitoring Team of the Security Council Taliban Sanctions Committee* (June 1 2021), https://www.undocs.org
14. Vahid Brown and Don Rassler. *Fountainhead of Jihad: The Haqqani Nexus, 1973-2012* (Oxford University Press, 2013), pp. 3-14.
15. For more information, please see: Celia Cook-Huffman. "The role of identity in conflict," in Dennis J.D. Sandole, Sean Byrne, Ingrid Sandole-Staroste, Jessica Senehi and Dean G. Pruitt (ed.) *Handbook of Conflict Analysis and Resolution* (Abingdon: Routledge, 2008).

9

Pakistan's Terror Machine and the Re-emergence of the Taliban

Sanchita Bhattacharya

Introduction

The re-emergence of the Taliban and the behind-the-screen act of Pakistan's terror machine is a long and gradual journey of Pakistan's ambition of becoming a major player in Afghanistan. It is a long-drawn-out and well-calculated strategy developed by Pakistan to continue with the process of disruption within the Afghan state and society. Post 9/11, the US-NATO backlash on the Taliban-*al-Qaeda* cohort did push the Taliban out of the political spotlight, but it was very much present in the big picture of the Af-Pak region.

The Taliban takeover in Afghanistan has given a strategic victory to Pakistan. Since the earliest stages, Pakistan has backed the Taliban fighters. It has nurtured the anti-Soviet *Mujahedeen* fighters who later morphed into the Taliban. Islamabad was amongst the three countries that recognised the Taliban government in Afghanistan and the last to formally break ties with it in 2001. Post 9/11, for two decades Pakistan provided shelter for the Taliban leaders and other facilities, including healthcare for its fighters. In a way, Taliban's dependence on Islamabad has enabled the Pakistani administration and various terror organisations based in Pakistan to apply a great amount of influence on the Taliban.[1]

Following a dubious policy, Pakistan was comfortable scheming with the then, (and now dead) supreme leader of the Taliban, Mullah Omar, even offering him safe haven inside Pakistan. This is the same Mullah Omar who had shielded Osama bin Laden as the *al-Qaeda* leader plotted the 9/11 attacks on the US that triggered the Afghan War. This is while Pakistan also signed up as an ally of the US in the "war on terror". Pakistan was taking American money to track down and kill the very Taliban leader it was hiding.[2]

Many were of the opinion that gradually foreign countries, especially Pakistan, would impose the Taliban on the Afghan people in order to deny self-determination to them, and keep them settled and divided across the artificial border drawn by the colonial power of Great Britain—the Durand Line.[3] But, on the downside, to ensure the Talibanization in Afghanistan and Islamist inertia at home, Pakistan sacrificed over 80,000 of its own countrymen, which the military establishment has loudly dubbed "collateral damage". Sadly, in the decades dedicated to sustaining an Afghanistan that suits the Taliban, the Pakistani Army has also created a Pakistan that suits the Taliban.[4]

Who are the Taliban?

The Taliban is an Islamist militant organisation established in 1994 during the civil war that followed the Soviet Union's withdrawal from Afghanistan. Although it was officially formed in 1994, its original fighters were the Mujahedeen, forces that fought the Soviet Union in Afghanistan from 1969 to 1989. In September 1994, Mullah Mohammad Omar, the future leader of the Taliban, left Sang-i-Hisar *Madarsa* in Maiwand, where he had been studying since the end of the Soviet occupation. Eventually, he gathered a small group of students and pledged to rid Afghanistan of warlords and criminals. With just 50 students supporting his campaign, Mullah Omar founded the group that would later become known as the Taliban.[5] The group, many of whom were *madarsa* (Islamic school) students, called themselves Taliban, meaning students. Many others who became core members of the group were commanders in other predominantly Pakhtoon parties, and former Khalqi People's Democratic Party of Afghanistan (PDPA) members.[6]

In 1997, the Taliban renamed the country the Islamic Emirate of Afghanistan and Mullah Omar assumed the title of *Amir-ul Momineen* (Commander of the faithful). In areas under their control, Taliban authorities enforced their version of Islamic law, enacting policies prohibiting women from working outside the home in activities other than health care, and ensuring corporal punishment for those convicted of certain crimes.[7]

The Taliban philosophy is based on Salafism. Interestingly, the ideology of the Taliban is considered a shift from the traditional Islamist views held by the Mujahedeen in the 1980s and early 1990s to a combination of strict anti-Western Pakhtoon tribal ideology mixed with radicalised Deobandi interpretations of Islam. The Taliban has an ideological commitment to a strict interpretation and enforcement of Shariah law.[8] Following the US offensive on Afghanistan, the Taliban regime unravelled rapidly after its loss at Mazar-e-Sharif on 9 November 2001. Over the next week, Taliban strongholds were crushed after Coalition and Northern Alliance offensives on Taloqan, Bamiyan, Herat, Kabul, and Jalalabad. Resultantly, numerous leaders, their families, and close aides shifted to neighbouring Pakistan.

The *Quetta Shura* is believed to be an important part of the Taliban structure. It was headed by Mullah Omar. The term '*Quetta Shura*' originated from Mullah Omar's relocation of the Taliban to Quetta in the Balochistan province of Pakistan during the year 2002. Mullah Omar and his group continue to refer to themselves as the Islamic Emirate of Afghanistan, despite being removed from power in 2001.[9] Currently, the *Shura* has a leadership crisis, as Mohammad Yaqoob, eldest son of Omar, is trying to exercise some control over the *Shura*, but not with incredible success.[10]

Also, the most lethal and sophisticated insurgent group, the Haqqani Network, functions both as an independent organisation and as a fierce branch of the Taliban. It officially affiliated with Taliban in 2007.[11] Based mainly in North Waziristan, Pakistan, the Network was created as a Sunni Islamist militant organisation. In Afghanistan, the group's stronghold spans the Loya-Paktia region, which includes provinces in Paktia, Paktika, Khost, and sections of Ghazni.[12]

Post 15 August 2021, the new Taliban government in Kabul announced on September 7 is headed by Prime Minister Mohammad Hassan Akhund, one of the close aides of Mullah Omar. Mullah Omar's son, Mohammad Yaqoob, is defence minister, while Sirajuddin Haqqani, leader of the Haqqani Network, heads the ministry of interior that is responsible for internal security. Abdul Ghani Baradar, who was the public face of the Taliban during negotiations in Doha, Qatar, is one of two deputy prime ministers.[13] The decision-making powers are with the *Rahbari Shura* (Leadership Council) and most of its members were part of the fighting inside Afghanistan.

It can very well be remarked that the Taliban has evolved into a military group capable of advancing along multiple lines of effort. The shadowy insurgent network skilful at executing rural ambushes and planting improvised explosive devices has been replaced by a complex organisation managing as many as 80,000 fighters who are even more skilled at using social media than AK-47s. Their operational art now combines information operations, including appeals from tribal elders alongside text messages and Twitter, with decentralized orders that permit local commanders who know the topography and politics in their areas to categorize prospects for taking the initiative. Most importantly, when Taliban forces achieve military success, they emphasize those advances with mobile reserve exploitation forces, hordes of commandos on motorcycles, allowing the group to maintain speed on the battlefield.[14]

Reasons Behind Effective Relations Between Pakistan and the Taliban

Post 9/11, Pakistan was also the first country that supported the war against terrorism that was launched by the then US President George W. Bush and stood beside him in the struggle against the Taliban. At the official level, Pakistan distanced itself from the remaining Taliban in Afghanistan. At the same time, parts of Pakistan's military and intelligence establishment, maintained links with Islamist groups in Afghanistan like the Taliban. Those links, it is claimed, at times turned into significant material and logistical support.[15] In reality, numerous Taliban leaders and fighters crossed the border in the northern tribal areas, as the paramilitary forces (Frontier Corps) based there created no problems for them. Apparently, the current Deputy First Prime Minister of Taliban's power structure in Afghanistan, Mullah Abdul Ghani Baradar fled to Pakistan and started preparing the re-launch of the Taliban.[16]

There is no doubt that Pakistan has provided a safe harbour to the Taliban militants, since the US-NATO offensive of 2001. Moreover, due to the predominant system, corruption and abuse of power is common which causes educational backwardness and socio-economic deprivation in Pakistan. Besides, the government has no control on the border with Afghanistan where the Taliban frequently cross it from Afghanistan. The administrative and structural flaws present in the tribal areas provide the justification for and sustainability to the Taliban movement.[17]

Besides, Pakistani army and intelligence wings retain substantial control over the Taliban despite its gains in Afghanistan. For instance, members of the Taliban's leadership council (*Shura*) safely reside in Pakistan. The Taliban can freely move men and materiel into Afghanistan, use Pakistani hospitals to treat their wounded fighters, and communicate with their operational commanders in Afghanistan; in some instances, they have even used Pakistani passports to travel overseas. They also apparently own lucrative real estate holdings and have significant business interests in the Pakistani cities of Quetta, Karachi, and Peshawar.[18]

Tribal Affinity

The Pakhtoon factor on both sides of the Durand Line helped in fructification of the Taliban's official comeback in Afghanistan. The Pakhtoons are based in the southern and south-eastern areas of

Afghanistan and have a presence across the border in the north-western tribal areas of Pakistan, where the core of the Taliban leadership is said to have moved following the US invasion in 2001.

The ethnic factors contributed to the role of the Pakistani tribal volunteers in the Afghan Taliban movement in the initial years. There is a long history of involvement of the border Pakhtoon tribes in conflict in Afghanistan. Also, Maulvi Jalaluddin Haqqani, the senior-most former Mujahedeen commander to join the Taliban, had for 25 years been based in Miranshah of North Waziristan. As the Taliban Minister for Frontiers and Tribes, he was the principal patron for Pakistani tribal fighters serving with the Afghan Taliban. However, the single largest movement of Pakistani Pakhtoon volunteers into Taliban-run Afghanistan occurred at the start of the US intervention in 2001. Sufi Mohammad, leader of the Tehreek-e-Nafaz-e-Shariat-e-Mohammadi (TNSM) in the Malakand area of Khyber Pakhtunkhwa, led a force of some 10,000 men pledged to guard against US attack.[19]

The Taliban rely on tribal ties to set up bases in the Federally Administrative Tribal Areas (FATA), which is now part of Khyber Pakhtunkhwa province. Here, it benefits from the tribal loyalties, even from the lower ranks of the Frontier Corps, who are often members of the same Wazir or Daur tribes.[20] The tribal kinship works as a shield for the Taliban, as they get support at the household level in these areas, and it becomes difficult for security forces to differentiate between a Taliban fighter and a common resident.

Religion

The driving force behind Taliban ideology and Pakistan's support to it is Islam. Establishment of an Islamic Emirate adhering strictly to Sharia-based laws was and is the fundamental aim of the Taliban. At the heart of this Islamic quest is the Deobandi ideology. This particular school of Islamic thought had a very precise understanding of the faith. The Deobandi brand of Islam observes an orthodox Islamism, claiming that the adherence to Sunni Islamic law, or Sharia, is the path to salvation. It insists on the revival of Islamic practices that go back to the 7th century, the time of the Prophet Muhammad. It also upholds the concept of global *jihad* as a sacred duty to protect Muslims across the world, and is opposed to any non-Islamic concepts and ideas.[21]

Accordingly, several prominent Islamic seminaries (*madarsas*) of Pakistan, following the Deobandi path have been a constant support for the Taliban since the time they were fighting as Mujahedeen. It is true that many clerics and Islamist groups are sympathetic to the Afghan Taliban and support them covertly. They are accused of intensifying efforts and encouraging the militant groups. The Afghan Taliban is banned in Pakistan, but some clerics as well as Islamist groups are sympathetic to these militant groups and engage in recruitment activities on their behalf. This is not the first time that clerics and religious leaders within Pakistan have supported the cause of the Taliban across the other side of border.

These seminaries have often championed the cause of Taliban militants and post 15 August 2021 are in a celebratory mode. In a way, it is the victory of Deobandi ideology over the infidel 'occupying' forces of West. In one such instance, the Jamia Hafsa, a women's *madarsa*, linked with Lal Masjid, hoisted the flag of the Islamic Emirate of Afghanistan causing a recent spate of controversy in Pakistan. The Jamia Hafsa students in a celebratory event were seen singing the song—*Salaam Taliban*—in praise of the regime.[22] Moreover, Balochistan has become a hub of Taliban ideology in the form of the *Quetta Shura*. There are over 15,000 *madarsas* being run on the Pak-Afghan border out of which Balochistan has more than 60 per cent.[23]

Interestingly, the entire cadre base of Taliban during the 1990s was supported by Darul Uloom Haqqania *Madarsa* situated in the Pakistani province of Akora Khattak. The Darul Uloom Haqqania seminary has repeatedly churned out the 'who's who' of Taliban top brass including many on the hardliner group's negotiating team that held talks with the Kabul government to end the 20-year war. The seminary's late leader, Sami-ul-Haq, boasted of advising the Taliban's founder, Mullah Omar, earning him the nickname of "the Father of the Taliban". Haq later sent students to fight for the movement when it issued a call to arms during its rise to power in the 1990s. The

Haqqani network, the Taliban's ultra-violent faction, is named after this seminary where its leader was taught, raised, and subsequently followed by numerous other members.

Post 2001, the Taliban needed to recruit new fighters to reinforce their ranks in campaigns against the coalition forces and the Afghan state. Since it was not possible for the Taliban to recruit new members for their armed opposition within Afghanistan, as coalition forces and the security forces together with militia forces have an overriding presence, consequently they chose a substitute strategy. The Taliban began to encourage young students in Afghan refugee camps and religious schools in Pakistan to join them in their campaign.[24]

The Taliban thus, enjoys not only the support of Pakistan's prominent *madarsas* but also, mainstream Islamic parties such as the Jamiat-ul-Ulema-Islam (JUI) and Jamaat-i-Islami. Shuja-ul-Mulk, a leader of the JUI, who has served in the National Assembly of Pakistan, stated, "...who have made many sacrifices, and with whom we share a common ideology."[25] JUI Nazriati, which broke away from the JUI after 9/11, remains among the Taliban's most loyal supporters. The group's leader, Maulana Abdul Qadir Luni, openly supports Afghan *jihad* in speeches, rallies and videos.

Geography

Not only religion and ethnicity, Pakistan's geography also played a great role in sustenance of the Taliban ideology within Pakistan that finally helped in the Taliban gaining power and control in Afghanistan. The safe havens located in and around Waziristan and Quetta did facilitate Afghanistan's Taliban movement.

Since the tribal areas are the natural geo-strategic gateway to Afghanistan, South Waziristan was a particularly important supply route for the *Mujahedeen*, helped by the fact that the same tribe (*Wazir*) live on both sides of the border. After the toppling of the Afghan Taliban regime in late 2001, Pakistani, Afghan, and foreign militants fleeing from US forces gathered in strength in Waziristan due to the naturally porous borders.[26] The inhospitable terrain of these mountainous regions helped scores of Taliban fighters and their family to escape from Afghanistan and eventually settle in Pakistan. Regions in line with the Afghan provinces of Paktiya and Paktika have many passages and routes to which security forces have no access. Angur Ada and Baghar China (South Waziristan) and Sara Kandaw and Shawal (North Waziristan) were regions where multiple routes and passages were accessible.[27] Supporters of the Taliban in Waziristan before 9/11 were present but they had no group except the Haqqani Network. After 9/11, all the existing ground realities like terrain, tradition, administrative system, lack of political power, religious feelings, and socio-economic deprivation prevalent in Waziristan provided favourable and feasible ground for the rise and spread of Talibanization.[28]

Also, the geographical proximity and connectivity of Quetta with the Taliban stronghold of Kandahar, worked in favour of the militants. These two cities have historical trade and cultural relations exploited by the Taliban. Not only Kandahar, adjoining areas of Chaman and Pishin in Balochistan have also witnessed Taliban presence since many years. The name '*Quetta Shura*' is self-evident in this context. Taliban graveyards are also visible in the area, along with their flags over homes and shops. Chaman has acted as a major entry point of the Taliban into Pakistan. Donation campaigns organised for the Taliban war chest at Pishin's main bazaar is a commonplace event in Balochistan, especially during the month of Ramzan.[29]

Taliban Funding

The annual Taliban income from different sources is estimated to be between \$300 million and \$1.6 billion, according to *Letter dated 19 May 2020 from the Chair of the Security Council Committee established pursuant to resolution 1988 (2011) addressed to the President of the Security Council*.[30] Pakistan acted as a fertile catchment area for collecting funds for Taliban activities. The importance of Pakistan in raising funds can be derived from a statement of Mulla Rahmatullah Kakazada, a senior Taliban diplomat of 2016, in which he said that while the territory under control of the Taliban in Afghanistan was expanding, fundraising was not keeping pace. Despite the alleged availability of a lot of territory in Afghanistan, he stated that "if we left Pakistan, we would not survive one week."[31]

Narco trade is another source of stable income for the Taliban. Pakistan along with Iran and Afghanistan constitute the Golden Crescent, one of world's biggest drug-producing regions. Drug smugglers call it the golden route: from Afghanistan into Pakistan and then into eastern Iran. The general route for smuggling Afghan-produced opiates from Karachi, Pakistan goes overland from Balochistan province across the border into Iran and finally into laboratories in Turkey.[32] Officials described a system of heroin smuggling and taxation organised by the Taliban that stretched across Nangarhar's southern districts on the border with Pakistan. Heroin produced in the western-most area of Nangarhar was trafficked eastward. Once across the border, narco bosses could take the equivalent of $6 per kilogram of heroin as profit, a portion of which was again redirected back to the Taliban via security officials. The same process was replicated through lesser border crossings, such as those over the Spin Ghar mountains towards Tirah Valley and Khyber in Pakistan.[33]

Afghan Taliban militants stay with coal miners in the mountains near Quetta and come to the bazaar area every Friday to solicit 5,000-10,000 Pakistani rupees ($50 to $70) from shopkeepers. They generally travel on motorbikes and ask larger stores for contributions. They say that they belong to the Taliban movement and that they are fighting in Allah's path. The Taliban openly holds fundraising campaigns in several places of Balochistan: Quetta, Kuchlak Bypass, Pakhtoon Abad, Ishaq Abad, Farooqia Town etc.[34] Local sources reported that mining companies in Balochistan were involved in quarrying precious minerals and marble that was later refined in Karachi and sold as products of Pakistan. Taxation and revenues from mining contracts were reportedly overseen by the Taliban's "Dabaro Comisyoon" (Stones and Mines Commission).[35]

Logistic Support

Since Pakistan is an industrial country with many legal gaps on control over dual use materials, it is easy to have access to every single kind of goods. As the Taliban began to produce remote control devices and electric circuits, raw materials they needed were provided from Pakistan or through Pakistan as the importing country. Furthermore, the Taliban also needed chemicals and ammonium nitrate to make explosive devices to be placed on highways. These items could be bought in large quantities on the free market in Pakistan without any legal procedure.[36]

Interestingly, as reported on 9 August 2021, just a few days before the Taliban 'takeover', the then head of international affairs in Afghanistan's National Security Council, Ahmad Shuja Jamal (now in exile), said that many, about 80 per cent, of the explosive devices that were used to kill American soldiers in Afghanistan, used ammonium nitrate which is a fertilizer but also a precursor for explosives, produced in two Pakistani factories.[37]

Pakistani companies, Pakarab Fertilizers Ltd. and Fatima Fertilizer Co. have been very active in supplying raw materials for explosives. Fatima and Pakarab were not normal corporations engaged in routine business. Instead, they were widely understood to be active co-conspirators with the Haqqani Network terrorists. The IEDs planted by the Taliban in Afghanistan targeting US-NATO forces used ammonium nitrate derived from the Fatima Group CAN Fertilizer, manufactured, sold, and distributed by Fatima and Pakarab.[38]

ISI Network and the Taliban

While discussing the role of Pakistan's terror structure in the re-emergence of the Taliban, we cannot deny the role played by the Inter-Services Intelligence (ISI), Pakistan's infamous spy agency. The ISI Directorate, formed in 1948, has dramatically augmented its capacities, both within Pakistan, and across expanding theatres abroad.[39] It officially has seven sections: Joint Intelligence X (JIX), Joint Intelligence Bureau (JIB), Joint Counter Intelligence Bureau (JCIB), Joint Intelligence/North (JIN), Joint Intelligence Miscellaneous (JIM), Joint

Signal Intelligence Bureau (JSIB) and Joint Intelligence Technical Division (JIT). Of these, the JCIB oversees intelligence operations in Afghanistan, along with Israel, Russia, Middle East, etc.[40] The ISI also has four wings: A, T, C and S for better functioning. Among the four, it is also well known that the S-Wing is involved in arming the Taliban. It is the main provider of funding, training, protection, and intelligence to the Taliban and other militant organisations. S-Wing operatives search radical *madarsas* in Pakistan to find new recruits for terror groups.[41]

The Taliban, over a period of considerable time, has developed a symbiotic relationship with Pakistan's ISI, both inside Pakistan and across its borders with Afghanistan. During the Soviet occupation of Afghanistan in the 1980s, the US's Central Intelligence Agency (CIA) and ISI were instrumental in supporting seven Sunni Muslim mujahedeen groups in their *jihad* against the Soviets, and was the principal conduit for covert US and Saudi funding. It subsequently played a pivotal role in the emergence of the Taliban.[42] This support comprised not only arms, ammunition, fuel, equipment, and other essential supplies, but also military advisers and trainers, as well as economic support.[43] During the mid-1990s, unquestionably, the Pakistani army and intelligence agencies, with the ISI at the front, made a vital contribution for the Taliban to become a highly effective military force. The covert support and backing of the Taliban by the ISI came from the corps headquarters in Peshawar.[44]

Even following Pakistan's change of President in 1999, when Pervez Musharraf led a coup d'état, the Taliban still flourished with the backing of the Pakistani government and the ISI. After 9/11, the Pakistani government suddenly switched sides and appeared to be a US ally. Whereas, on the surface, Pakistan's ISI pledged to fight the Taliban alongside US troops, in reality, the agency continued to send weapons and fuel to the Taliban in Afghanistan.[45] Unsurprisingly, even in 2001, in breach of UN sanctions, up to 30 ISI trucks a day were still crossing into Afghanistan.[46] The Taliban were even allowed to re-settle in Pakistan's restive province of Balochistan. Meanwhile, the ISI assisted the Taliban to create disturbances in Afghanistan post

2001. US and NATO intelligence shows a methodical and persistent system of ISI collusion. The ISI held training camps for Taliban recruits north of Quetta, handing out money and weapons from the Gulf states and planned shopping tours in Quetta and Karachi, where the Taliban were able to stock up on material, buying hundreds of motorcycles, pickup trucks and satellite phones.[47] Also, the Taliban, along with the ISI and the *madaris* of the JUI were recruiting and training young students to fight in Afghanistan.[48]

The ISI has also been very dominant in asserting its control over the Taliban. Mullah Abdul Ghani Baradar (current Deputy PM of the Taliban 'government') was arrested by the ISI in 2010. Ironically, he was arrested because he engaged in unauthorised talks with then Afghan President Hamid Karzai. The ISI, in a way, was sending a very clear message to the Taliban leadership: don't engage in talks without our say-so. In 2018, the ISI gave its nod to the talks. In short, without Pakistan's support of the Taliban, the discussions in Doha would have folded up years ago.[49] Also, the death of Mullah Akhtar Mohammed Mansour, the leader of the Taliban after Mullah Omar, in an airstrike in Pakistan is believed by many to be engineered by the ISI to remove a leader who had lost their trust.[50]

As the Taliban formed its 'government' on 6 September 2021, the mind the screen role of the ISI is very much evident as two ISI favourites, Sirajuddin Haqqani, a designated global terrorist, and Mullah Yaqoob were made the next Interior and Defence Ministers in a cabinet of over two dozen men. Reports also suggest that ISI Chief Lieutenant General Faiz Hamid's visit caused a reshuffle in the Taliban cabinet.[51] There are reports suggesting that Taliban operations are being controlled from two command centres of the ISI located in Chaman (Balochistan) and Jalalabad in Nangarhar province of Afghanistan, which are manned by Brigadier-rank officers of the ISI.[52]

The Taliban-ISI relationship is based on mutual benefits. The Taliban need external sanctuary, as well as military and logistical support to sustain themselves; the ISI believes that it needs an important allied force in Afghanistan to uphold and preserve regional strength and 'strategic depth' in their rivalry with India.[53] Also, in a way, the homecoming of the Taliban in Afghanistan reinforced Pakistan's control on the overall affairs of Afghanistan, and the ISI indeed played a vital role.

Pakistan and the 'Good' Taliban

The devious policy of justifying terror according to Pakistan's own whims and desires has resulted in sustenance of the Taliban movement on both sides of the Durand Line. The Pakistani side provided support and refuge to the Afghan side; in return, the overt state distinguished the Afghan Taliban as the 'good' ones (as they caused disruption within Afghanistan, creating further chaos and setting straight Pakistan's design) and the 'bad' ones (attacking Pakistani establishment and security forces to establish a Sharia-based Pakistan).

In every way, Pakistan Army's "good Taliban, bad Taliban" strategy has been ingrained in distinguishing between *jihadist* groups that target Pakistan and those that can be controlled to accomplish the geostrategic objectives of the military establishment. The return of the Taliban to power in Afghanistan is naturally considered the conclusion of two decades of Pakistan providing the group, and its affiliates with havens to endure themselves until the withdrawal of the US-NATO forces.[54]

Behind Pakistan's efforts to shield the so-called 'moderates', (the good ones) has been an intent to preserve its dominant influence in Afghanistan and avert the complete elimination of the Afghan Taliban, which it created as a strategic asset. It is almost impossible to make a distinction between 'good' and 'bad' Taliban and trying to do so is not only misleading but could further complicate the situation in both Afghanistan and Pakistan.[55] The policy has not only given legitimacy to violence perpetrated by the Taliban in Afghanistan, but also worked against Pakistan's motive of keeping the bad ones in control. The TTP with the stated aim to overthrow the government in Islamabad by fighting a violent military campaign against the state is very much present in the tribal belt of Pakistan, and violence will increase in the coming months.

Crucially, it needs to be understood that Talibanisation is a

Pakistani notion and construct that was exported to Afghanistan and not the other way round. In other words, the Taliban are inherent to Pakistan and the good Taliban are only an extension of Pakistan's political ambition.

Pak-based Terror Groups Supporting the Taliban

Various terror organisations working in tandem with the Taliban or at times merging with them at operational levels have in a way sustained the spirit and relevance of the Taliban, even after 2001. These affiliations greatly helped in continuation of the Taliban and inter-generational transmission of its ideology among the fighters. During the reign of the Taliban in Afghanistan, groups from Pakistan's tribal belt, as well as Punjab and Sind, served in the ranks of the Afghan Taliban. Following the collapse of the Taliban regime in Kabul in late 2001, Taliban and foreign fighters sought safe haven in the Pakistan/ Afghanistan border areas.[56] Few of the notorious groupings are discussed below:

Tehreek-e-Taliban Pakistan (TTP)

Tehreek-e-Taliban Pakistan (TTP) has mutual relations of support with the Taliban movement in neighbouring Afghanistan. Moments after taking charge in Kabul, the Afghan Taliban released leaders of the TTP, including former 'deputy chief' Faqir Mohammad. The Afghan Taliban reportedly also released around 2,300 leaders of the TTP, who have duly felicitated the former for taking over Kabul, after having already sworn loyalty to Hibatullah Akhundzada.[57]

The TTP leadership in both the tribal areas of Khyber Pakhtunkhwa (KP) has many a time publicly sworn allegiance to Mullah Omar. Indeed, the Pakistan and Afghan Taliban could be said to be Siamese twins—two heads of the same body. Despite differences in opinion and agendas between the Afghan Taliban and (parts of) the TTP, for instance, over where the battlefield should be, it is difficult to deny that the Taliban has profited significantly from cooperation with its Pakistani counterpart.[58] In 2001, before the TTP's official formation, many of its current members operated independently in

KP. These groups supported the Afghan Taliban's fight against the US-led coalition operations in Afghanistan by providing additional soldiers, training, and logistical backing.[59] They also operated as supplementary groups for the Afghan Taliban until 2002, when the Pakistani military began to conduct operations in the FATA against militant groups fleeing the war in Afghanistan.[60]

Reportedly, in 2007, TTP commander Baitullah Mehsud fought alongside the Taliban in Afghanistan before the formation of this terror organisation. Also, the two groups shared a goal of using violence and terror to establish a government following Sharia law.[61]

In 2008-2009, Osama bin Laden and Mullah Omar met the three dominant TTP commanders: Hafiz Gul Bahadur, Baitullah Mehsud, and Maulvi Nazir. They encouraged the leaders to sink their differences and reduce their operations in Pakistan in order to help the Afghan Taliban counter the impending increase of US-led coalition forces in Afghanistan. The three commanders agreed and formed a temporary coalition known as the *Shura* Ittihad al-Mujahedeen (Allied Mujahedeen Council) in February 2008.[62] Nevertheless, the Council was disbanded in 2009 due to fighting among the three leaders.

Jamaat-ud-Dawa + LeT Cohort

The Taliban relied not only on members of *madarsas* in the Deobandi network for getting assistance from non-official sources. The Jamaat-ud-Dawa and the Lashkar-e-Taiba (LeT) affiliated with non-traditional elements also supported them widely. The Jamaat-ud-Dawa has also been involved in recruitment of fighters and providing weapons for the Salafi Mujahedeen nominally aligned with the Taliban operating in the provinces of Nuristan and Kunar.[63] Many LeT members are Pakistani or Afghans. It was believed that the group had ties with Afghanistan's Taliban government and with Osama bin Laden. Reportedly, fighters from the Lashkar-e-Taiba were killed in August 1998 when US Cruise missiles struck bin Laden's training camps in Afghanistan, and a senior *al-Qaeda* official was captured in a Lashkar-e-Taiba safe house in Pakistan in March 2002.[64]

Besides, the leadership of the Jamaat-Lashkar has close ties with the Taliban. Abdul Rehman Makki is the brother-in-law of LeT founder Hafiz Muhammad Saeed and is also the second-in-command of the group. The US put a $2 million bounty on his head due to his close relationship with the late Taliban leader, Mullah Omar, and *al-Qaeda* leader, Ayman al-Zawahiri.[65]

Lashkar-e-Jhangvi (LeJ)

The LeJ, along with Siphah Sahaba Pakistan, the suspected militant wing of Ahl-e-Sunnat Wal Jamaat (ASWJ), has been orchestrating Shia killings all over the country with Balochistan's capital, Quetta, the most prominent stage for what many are labelling as an ongoing Shia genocide.[66] The Pakistani government banned the LeJ in 2001. After the ban, a few LeJ militants fled to Afghanistan for Taliban protection and used the region as a base to plot attacks in Pakistan. The group continued to carry out sectarian attacks throughout the 2000s, and likely worked together with other Sunni militant groups, such as the Afghan Taliban, in those attacks. Some analysts believe that many attacks claimed by the Afghan Taliban in the late 2000s were actually carried out by LeJ militants.[67] In comparison to the TTP or LeT, the LeJ is a Punjab-based terror organisation, with sectarian underpinnings. The linkage between the LeJ and the Taliban show the extent of Talibanisation within the non-tribal areas of Pakistan.

Conclusion

Pakistan is trying very hard to publicize the Taliban cause in the United Nations in an effort to get recognition for it on the global platform. It is a brazen act showcasing the stand and aspiration of the Pakistan establishment vis-à-vis the Taliban regime of Afghanistan. This effort in the United Nations has unfortunately, coincided with the Taliban's Maulana Nooruddin Turabi, in charge of jails, announcing that brutal Sharia-based punishments like cutting off one's hand and whipping and beheading of the guilty would be soon re-imposed.

Also, Pakistan's 'appeal' to the Afghan Taliban urging it not to support the TTP cause, will prove a failure. Pakistan needs to gear up its security agencies to tackle upcoming terrorist and sectarian conflicts not only in the tribal areas, but also in the provinces of Sindh and Punjab, where Taliban ideology has entrenched been deeply within the social structure. More worryingly, post 15 August, various religious groups are demanding imposing of the Sharia within Pakistan.

Pakistan in its age-old scheme of creating chaos in the neighbourhood has in a way become obsessed with the 'Afghan Question'. So much so that instead of fighting the fire in its own territory, the state agency is requesting the Islamist regime of Afghanistan not to assist their fellow militants inside Pakistan. As the Afghan and Pakistani Taliban share close tribal, religious, ethnic and organisational connections, there is hardly any hope of sustainable peace in Pakistan.

Afghanistan is going the Sharia way, may be slowly. The existence of a strict Sunni Islamic country sharing a common international border will have a grave ramification on the socio-political edifice of Pakistan. This re-emergence of the Taliban will further diminish democratic ideals and the ethos of parliamentary politics within Pakistan. There is no doubt that the Taliban will bring in an era of instability and viciousness on both sides of the Durand Line.

NOTES

1. Michael Kugelman. "Pakistan's Friendship with the Taliban Is Changing", *Foreign Policy*, September 13, 2021, https://foreignpolicy.com/2021/09/13/pakistan-taliban-ties-afghanistan/
2. Stan Grant. "'Good' Taliban, 'bad' Taliban and IS-K: For Afghanistan, it's never a simple story," September 5, 2021, https://www.abc.net.au/news/2021-09-05/taliban-is-k-afghanistan-never-simple-as-good-or-bad/100425728
3. Khalilullah Safi. "The Afghan Taliban's Relationship with Pakistan," *LISD White Paper*, No. 4, September, 2018, https://docplayer.org/199063403-The-afghan-taliban-s-relationship-with-pakistan-lisd-white-paper-khalilullah-safi-translated-and-edited-by-joesph-mohr.html
4. Kuwar Khuldune Shahid. "How the Taliban Used Pakistan," *The Diplomat*, August 19, 2021, https://thediplomat.com/2021/08/how-the-taliban-used-pakistan/
5. Centre for International Security and Cooperation, "The Afghan Taliban", https://cisac.fsi.stanford.edu/mappingmilitants/profiles/afghan-taliban
6. Human Rights Watch. "Backgrounder on Afghanistan: History of the War," October, 2001, https://www.hrw.org/legacy/backgrounder/asia/afghan-bck1023.htm
7. Ibid.

8. Ibid.
9. Institute for the Study of War. "The Quetta Shura Taliban in Southern Afghanistan: Organization, Operations and Shadow Governance," December 21, 2009, https://www.understandingwar.org/sites/default/files/QuettaShura Taliban_1.pdf
10. Synovitz, Ron. "Will the Taliban Stay United to Govern, or Splinter into Regional Fiefdoms?," August 25, 2021, https://gandhara.rferl.org/a/taliban-govern-regional-factions/31428069.html
11. Khalilullah Safi, op. cit.
12. Devin Lurie. "The Haqqani Network," American Security Project, September, 2020, https://www.americansecurityproject.org/wp-content/uploads/2020/08/Ref-0241-The-Haqqani-Network.pdf
13. Trofimov, Yaroslav. "Who are the Taliban and what's next for Afghanistan?," September 28, 2021, https://www.livemint.com/politics/news/who-are-the-taliban-and-what-s-next-for-afghanistan-11632751216348.html
14. Benjamin Jensen. "How the Taliban did it: Inside the 'operational art' of its military victory," *Atlantic Council*, August 15, 2021, https://www.atlantic council.org/blogs/new-atlanticist/how-the-taliban-did-it-inside-the-operational-art-of-its-military-victory/
15. James Landale. "Afghanistan: What rise of Taliban means for Pakistan," *BBC*, September 3, 2021, https://www.bbc.com/news/world-asia-58443839
16. Khalilullah Safi, op. cit.
17. Khan Zeb Burki. 'Rise of Taliban in Waziristan', *The Dialogue*, vol. 3, (2010), pp. 188-211.
18. Aqil Shah. "What Will Happen to Afghanistan and Pakistan's Uneasy Border?," *Carnegie Endowment*, August 13, 2021, https://carnegieendowment.org/2021/08/13/what-will-happen-to-afghanistan-and-pakistan-s-uneasy-border-pub-85152
19. Michael Semple. "The Pakistan Taliban Movement: An Appraisal," *CIDOB*, November, 2014, https://www.cidob.org/en/publications/publication_series/project_papers/stap_rp/policy_research_papers/the_pakistan_taliban_movement_an_appraisal
20. Shuja Nawaz. "FATA-A Most Dangerous Place," *CSIS*, 2009, https://csis-website-prod.s3.amazonaws.com/s3fs-public/legacy_files/files/media/csis/pubs/081218_nawaz_fata_web.pdf
21. Sohel Rana and Sumit Ganguly. "Taliban's religious ideology–Deobandi Islam–has roots in colonial India," August 25, 2021, https://theconversation.com/talibans-religious-ideology-deobandi-islam-has-roots-in-colonial-india-166323
22. *India Today*, "Pakistan students sing 'Salam Taliban', hoist flag at women's madrasa," August 22, 2021, https://www.indiatoday.in/world/video/pakistan-students-sing-salam-taliban-hoist-flag-women-madrasa-1844012-2021-08-22
23. Amit Bansal. "Taliban: A strategic analysis of the Islamist group's historic rise", *The Economic Times*, August 15, 2021, https://economictimes.indiatimes.com/news/defence/taliban-a-strategic-analysis-of-the-islamist-groups-historic-rise/articleshow/85344522.cms?from=mdr
24. Devin Lurie, 2020.

25. Roshan Noorzai. "Taliban Donations Soar in Pakistan Ahead of US Pullout from Afghanistan", *VOA*, June 18, 2021, https://www.voanews.com/a/extremism-watch_taliban-donations-soar-pakistan-ahead-us-pullout-afghanistan/6207199.html
26. M. Syed, Abass Zaidi and Syed M. Abbas. "A Profile of Baitullah Mehsud", *The Long War Journal*, September 2008, http://www.longwarjournal.org/multimedia/Baitullah-profile-Manzar-LWJ09302008.pdf.
27. Khalilullah Safi, op. cit.
28. Khan Zeb Burki, op.cit.
29. Abdul Hai Kakar and Abubakar Siddique. "Pakistani Support Base Bolsters Taliban As U.S. Exits", *Gandhara*, June 21, 2021, https://gandhara.rferl.org/a/afghan-taliban-support-base-pakistan/31318820.html
30. United Nations Security Council, "Letter dated 19 May 2020 from the Chair of the Security Council Committee established pursuant to resolution", 1988 (2011) addressed to the President of the Security Council', May 27, 2020, https://www.securitycouncilreport.org/atf/cf/%7B65BFCF9B-6D27-4E9C-8CD3-CF6E4FF96FF9%7D/s_2020_415_e.pdf
31. Jon Boone and Sami Yousafzai. "Taliban facing financial crisis as civilian deaths deter donors", *The Guardian*, November 20, 2016, https://www.theguardian.com/world/2016/nov/29/afghan-taliban-facing-financial-crisis-as-civilian-deaths-deter-donors.
32. Sanchita Bhattacharya. "Narco Terror: A Thriving Industry of Pakistan", *Journal of Counterterrorism & Homeland Security International*, vol. 20, No. 2 (2014), pp. 26-30.
33. United Nations Security Council, op. cit.
34. Roshan Noorzai, op. cit.
35. United Nations Security Council, op. cit.
36. Khalilullah Safi, op. cit.
37. *The Statesman*, "Taliban received men, weapons, explosives from Pakistan", August 9, 2021, https://www.thestatesman.com/world/taliban-received-men-weapons-explosives-pakistan-1502991987.html
38. The United States District Court for Eastern District of New York, "Complaint under the Anti-Terrorism Act", August, 2021, https://terrorismcase.com/wp-content/uploads/2021/08/Wildman-v.-Deutsche-Bank-ATA-Complaint.pdf
39 Grant Holt and David H. Gray. "A Pakistani Fifth Column? The Pakistani Inter-Services Intelligence Directorate's Sponsorship of Terrorism", *Global Security Studies*, vol. 2, no.1 (2011), pp. 55-68.
40. Sanchita Bhattacharya. "ISI: Twisted Shadows", *South Asia Terrorism Portal*, vol. 11, no.16 (2012), http://www.satp.org/satporgtp/sair/Archives/sair11/11_16.htm#assessment1
41. Rajeev Sharma. "Mullah Omar disclosure is yet another case for the closure of ISI Special Wing", *Firstpost*, September 5, 2015, https://www.firstpost.com/world/mullah-omar-disclosure-is-yet-another-case-for-the-closure-of-isi-special-wing-2422282.html
42. Steve Coll. "Ghost Wars: The Secret History of the CIA, Afghanistan and Bin Laden, from the Soviet Invasion to September 10, 2001", London: Penguin 2005

43. Ahmed Rashid. "Descent into Chaos. How the War against Islamic Extremism is Being Lost in Pakistan, Afghanistan and Central Asia", (London: Allen Lane 2008).
44. S.M. Gabbay. "Networks, Social Capital, and Social Liability: The Case of Pakistani ISI, the Taliban and the War against Terrorism", *Social Networking*, vol. 3 (2014), pp. 220-229.
45. *Small Wars Journal*, "The Pakistani Godfather: The Inter-Services Intelligence and the Afghan Taliban 1994-2010", April 2, 2013, https://smallwars journal.com/jrnl/art/the-pakistani-godfather-the-inter-services-intelligence-and-the-afghan-taliban-1994-2010
46. Ahmed Rashid, op. cit.
47. *Small Wars Journal*, op. cit.
48. Ahmed Rashid, *op. cit*.
49. Rudra Chaudhuri and Shreyas Shende. "Dealing With the Taliban: India's Strategy in Afghanistan After U.S. Withdrawal", *Carnegie India*, June, 2020, https://carnegieendowment.org/files/Chaudhuri_Shende_-_Afghanistan.pdf
50. Carlotta Gall and Ruhullah Khapalwak. "Taliban Leader Feared Pakistan Before he was Killed," *The New York Times*, August 9, 2017, https://www.nytimes.com/2017/08/09/world/asia/talibanleader-feared-pakistan-before-he-was-killed.html
51. Sandeep Dikshit. "ISI favourites make it to Taliban govt, Hasan Akhund acting PM", *The Tribune*, September 8, 2021, https://www.tribuneindia.com/news/nation/isi-favourites-make-it-to-taliban-govt-hasan-akhund-acting-pm-308010
52. Amit Bansal, op. cit.
53. Matt Waldman. "The Sun in the Sky: The relationship between Pakistan's ISI and Afghan insurgents", June, 2010, https://www.files.ethz.ch/isn/117472/DP%2018.pdf
54, Kuwar Khuldune Shahid, op. cit.
55. Sanjeeb Mohanty. "Negotiating with the Taliban: an Indian perspective", 2010, https://www.iias.asia/sites/default/files/nwl_article/2019-05/IIAS_NL55_09.pdf
56. Qandeel Siddique. "Tehrik-e-Taliban Pakistan", *DIIS Report*, 2010, https://www.files.ethz.ch/isn/125545/RP2010-12-Tehrik-e-Taliban_web.pdf
57. Kuwar Khuldune Shahid, op. cit.
58. Qandeel Siddique, op. cit.
59. Hassan Abbas. "A Profile of Tehrik-i-Taliban Pakistan", *CTC Sentinel*, vol. 1, no. 2 (2008), https://ctc.usma.edu/wp-content/uploads/2010/06/Vol1Iss2-Art1.pdf
60. Centre for International Security and Cooperation, 'Tehrik-i-Taliban Pakistan', https://cisac.fsi.stanford.edu/mappingmilitants/profiles/tehrik-i-taliban-pakistan
61. Michael Kugelman, op. cit.
62. Carlotta Gall. "Pakistan and Afghan Taliban Close Ranks", *The New York Times*, March 26, 2009, http://www.nytimes.com/2009/03/27/world/asia/27taliban.html.
63. Khalilullah Safi, op. cit.

64. *Britannica*, "Lashkar-e-Taiba", https://www.britannica.com/topic/Lashkar-e-Taiba
65. CISAC. "Lashkar-e-Taiba", November 2018, https://cisac.fsi.stanford.edu/mappingmilitants/profiles/lashkar-e-taiba#text_block_25834
66. Kunwar Khuldune Shahid. "Pakistan: No More 'Good Taliban'?", *The Diplomat*, January 19, 2015, https://thediplomat.com/2015/01/pakistan-no-more-good-taliban/
67. CISAC. "Lashkar-e-Jhangvi", July 2018, https://cisac.fsi.stanford.edu/mappingmilitants/profiles/lashkar-e-jhangvi-lej#text_block_25826

10

Afghanistan's Inevitable Fallout on J&K

Syed Ata Hasnain

Over the years, the question about Afghanistan's effect on Jammu & Kashmir (J&K) was invariably raised by many scribes all over India. It always elicited a stock answer—that the ripple effect of the waves moving outwards from Afghanistan's violent turbulence always touches J&K. No one was too sure what this really meant but it kept the scribes happy. Post July 2021, as Afghanistan commenced a meltdown and this statement was revisited and analyzed a little deeper. Turbulence of any kind, especially political and social, has a nasty way of travelling through the mode of inspiration especially if there is even a remote similarity among neighbouring regions. We are now witnessing a return to violent days once again in J&K. Those who predicted that events in Afghanistan would have a marginal effect on J&K and a return to the situation of the Nineties may be disappointed. It is an interesting study to examine how the effect of the successful takeover of Afghanistan by the Taliban and the return of Pakistani influence has affected J&K.

Pakistan's grand strategy since 1977 has always included the introduction of political Islam into the region in a manner that it unites the Islamic community for strategic causes and allows Pakistan to hold sway and dominant influence. Its attempts to introduce the same in J&K through almost 30 years have only partially succeeded. The peaceful coexistence of communities in J&K is anathema for the grand design of Pakistan that perceives that this phenomenon replicates India's secular model. It believes that as long as this replication exists with the presence of symbols of tolerance and pluralism, the desire of the people towards affinity with Pakistan is unlikely to manifest itself. This belief extends from the idea that Islamic nations must be united under the ideology of political Islam stretching from the Middle East through Afghanistan to Pakistan and that the only way to wrest J&K and integrate it with Pakistan is by extending political Islam's ideological influence into it. It is good to take note of the fact that in January 1990, at the beginning of its proxy campaign in J&K, Pakistan chose to target the minority of Kashmiri Pandits and other Hindus. It was also a symbolism to attract the region's Muslim community away from its well-established middle path ideology. In 2021, it is attempting to do the same almost as if a fresh campaign is beginning.

Pakistan's actions in 1990 and subsequent years created a false hope of sub-regional aspirations with the embedding of an obscurantist strain of Islam. With this, it continued on the path of cultivating separatism and followed a hybrid strategy of different means of sowing dissension and promoting instability in J&K. Infiltrating ideologically motivated Pakistani terrorists to keep control over the movement, sowing dissension through ideologues and promoting radical ideology, besides establishing a plethora of networks—financial, ideological, media, legal, academic and even media—has been Pakistan's broad strategy. Through a combination of controlled violence, promotion of separatism and linking it all with the faith of Islam this movement has flourished over thirty years. Minority targeting was also interspersed in the course of this period, as a part of the strategy.

The strategy has never been static; always dynamic, attempting many times to remain ahead of the loop of response of the Indian establishment. That is why the 5 August 2019 decisions by the Indian

Government that amended Article 370 and abrogated Article 35A, besides other administrative decisions, resulted in the Pakistani strategy being stymied to an extent; it actually took Pakistan's deep state by utter surprise. The networks were addressed effectively by the Indian agencies and although separatist and radical ideology may not have been substantially impacted, the Indian narrative started to make a difference. A worried Pakistan knew that time was against it and that if allowed to continue in the way J&K was progressing then all the time and energy invested over 30 years would be wasted.

All this comes with the backdrop of a progressively improving security situation over the last two years and more, especially after the amendment of Article 370. It also refocused security efforts to stabilise the environment and deny Pakistan-sponsored terror groups and overground workers (OGWs) the leeway to operate in a calibrated way. In recent times, there was a comparative reduction in recruitment of local terrorist cadres and infiltration from Pakistan-occupied Jammu & Kashmir (PoJK) which reportedly diluted the strength of terrorists in Kashmir to less than 100 in number. Although street turbulence has remained almost negligible, there have been encounters between terrorists and security forces in the hinterland; almost 120 terrorists have been gunned down through 2021 as compared to 225 in 2020.

In terms of integration efforts, the UT government of J&K has been working hard and bringing serious development efforts to the region. An improvement in the power situation is evident and innovations to increase horticultural produce are rife. Tourism has received an upward tick although the pandemic yet remains an obstacle to further increase. Recent efforts at promoting patriotic fervour with symbolic gestures such as placement of the tricolour at Hari Parbat and Gulmarg, as also Lal Chowk being lit in national colours replete with a military band display, are things not witnessed in Kashmir for long.

The above progression in the environment was cause for celebration in India but must equally be causing consternation among the deep state in Pakistan—the sponsors of the proxy war in J&K. Thirty years of investment seemed to be going up in smoke. Yet any security analyst will tell you that these situations of normalisation and lower intensity of violence in a counter-terror environment are usually temporary. External sponsors who remain adversaries will make every effort to retrieve and turn the situation in their favour. That happens when the networks on which terrorism relies remain intact and the counter-terrorism efforts focus solely on the elimination of terrorist cadres.

Clandestinely, OGWs run networks in the domains of financial, media, ideological, safe havens, and the legal profession, through social media, and support terror and separatism. It took long before our agencies finally pursued these and succeeded in greatly marginalising them. However, they still exist and more work on neutralizing them will be needed. They lie low to escape the security forces dragnet but raise their heads based on directions from across the LoC. One of those moments is upon us now for a couple of reasons.

The developing situation in Afghanistan from March 2021 made it evident that the USA would withdraw completely but it was expected that the Afghan National Security Forces (ANSF) would hold the fort and that the government of Ashraf Ghani would continue to rule. From 15 August onwards, this assumption took a back seat as it became evident that the Taliban in its new avatar would rule Afghanistan. The advantage for Pakistan was rapidly advancing. It had hosted the Taliban for over 20 years and more importantly had actually aided its foundation. The Taliban rose in the refugee camps on the Pak-Afghan border through the Eighties and Nineties until it came to power in 1996. For Pakistan, it was evident that events could largely progress as per its own agenda in Afghanistan, even though Taliban 2.0 is no monolith and there is no guarantee that it would toe its line. Yet, J&K on the other front was becoming more important. It could not afford to await more brainstorming and preparation to trigger substantial instability there. Oct-Nov 2021 was the period when something could be done, otherwise the plan would have to wait until April-May 2022, and six months is a long time in such situations.

The full withdrawal of the USA from Afghanistan, the takeover by Taliban 2.0 and restoration of Pakistan as the key state in control of the situation there, gave Pakistan the leeway and flexibility to experiment on ways of returning to relevance in J&K after the 5 August 2019 decisions of the Indian Government. In J&K, everything remains seasonal. Delay beyond October 2021 would have meant that the efforts at revival of radical ideology, terror, and separatism, the three core elements of remaining relevant, would have been pushed to the next summer. Big terror acts are risky due to the current Indian Government's propensity to respond in trans-LoC mode. Even *Fidayeen* type suicide actions take time to plan and activate resources. Consequently, the choice fell only on low risk, high dividend actions against the softest possible targets, which are either minorities or soldiers and policemen on leave. We witnessed targeting of the latter in 2017-18 when among others Lt Umar Fayaz and Rifleman Aurangzeb were kidnapped and killed. Through the years after the Kashmiri Pandit holocaust in January 1990, we also witnessed targeted killings of minorities. This time non-Kashmiris of all faiths are also experiencing the threat with migrant labour making an exit in droves.

Given the resounding but far from permanent success that Pakistan has achieved in Afghanistan with the coming of Taliban 2.0 and the attainment of perceived strategic depth, Pakistan has not lost time. It is strategizing with two factors in mind. First, the need to once again gain traction in Kashmir after the severe loss that has come its way after 5 August 2019, and initiate this before the coming winter. Second is to exploit the inspirational, ideological winds flowing from the events in Afghanistan. The strategy appears to harp on enhancing the strength of terrorists through infiltration from multiple directions in the hope of success somewhere. It also looks at targeting some shallow objectives in the vicinity of the LoC (recall the recent Uri infiltration). The strategy progresses with the flagship measure of attacking the softest target in Kashmir, the minorities. Almost 800 Kashmiri Hindu families still reside there along with 1.5 lakh Sikhs. Pakistan realises that India's Achilles Heel is this—it has ramifications across the length and breadth of the nation. There is also a prevailing perception among Pakistani sponsors that eviction of minorities from Kashmir helps to link its majority populace to Pakistan through a common religious ideology that harps on an obscurantist form of Islam.

People like Makhan Lal Bindroo, the Srinagar-based chemist who fell to terrorist bullets, spelt courage of the highest variety. As a Kashmiri Pandit, he had witnessed the virtual holocaust of January 1990 when almost the entire community had chosen to move out of Kashmir due to targeted killings and threats. Yet, he had decided to stay back and run his business. Supinder Kaur, the Prinicipal of the Government School Eidgah, Srinagar was identified by gunmen by checking of identity cards and then targeted because she was a member of the minority Sikh community, which at various stages of the terror campaign and proxy war has been targeted with the purpose of virtual ethnic cleansing of the Kashmir Valley. The most prominent of these attempts was at Chittisinghpura in South Kashmir in March 2000 when 36 members of the Sikh community were targeted. An organisation calling itself the 'The Resistance Front (TRF)' claimed the recent killings. The latter is a crude effort to provide a cover name for an umbrella organisation that Pakistan's ISI runs to avoid the scrutiny and surveillance of the Financial Assistance Task Force (FATF) of the UN, which examines the role of nations in terror financing in various terror-stricken regions of the world. Its observations and classification of nations can lead to all kinds of international sanctions against them. The TRF is reported to have the Lashkar-e-Taiba (LeT), Jaish-e-Mohammed (JeM), and even the Hizbul Mujahideen (HM) under its wings.

The immediate impact of the targeting of minorities in Kashmir is social pressure for many of them to leave their home and hearth. That would be a victory of sorts for the perpetrators. It is at this time that the political and security communities in J&K must rise to give comprehensive assurances and work towards minority security. A social movement within the Kashmiri Muslim community must emerge to display courage and empathy with the unfortunate members of their society. They cannot be seen to be resigning themselves to the situation and succumbing to the diktat of terrorists and separatists. Political parties must set aside differences and the

Army must make use of its outreach network. Kashmir cannot be surrendered to the will of murderers and terrorists.

Pir Panjal South

In what some consider as an unconnected set of events south of the Pir Panjal we witnessed a major operation by the Army to flush out terrorists from the Bhata Durian forest area between Rajouri and Poonch, near Surankote. In a series of contacts, the Army lost nine soldiers leading to the build-up of a major force to clear the area. The terrorists appear to have infiltrated through the Poonch-Rajouri sectors in August 2021 and were logistically sustained with the help of local networks, which are always existent for the sake of making a quick buck. The concentration in an area in heights above which we witnessed Operation Sarp Vinash in 2003, gives rise to speculation of a potential repeat of the age-old strategy of Pakistan.

Pakistan has a propensity to keep repeating ad nauseum the same old operational strategy to build the strength of terrorists inside J&K that can instigate an uprising by the people to internally defeat the Indian security forces. The Bhata Durian forest is so thick that even helicopters and drones cannot penetrate the cover for effective observation; it is an ideal hiding ground and an area to train locally recruited terrorists so that they do not have to exfiltrate to PoJK for training. A sizable contingent of local terrorists can be concentrated at different camps away from the gaze of the Army in preparedness. Only major contact with terrorists will confirm this.

In Operation Sarp Vinash in 2003, the effects of operations south of Hilkaka were felt on the Valley side of the Pir Panjal with large groups attempting to escape the pressure. Ambushes by the Army had a field day cleaning out the escaping groups. That is why the Army for sure would be placing such ambushes. Now that the first snow of the season has arrived, the terrorists will find it difficult to move over the meadows of the Pir Panjal into the Valley and footmarks on fresh snow will spell their doom if they try. Under these circumstances, Winter Aerial Surveillance and Observation (WASO) sorties by Army Aviation helicopters should ensure the nailing of the terrorists.

The lesson coming through loud and clear is that Pakistan will often repeat the area and methodology of its conduct of the past. This time it obviously fits into the strategy of Fifth Generation Hybrid War that General Qamar Bajwa, the Pakistan Army Chief spoke about on 6 September 2021 at the fake Victory Day celebrations.

Fifth Generation Hybrid War by Pakistan

What exactly is Fifth Generation Hybrid War? There is no universally accepted definition of Hybrid War itself. Usually a combination of conventional and irregular methods of war is the broadest understanding. Methods and tactics may include conventional capabilities, irregular tactics, irregular formations, diplomacy, politics, terrorist acts, indiscriminate violence, criminal activity, and anything that can adversely affect the status of the opposing party or state. The manpower for this could be state or non-state or state sponsored non-state. Once again, Fifth Generation Hybrid War finds no definition but the ambit of hybrid war fought with the exploitation of all modern technological means of the information domain, which extends to psychological and media propaganda and off late political warfare is the larger understanding. Consensus is difficult on definitions but much easier on application. Pakistan has fought a hybrid war campaign in J&K for the last thirty years. For the last two years and a little more its ability to pursue that path had become difficult after India decided on a strong clampdown on violence in the Valley and a recourse to constitutional decisions on J&K's status. Afghanistan has changed that and October this year offered unique opportunities, which Pakistan has exploited to the hilt.

One of the most important things regarding rekindling the turbulence in J&K is to recreate among the people an empathy towards the Pakistan narrative and neutralisation of all Indian efforts at outreach to the people. Some of this flows naturally from the Taliban victory in Afghanistan and Pakistan's deep involvement there. The direct trigger to change the discourse of the improving security situation has been the minority and migrant targeting. Fence-sitters in Kashmir start gravitating away from India whenever such acts occur. The hard response involving detention of youth and interrogations is never helpful and the gains of a few months of positive outreach are probably negated by this. However, that is the response expected by Pakistan and it works to promote it. The method of executing minority and migrant targeting has also been tweaked to bring pairs of terrorists or lone wolves with only pistols and go for the most unexpected targets.

Simultaneously, efforts have been afoot to enhance terrorist strength through a relatively safer area as compared to Kashmir's counter infiltration grid. In its wisdom, Pakistan has chosen to revisit a strategy of the past; the concentration of foreign fighters and caches of weapons and wherewithal. The Pir Panjal acts as a midway point and the selected area of concentration appears to be somewhat similar to Hilkaka, the group of nomad hutments, which saw much action for almost three months in 2003. It could also act as a clandestine training area for local recruits. It seems obvious that reserves of terrorists would be held in such a location waiting to launch into a situation where expansion of terrorist activities could be swift without awaiting infiltration. Even if this preparation for concentration was discovered early, it would draw the Indian Army into large-scale operations in an area, which had been relatively quiet for some years. That activation itself would probably be considered a success by Pakistan since the areas south of Pir Panjal have been without action for long.

The Fifth Generation Hybrid War elements would probably have been the subject of research for some time. The Inter Services Public Relations (ISPR) wing of the Pakistan Armed Forces would have been tasked to draw up the means of execution of a program involving various resources of strategic communication. With political warfare the new mantra in the world of hybrid warfare, it is grey zone war which begs entry. The social and political environment in India is in a flux and exploitable particularly in a pre-electoral scenario. The communal situation in India and the then upcoming T-20 World Cup match between India and Pakistan in combination offered much scope.

Countering Pakistan's Revival Game

Enough has been said about the reasons for these killings but not enough on how we can counter this newest phase in Pakistan's strategy. There is an internal and an external dimension to the counter campaign. Internally, all the security, social and political domains must be activated. Sharpening of intelligence, pick up and interrogation of overground workers (OGWs) besides full view and high energy domination operations by all forces. The modus operandi of the terrorists is going to make the task of security organisations extremely difficult. The use of pistols by a single terrorist or a pair of them is smart thinking on the part of the sponsors. These terrorists know how to merge with the public and pose very small targets unlike the erstwhile ones. Intelligence in this case needs much more leg work. Migrant labour has reportedly largely left the Valley but those yet present may have to be housed collectively in selected camps after a certain time of the day/evening under escort, thus curtailing their freedom and causing more discomfort; essentially a defensive step. This is possible for short periods if the threats do not run the full course. Usually such trends last a year or so in Kashmir but revisit again when such options give dividends as they are currently giving.

It is the political and social domains that are equally important as they provide indirect security; after all, this proxy conflict is hybrid in nature. We have seen a display of disgust by some select members of the majority community who form part of civil society. There has been insufficient condemnation although voices like those of Junaid Mattoo, the Mayor of Srinagar, and of Sajjad Lone have been loud and clear against the atrocities. Kashmir's Muslim majority must clearly project its inclusive and non-obscurantist belief. It must rise against radical thinking and stop its children supporting anti-national ideologies. There should be voices from the rest of India which must be reassuring for Kashmiris and the many nationalist young Kashmiris who are risking themselves must in turn get local support.

Clearly, a societal movement to marginalise those who act against innocent minorities and migrant labour is needed but there is no leadership for the same. Politics is currently not active in Kashmir and the old world political leadership appears out of sync making impassioned appeals for talks with Pakistan. It is a challenge for young leaders not yet infused with political savvy to make a difference; and there are many of them. It is also for the establishment to help create such a network that can counter the networks of the OGWs. Unfortunately, too many people sit on the fence in Kashmir and therefore urging them to move beyond positively is contingent upon how long the support can be sustained. This influence campaign cannot be done from Delhi. It needs people in Kashmir to lead and ownership must be taken by the Kashmiri Muslim community to defeat the obscurantist elements. Without leadership, it may remain just an expectation.

It is not just defensive measures that are important. Targeting networks must continue as this is a laborious process of painstaking intelligence work. Intelligence must be stepped up and domination operations around pockets of minority settlements must be energized. This is a great opportunity to show resolve through strong and patient messaging. What happens now will set the tone for the future. Anticipating the next steps by the terror elements is also important. There is a need to warn all soldiers and policemen on leave and their families, as they too offer soft targets.

Home Minister Amit Shah's Visit

Home Minister, Amit Shah broke all norms in October 2021 by visiting J&K for a full three days and ticking off almost all the boxes that make up the desire for India to play out a strategy in J&K. Without addressing details, it is important to note the tone and tenor of the Home Minister's speeches; firm yet very compassionate. His speech to the youth reinforced all the efforts going on ground to reach out and bring the youth on board India's march towards better education and opportunities. Pakistan's efforts at Hybrid War will dent these efforts from time to time but more frequent visits by important functionaries and making the right statements while speaking on behalf of the Government of India will go far in ensuring that what commenced on 5 August 2019 is eventually completed.

11

Thriving in the Graveyard of Empires

Devyani Rao

The flight from Delhi to Kabul is nothing less than in a time machine. The 1-hour, 55-minute journey transports one to not just a different place but to a parallel reality; a land living in a century past, isolated from life as we know it and having only the strangest connections with the rest of the world.

Circa 2006, the Afghanistan I knew and which I learned to mostly love and sometimes hate, was a country on the upward incline. It had its fair share of problems, but the situation was looking up. There was promise and hope that the worst had been left behind. I'm not sure what I expected, but I was pleasantly surprised to find perfectly comfortable dwellings and a fully functional society within the context of the country. It most certainly wasn't like any other trip that I had made anywhere else and yet, there was a sense of utter normalcy. The sight of tanks cruising around the city, soldiers pointing their automatic weapons at approaching vehicles, barricades of sand-filled sacks and rings of barbed wire, soon became mundane sights, a par for the course as one quickly was enveloped in the Afghan way of life.

My first few articles spoke of the joy and wonder I had felt in my initial outings and interactions with all manner of people. Officers from the International Security Assistance Force (ISAF), Members of Parliament and Governors, my former colleagues who had now taken on the responsibility of looking after me and keeping me safe, the young staff at my hotel...they all welcomed me warmly and spoke of their ambitions for themselves and their bruised and battered country.

There was a curious sense of camaraderie; we were all on the same team—the "good guys" united for a common cause. Every person there had a mission, not just a job. The hotel staff had the mission of keeping guests like me safe; the sweeper at Kabul University, which I visited several times, was willy-nilly a part of the mission to educate and emancipate Afghan youth; the mission of every soldier and security guard was to provide an umbrella of safety for people to go about their lives and conduct their work; every aid worker, advisor, journalist.... At the end of the day, it all tied up in to a single cause that each and every one of us contributed to in our own way—rebuilding Afghanistan.

One day, I was invited to a friend's house for dinner and since the couple were considerably older than me, I had covered my head with a *chador*. The lady of the house immediately asked me why I was wearing it and I replied awkwardly, "Out of respect for you..."

"Please don't", she replied.

I was taken aback. She went on to explain that this, along with numerous other so-called "norms", were actually completely alien to their culture. She spoke of the liberal 20s under King Amanullah Khan and later the 60s under King Zahir Shah, of the time when Afghanistan was the cultural Mecca of Central Asia where women wore miniskirts and people flocked to Kabul from Pakistan and Iran to watch movies in Kabul's cinema halls. She begged me to set an example for other Afghan women and defy these Taliban-imposed customs, which sought only to repress, silence, and create divisions. I gladly agreed, realising then that if my behaviour sent a message, I wanted it to be a positive one.

As an Indian girl, I didn't quite fit into the usual brackets: my "foreignness" meant I was free from the usual social restrictions and expectations of a local girl. My interactions with male friends, colleagues and acquaintances were not judged by the same yardstick as those used for Afghan women. I was, for the most part, "one of the boys". At the same time, ironically, I was a foreigner, yes, but I was an *Indian*. That's hardly "foreign" in Afghanistan, where people have grown up watching Bollywood movies and where many, I daresay, were far better versed in Indian cinema than I was. India was considered an age-old friend whose relationship had withstood the test of time and Indians were widely and warmly welcomed.

Contrary to that was the equally widespread disdain with which the Afghan populace regarded Pakistan. "But you lived there as a refugee", I once asked someone, "Don't you have *any* affection for the country despite that?" "Sure, it was nice, and people were good to us, for which we are grateful. But we didn't seek refuge by choice. It was, after all, Pakistan that brought the Taliban to power. After the Soviets, Pakistan made it *necessary* for us to run away as refugees", was his answer that was echoed by many others.

In the course of my tenure in Kabul, besides the usual stories pertaining to the security situation, I was fortunate to be able to meet and write about extraordinary, ordinary people, such as the brave young journalist who had been the victim of terrible domestic violence resulting in a large scar on her face. I had been seeing her at various press conferences and a colleague from Agence France-Presse (AFP), a young man by the name of Sardar Ahmad, suggested that I interview her. Hers turned out to be an incredible story of valour, given what she had overcome and the hardships she had undergone in the pursuit of her passion and commitment to journalism. Then there were artists whose paintings I fell in love with and who had struggled to keep their works safe and their art alive during the Taliban reign of 1996-2001; designers giving liberating opportunities to talented local artisans while keeping Afghan handicrafts alive and flourishing, reaching runways around the world; film-makers, musicians, people returning to complete their university degrees after a long hiatus, young, local journalists, translators, and fixers.

Afghanistan's fledgling media reflected the country's progress. Newspaper editors worked out of tiny, inconspicuous offices in some of the poorer locales of the city. For a time, I was glad to be invited to help edit some stories in English for the Pajhwok News Agency, which bravely continues to report from all over the country today. Afghan radio stations had launched some innovative, new programmes including an "Agony Aunt"-style talk show, where listeners called in with their problems and were advised on how to deal with them. The problems themselves were indicative of a society trying to make its way out of the quagmire of repressive customs and norms, in terms of relationships, work and education.

After abandoning their studies midway when the Taliban took over the country in 1996, many of the urban, aspirational youth were returning to complete their degrees at Kabul University; among them, several of my Afghan colleagues. The university had a large, open campus, which would be blanketed with snow every winter. It made for a refreshing walk. I once asked a friend whether they had the freedom to express dissent or at least question some of the teachings on sensitive subjects such as religion. I was told they seldom did, because it was believed that several students were "sponsored" and raised by warlords such as the infamous Abdul Rashid Dostum, and no one wanted to risk word reaching them of people questioning traditional *Shariat* teaching. Indeed, another warlord, Gulbuddin Hekmatyar, as a young student at Kabul University, had once shot a dissenter in the mouth for precisely that reason. At any rate, there were bound to be some students who were already predisposed to extremism and could turn violent. The answer, therefore, was clear—education even now, was not as liberal as people thought.

My days were mostly busy, attending press briefings at ISAF Headquarters, the United Nations Assistance Mission in Afghanistan (UNAMA), and occasionally at the Arg or Interior Ministry. Besides that, there was ground reporting to be done from the scene of an attack or interviews with officials and representatives of aid organisations to talk about various aspects of development, the nefarious opium trade, social issues, etc.

In the evenings, there was often a get-together somewhere or a restaurant to go to. Yet, within that busy schedule there were also several moments of intense loneliness and quiet reflection, when the reality of it all would actually sink in. There was not much social media to speak of at that time and international phone connections were poor and costly. I found comfort and solace in local music, which I listened to for hours at night, losing myself in quiet thought. *How could such a beautiful land be the scene of so much violence? What would be its future?*

Much of Kabul's history lay in plain sight, allowing one an experiential understanding of it. From the great walls built by the *Kabulshahan*, the bombed ruins of the once-ethereal Darulaman Palace, the bullet-ridden metal containers that had obviously failed to protect those who had hidden inside them during Afghanistan's Civil War, the Ali Abad mountain from where Ahmed Shah Masood and his men descended on Soviet troops seeking to invade the capital, to the curiously juxtaposed tranquillity of the Bagh-e-Babur, chosen by the Mughal emperor to be his final resting place in the city he most loved, all stood as testaments to Afghanistan's past. At the same time, shops in the city centre sold authentic, recently-launched models of mobile phones and other gadgetry, skilled techies repaired and vamped up laptops in their dingy offices and grocery stores sold well-known international brands of all kinds of food and dairy products. As night fell, the smell of freshly baked *naans* from traditional, roadside ovens wafted through the air, even as the dimly-lit Kabul city fell eerily dark, barring the odd, functional traffic light, or a lamppost here and there. In the distance, the lights of the houses along the mountainside in the east of the city twinkled against a black, star-filled sky.

There was a dark side to Kabul too. Prostitution, the contraband of drugs, domestic violence, forced marriages and social pressures were all too common. As indeed was corruption and the omnipresent security threat. One drove around uneasily, briefly glancing at the cars around. *Could that person be a suicide bomber? Or that one there?* Whether one was stuck in heavy traffic or cruising alone on an open road, the threat of an attack was very real. I wondered aloud why someone like me would be a target. I was promptly informed that while attackers primarily targeted foreign soldiers, in the event that they could not get to them, their next preferred target was any foreigner and maximum damage. And so, most people kept a low profile in public and tried their best to remain inconspicuous. No one was completely safe.

Behind high walls and heavy gates, restaurants of all kinds thrived in Kabul—Turkish, Lebanese, Italian, French and Indian. Some were located in large, beautiful compounds, allowing one to briefly forget where one was and enjoy some good food, a cheerful ambience and uplifting music. I discovered one evening, however, as I went to one of these restaurants with a group of Afghan colleagues, that some of these places did not permit Afghans to enter. I was indignant. The reason for this discrimination was that these places had liquor licences and were not permitted to serve liquor to Afghans. Although this was, I believe, endorsed by the government, I found it uncomfortably reminiscent of the British Raj's "Indians and Dogs Not Allowed" policy and could not, in good conscience, ditch those whom I had trusted to protect my life, for the sake of mere indulgence. The 'Foreigner's Life' for me, therefore, was effectively shut down. That meant missing out on experiences such as the Gandamack Lodge—the local watering-hole for expats, similar in many ways to Singapore's iconic Raffles Hotel, where intelligence was rumoured to be exchanged, heroin and hashish partaken of and where the insidious tensions and frustrations of living in a war zone temporarily melted away. But there was indeed an upside to forsaking the expat life—I got to live the Afghan life instead. The occasional few minutes behind the wheel of a colleague's car, travelling all around Kabul city and around the country, interviewing repatriated refugees at the Iran border, bargaining for wares on Chicken Street, all made for heady experiences of exhilarating defiance and liberation. So much so that on one occasion when a friend from the World Bank in Delhi was visiting and I called to check on her, I was surprised when she said it was such a dreary day.

"Dreary? Are you not in Kabul?" I asked.

On hearing that she was, I was even more puzzled.

"It's not dreary! The sun is shining, there's a beautiful breeze and the sky is a perfect blue!" I exclaimed.

For many, like my friend, who worked in large organisations, security restrictions meant that even when they ventured out, it was in an armoured vehicle that would drop them right at the door of their destination. There was no loitering about and that, inevitably, meant that many of the experiences I was fortunate enough to have, had been denied to them. Friends I made at the place I lived in, old colleagues, new colleagues whom one met several times a week at various press briefings and people whom I interviewed and subsequently got to know—all offered invaluable insights into local life, culture and, most importantly perhaps, their perspective. Defiant, hot headed, chauvinistic, egoistic, proud, and exasperatingly bullish, Afghans could be most frustrating at times. After 50 years of war, they were sick of politely asking and gratefully acknowledging the assistance that came their way in different shapes and forms. They had come to take it rather for granted and demand it unabashedly, as a right. I reckon a half century of war will do that to you, especially if you belong to patriarchal, tribal societies historically at loggerheads with one another, unconquerable, undisciplined, and disunited. Something like the Gauls of Goscinny and Uderzo, minus the humour. Family and religion were subjects not readily discussed, even amongst themselves and certainly as an outsider, one hesitated to probe beyond a point.

America, with the largest troop presence in the ISAF under Operation Enduring Freedom, and an additional 20,000 troops tasked with counter-terrorism operations and who operated independently of ISAF's counter-insurgency mandate, was seen as a necessary evil. What initially seemed like a total lack of gratitude on the part of Afghans, as they cursed the American troops, later became easier to comprehend. How would anyone feel having a foreign military presence in their country, aiming their guns at them, and telling them where they could and could not go? It was certainly an affront to Afghan pride, compounded every now and then by the heavy toll of civilian casualties—collateral damage in numerous military operations which more than once, brought President Hamid Karzai to near tears as he spoke to the press at the Arg. Afghans were also wary of the US commitment to their country having twice witnessed a disengagement from Washington at crucial junctures. The first, following the Soviet withdrawal in 1989 after which the US government left the radical, militant Taliban which it had nurtured via Pakistan's Inter-Services Intelligence (ISI), to their own devices, leading eventually, to their taking over the country; the second instance was when the USA invaded Iraq, redirecting both troops and focus away from Afghanistan, which allowed the ousted Taliban to regroup and reorganise itself enough to be able to wage a 20-year insurgency. Suicide attacks, which were on the rise, had never been the classic *modus operandi* of the Taliban, but rather something they had imbibed from *al-Qaeda*'s wars in Iraq and Syria. What if the Americans were to leave again? Some believed optimistically, that regardless, the Taliban could never come back to power. Others reckoned the return of the Taliban was inevitable, as and when the USA left.

Discussions on security were endless and incessant, with every newly-arrived journalist asking their 20 questions over lunches and dinners and drives and phone calls at all hours. At times it could be overwhelming but there was no denying that security was the greatest impediment to Afghanistan's progress, and it was hardly surprising then that it should be the dominant subject of conversation. What surprised me was how readily locals were willing to indulge them. Didn't they ever tire of it? Didn't they ever take a break? Their wild ambition bewildered me. They seemed to be in a tearing hurry to climb the professional ladder. In retrospect, I understand why. Those were the 'make or break' years. No one knew when America might abandon Afghanistan again and should the Taliban return, it would be all over for them. This was their shot at making their money which would buy them a one-way ticket out of their unfortunate country, and they weren't scared to lose a little sleep or to step on a few toes to make it happen. In the meantime, however, the USA bore the brunt of counter-terrorism operations, while ISAF struggled with caveats imposed by the governments of several countries, restricting the movements and operations of their troops. The hunt for Osama bin Laden was very much on and while he remained elusive till 2011, when he was eventually discovered and killed by US Special Forces in Abbottabad, a stone's throw from the Pakistani military headquarters in Rawalpindi, the allied forces, very much including the Afghan National Security Forces (ANSF), successfully eliminated several top leaders of the Taliban and *al-Qaeda*. Simultaneously, they worked to rebuild much of Afghanistan's broken or non-existent infrastructure and, under their security, schools and workplaces opened all over the country, including in the perilous South—the stronghold of the Taliban. Children played with real toys distributed by foreign troops and aid workers, unlike in the Soviet era, where spent weapons were the common playthings of toddlers. Kidnappings and assassinations by the Taliban, however, still continued and on one occasion, a foreign journalist was detained by the Taliban in the south, where he had been reporting from with the assistance of his Afghan interpreter. He was subsequently released and went on to relate how every day, a cute, little Talib boy would look at him and say something to his father, pleadingly. One day he asked his interpreter what the boy was saying.

"He is asking his father if he can be the one to shoot the foreigner...", was the hesitant and chilling reply. It was a very revealing story of how sharply contrasting the childhood of those children under the umbrella of the security forces was even then, from that of the children under the Taliban.

At a certain point, the casualty figures, and statistics one reported on a daily basis, turned into names of people one knew, people among *us*. At about 8:30 am on the morning of 7 July 2008, a suicide attacker rammed into two official vehicles of the Indian Embassy, as they were entering the embassy gates. As I saw the breaking news, I instinctively picked up the phone to call Mr. Venkat Rao, the Press Officer with whom I was in regular contact. Seconds later, his name flashed across the screen as one of the victims, along with Brig. R.D. Mehta. Both of them were riding in the vehicles that had been targeted.

A few years later, as Afghans celebrated Nowroz, several teenage Taliban fighters, having smuggled numerous small firearms into the high-security Serena Hotel, opened fire hours later at guests dining in the hotel restaurant. Among them was Sardar Ahmad, the friendly, kind AFP journalist with a sense of humour, who had once suggested a story to me. He was shot at close range, along with his wife, his 7-year-old daughter and 5-year-old son, while his youngest son, aged 3, was shot multiple times but somehow survived and was subsequently taken abroad to live with relatives. One didn't need to know Sardar well to grieve his death in that particularly heinous incident. In fact, the outpouring of grief for his family was so strong and universal that when his surviving son arrived in his new home, he was welcomed at the airport by dozens of strangers with offerings of gifts and toys.

Finally, my home in Kabul, where I was wonderfully looked after and where I felt safe, was razed to the ground in another suicide attack, some years after I had left Afghanistan.

The increase in the number of attacks invariably bred greater caution amongst foreign troops, who were generally the primary targets. This in turn resulted in more innocent Afghans being killed for pulling up too close to a military convoy or violating other such similar directions. The foreign forces then became enemies to the families of victims, so much so that in an interview conducted by a fellow journalist, a grieving father sought revenge for the killing of two of his sons by US forces. He declared angrily that he intended to send his other sons to the Taliban to train to be suicide attackers. Whether or not he actually followed through on that initial rage, the gap between the foreign troops and the people they were there to actually assist, widened. The classic "hearts and minds" pitch often went the wrong way.

The drawdown of US troops began with President Barack Obama and was continued by Donald Trump, during whose term formal negotiations began between the USA and representatives of the Taliban in Doha, for the complete withdrawal of foreign forces in Afghanistan. Joseph Biden, known to be against the US war in Afghanistan, sought to hasten the USA's departure from the country and decided to complete the withdrawal well before the negotiated deadline of 11 September 2021—the 20th anniversary of the 9/11 attacks.

On 15 August 2021, the world watched in horror as Taliban fighters entered the Afghan capital, having overrun the rest of the country at a stunning pace. For the Afghan people, women particularly, it signalled a return to their very worst memories; for soldiers, both Afghan and foreign, it prompted them to demand answers and apologies from the US government, for what they saw as an acknowledgement of defeat and a nullifying of their sacrifices and those of their comrades who lost their lives in the course of their missions; for the countless aid workers, entrepreneurs, journalists, advisors and anyone with any connection to the country, it felt like a stab in the back from the USA, who having begun this round of the Great Game, had suddenly decided it didn't want to play it anymore. Chaos unfolded in the final days of the American evacuation, with the image of desperate Afghans clinging to departing military transport aircraft and falling from the skies to their deaths, being ironically likened to the scenes of people jumping out of the windows of the burning twin towers.

While there may be scope for debate on the US decision to end its presence in Afghanistan, the manner in which it was done was criticised the world over, no matter which side of the debate one was on. Biden's decision to complete the withdrawal even as the Taliban advanced, even though the lives of those who had worked with foreign forces had not yet been secured, seemed more in keeping with Trump's idea of "America First" (and never mind the rest). In one of the early advances by the Taliban, a group of Afghan Special Forces were trying valiantly to defend their post and had called for air support which never arrived. Once they ran out of ammunition, they were called by the Taliban to surrender and promised amnesty if they did. In broad daylight, in a crowded marketplace, the soldiers came out with their hands in the air and as they did so, they were savagely gunned down one by one in true Taliban style. That single incident was probably enough to kill the morale of the rest of the troops. The CIA predicted that Kabul was likely to fall within three months of the US withdrawal, whereas it was abundantly clear to most that it was a question of a few days and indicative of a mass intelligence failure. The Afghan National Army (ANA) crumbled pathetically before the Taliban onslaught and soldiers often lay down their weapons and surrendered without firing a shot, knowing that their fate was sealed.

It would be unfair to squarely blame the USA for Afghanistan's fall. Various corrupt Afghan officials undoubtedly also played their part. However, the leaders of Afghanistan were hand-picked candidates put up by the USA. How could Washington not have known about the capabilities of the ANSF or indeed of the capability of the Taliban? As it later emerged, the strength of the ANA was far less than had been thought earlier. "Ghost soldiers" or fictitious entities numbered in thousands, their names reflected on the payrolls so that their salaries could be claimed by corrupt officials. How did the CIA miss this?

Some argue that America's longest war needed to be brought to an end and that it was time for the Afghans, who had been given a taste of democracy, to defend it and take control of their fate. Those people are right about just one thing—Afghanistan was given *a taste* of democracy and nothing more. In recent times, the world's greatest democracy, the United States of America, and the world's largest democracy, India, have found themselves on shaky ground, struggling hard to defend their democratic ideals. This is despite the fact that both nations have enjoyed a democratic way of life for several decades and many generations; both have a large intelligentsia, a burgeoning middle class, freedom of the press and civil rights and numerous institutions to safeguard all these. Yet, they have struggled. In the last 20 years, Afghanistan's own leaders and their foreign benefactors have failed to create such institutions. The last three generations of Afghans have known nothing but war. They have not had any real semblance of a "normal" life. For years they have been dictated to by foreign invaders, warlords, Taliban, and foreign soldiers—basically anyone with a gun. Few have had an uninterrupted education, if at all. With its foreign aid frozen and at the mercy of a Taliban government unrecognised by the rest of the world and which has yet to prove itself remotely capable of governance, Afghanistan is headed for a serious economic crisis. The Taliban, which violated basic principles of warfare as it killed those Special Forces, not three weeks before taking over the country, are the same Taliban as they were in the 1990s. More savvy perhaps, but at the core, the very same.

Brave Afghan women protest in the streets of Kabul, Herat, London and elsewhere around the world, refusing to be relegated to obscurity once again. At the same time, all those men and women, who could, fled. Others have perhaps resigned themselves to their fate. The greatest casualty resulting from the American withdrawal was hope.

Consequently, another chapter begins in Afghanistan's inglorious history. How it evolves will depend greatly on how much the Taliban can be coerced to fall in line with the norms of acceptability of the international community and also how far the international community is willing to go to ensure that it does. Its problems cannot remain its own for long. Wherever they might be, those who have ever lived or served there share the desperation of millions of Afghans. Because Afghanistan is a bit like Hotel California—you can check out any time you like, but you can never leave.

12

Afghanistan: Confronting the Humanitarian Catastrophe

Sanghamitra Sarker

"There's nothing low grade or low risk or low cost about any war. It's time to end the war in Afghanistan."[1] It is true that the longest war of the 21st century is over with the fall of Kabul to the Taliban. From being the 'Graveyard of Empires' to the Soviet invasion, *Mujahideen* chaos followed by Taliban rule, American involvement, and the recent takeover by the Taliban again, Afghanistan and its people have been victims of power contestations, violence and human rights abuses. With the American withdrawal and the Taliban once again holding the reins of power in Kabul, the nation-building in Afghanistan has primarily become the responsibility of the people of the land. This remains uncontested and there is no contradiction in this regard. However, it is important to understand what the status of human rights of the people in this part of the global village will be and what ought to be the safeguards to protect the human rights. This holds true especially due to the nature of the conflict and the trauma the people of Afghanistan have been subjected to.

Since the end of July 2021, the discourses on Afghanistan became an important area for all the stakeholders—the people of Afghanistan, state and non-state actors and the global media. This importance reached its peak in August when finally, the capital of Afghanistan—Kabul fell into the hands of the Taliban and the American withdrawal made it clear that there would be no immediate foreign contestations against Taliban rule. However, the manner in which the Afghanistan situation unfolded has brought most people at a loss for words. What can one write after watching the horrific images and reading accounts of the desperation of Afghans that was seen at Kabul airport and its adjacent areas? The images of the baby who was handed over by her young mother to an unknown US army official to save its life or the Afghan man who was clinging to the US military's massive C-17 cargo plane will continue to haunt human memory for years. It will be a while before they fade, but will never be forgotten.

Before diving into the crossroads created in Afghanistan, it is important to explore its periphery—the neighbourhood. When the history of South Asia is considered, the month of August would be especially important for the South Asians. Geographically, today's South Asia is more or less equivalent to the former British India. August 1946 flagged off a new format of communal riots in Calcutta, the city known for its pluralism and multiculturalism even in British India and the next twelve months had seen almost continuous communal rioting between the communities. According to many works of literature, the 1946 riot can be considered as the first experience of organised community conflict as a political weapon to settle political demands in South Asia. In August 1947, two important republic nation-states were born in South Asia. Against the backdrop of the partition of British India with its bloody cost of massive migration, the Islamic Republic of Pakistan and the Democratic Republic of India became sovereign members of the world community on 14 and 15 August, respectively, as was desired and designed by the British colonial masters.

The month of August 1947 gifted the people of South Asia two new notions, one is the republic political system, and another is a refugee. Without any question, women, irrespective of their Hindu,

Muslim or Sikh identity, were the main victims of the partition exercise. A divided India augurs ill not only for the Indian people but also for all of Asia and world peace.[2] Since its inception, much has been written and spoken about many aspects of the India-Pakistan bilateral relationship. Even today, it is hammering on one odd question. Do we believe in a nation state that includes people of all religions and different shades of opinion and is essentially secular or do we believe in the religious, theocratic conception of states that considers people of other faiths as something beyond the pale?[3] For the world community, despite many shortcomings, India represents the first model whereas Pakistan represents the second. *The idea of a theocratic state was given up some time ago by the world and it has no place in the mind of a modern person.*[4] Unfortunately, the last century, especially the Cold War era, has witnessed many incidents where the political representatives of the modern world have sponsored several theocratic states and their leadership, which promotes practices reflecting medieval mindsets.

The month of August again became the talk of the global village in 1975 when a military coup took place on 15 August in the Peoples' Republic of Bangladesh. Military officials killed Sheikh Mujibur Rahman, the then-Prime Minister of Bangladesh along with his entire family. The secular, parliamentary democratic, unitary, republican political system of the country was replaced by a military state structure in Bangladesh in August 1975.

Coming to the core issue of Afghanistan, the Taliban established their control over Afghanistan on 15 August 2021. The democratic political system with many limitations was replaced by medieval politics. More than two months have passed since then but the political status of Afghanistan remains unclear. Till now, official legal recognition by the international community (including Qatar and Pakistan) has not been forthcoming for the Taliban-led government. The People's Republic of China and Russia also remain sceptical on the issue despite having shown an interest to establish communication channels with the Taliban.

Looking back in history, it was in the year 1921 that Kabul and the

USA developed their first formal political relationship by bringing Amanullah Khan to power. In 1929, he was forced to flee to British India due to the volatile situation that had developed as a counter-reaction to a number of his progressive policies including the granting of voting rights to women. In the last hundred years, the world has witnessed a number of changes in all fields of life, but time has stopped for the lives of the Afghans. In August 2021, Ashraf Ghani, the last President of Afghanistan before the Taliban takeover, was forced to flee to Tashkent and finally to the United Arab Emirates. During this period, the Afghan population faced various forms of barbaric violence. In most of the violent incidents, the international community was apathetic to these incidents as long as their own subjects were not threatened or became victims. The brutal killing of the former head of state, Nazibullah and his brother also drew mere statements of condemnation from the world community, while, in the last twenty years, a large section of the Afghan population has also fallen victim to airstrikes.

While the Afghanistan buzz was a common topic of global discussions, the international media and the fraternity at large have rarely expressed their concern for the sufferings of the common Afghan people. There had been a few exceptions like the Indian film titled 'Kabul Express'[5] where the pain and agony of the people of Afghanistan was depicted as the central theme. Over the past 50 years, the flag of medieval barbarism carried out under any name or title, has been successful in getting sponsorships from the modern world using the garb of the sponsors' geopolitical compulsions. The flag has marched from Saqqawist to *Mujahideen*, *Mujahideen* to Taliban and, in the future, it may march from Taliban to something new.

The developments post the 15 August 2021 Taliban takeover vis-a-vis global power reactions are not an exception although today, in the globalised world, the desired role of the international community is different. Until 31 August 2021, most of the internationally recognised news agencies covered various incidents of misery in the lives of the people of Afghanistan but only as a part of extended coverage of the threats to the lives of Western citizens. The Indian media is no exception. While in the pre-digital age and with virtual connectivity, there was dependable information from the warfield for attentive stakeholders as well as the world community today, unfortunately, such coverage on Afghanistan is missing, especially after 31 August 2021. As a primary issue, the misery of the people of Afghanistan especially its women, children, and progressive sections, including members of the former Afghan National Army, are yet to draw the attention of the world media. On one hand, the focus of the present international media is concentrated on the apprehension of threats to the region and to the world, while on the other, it is focused on different initiatives of world power lobbies to reorient the power adjustment to use this region as a buffer or as a passage for their own interests. Against this backdrop, there is always a chance of error in assessing the recent Afghan politics and its humanitarian impact. In order to make sense of it, it is important to revisit the recent five important developments.

Afghanistan is facing a breakdown of the economic and social system that risks turning into a humanitarian catastrophe.[6] According to Joseph Borell's blog, the 27-country European Union has increased its humanitarian aid to Afghanistan since the Taliban took over control but has halted developmental assistance—a move taken also by other countries and the World Bank. Borell added that avoiding the worst-case scenario would require the Taliban to comply with conditions that would enable more international assistance.[7] Furthermore, United Nations representatives made a visit to Herat, Afghanistan, and carried out a survey that suggested that the large group of children below five years old are victims of severe food shortage. Due to hunger, the health condition of many mothers are too fragile to breastfeed their newborn babies.[8]

The global community had expected that the US Administration would be the most reliable provider of information to them regarding day-to-day political developments in Afghanistan. The expectation remains a disappointment. Washington, under the Biden Administration, is firm on its commitment of treating the Afghanistan issue as part of history and the extended Cold War.[9] The People's

Republic of China, Russia, Iran, and Turkey which may have different perceptions or compulsions of assessment while engaging with the Taliban-led government are in a wait-and-watch mode. They prefer to follow the Taliban's actions rather than depend on their words.[10]

From the above-mentioned five points, the rational conclusion derived is that the common people of Afghanistan are in deep trouble. Arguably, this may be worse than any of the previous years. Women including lactating mothers and children are in their worst situation. The global powers are aware of the deplorable situation of Afghanistan. However, as international power politics would have it, they agree to support and engage on the basis of their own interests and terms. The state is not synonymous with the government. A state is composed of land, population, government, stability, and sovereignty. Therefore, the change in the nature of the government cannot be the justification for denying the extension of support to its population in dire need. Even if stability is absent in the government machinery or recognition for external sovereignty is not managed, the needy population cannot be barred from support by the world body.

As a matter of fact, this international support is much more crucial in times like these to protect the human rights of the common Afghan citizenry in terms of dignity and to protect their lives from medieval brutality. The absence of law has been the main characteristic of the most medieval form of rule or governance. Without codification, neither justice nor law is possible. It is no secret that the Taliban swears to establish a puritan Islamic society based on the medieval Sharia law. However, this law, as quoted by Taliban leaders, is not codified in available resources, thus leaving ample scope for ambiguity and exploitation to promote self-interests. Even during the tenure of the first Taliban-led rule of Afghanistan during 1996-2001, the massive human rights violations were known to all. Moreover, the ruthlessness of atrocities against women, children, and ethnic minorities is beyond any sense of verbal expression. Given the state of the economy and society that has been inherited by the Taliban, an outfit know for brutal medieval practices of governance, justice, and law and order, the situation of the Afghan people will only become more deplorable.

The global village is for global cooperation and assistance for the sake of human lives and dignity. Women and children are not exceptions. This is not only the idealist approach to politics but is essentially realistic politics. The COVID-19 pandemic has taught that the world is one and we cannot let someone suffer ideally and realistically for their own safety and benefit. The people of Afghanistan cannot be treated as non-existent entities. In this moment of crisis, land-locked Afghanistan needs to be made land-linked as early as possible. Former President Hamid Karzai once promised the people of his land, *"We are rising from the ashes of invasion and will live forever..."*.[11] That promise has failed miserably. However, the United Nations, the European Union, and other regional organisations should not fail to follow their own unconditional promises to protect the human rights of the global citizens.

NOTES

1. US President Biden defended his decision to end the 20-year war in Afghanistan a day after the USA closed a two-week evacuation of 125,000 people from Kabul, *New York Times*, 31 August 1961.
2. Aung San. Burmese nationalist leader, in June 1947.
3. J.L. Nehru. Convocation address at Aligarh Muslim University, January 24, 1948.
4. Ibid.
5. A 2006 Hindi film produced by Aditya Chopra and directed by Kabir Khan who has made a number of documentaries on Afghanistan and is loosely based on the Director and his friend's experiences in post-Taliban Afghanistan.
6. 'Afghanistan on verge of socio-economic collapse: Mr. Joseph Borell, the Foreign Policy Chief of EU, said in Brussels, *The Times of India*, October 3, 2021.
7. Ibid.
8. 'Half of Afghanistan's under-5s expected to suffer acute malnutrition', *UN News*, United Nations, October 5, 2021.
9. US President Biden at UNGA, September 21, 2021.
10. British Prime Minister Boris Johnson in conversation with Pakistan Prime Minister Imran Khan, *Reuters*, August 18, 2021.
11. President Hamid Karzai in his inaugural speech to the National Assembly, Islamic Republic of Afghanistan, December 19, 2005.

13

Pakistani Aggression Perpetuates Humanitarian Crisis in Afghanistan

M. Ashraf Haidari

This chapter is dedicated to the loving memory of my dear friend, Late Shakti Sinha, who would often tell me, "Government policies come and go, but I care about our peoples. Afghans have suffered the most in South Asia."

Introduction

Afghanistan is facing one of the most complex humanitarian crisis of its recent history. This has stemmed from a convergence of the past four decades of imposed conflicts of geopolitics, the adverse effects of climate change, the impact of the global economic recession due to COVID-19, endemic poverty, as well as chronic foreign aid dependency at 40 per cent. The past six months of external aggression by proxy have further compounded the grim humanitarian landscape across Afghanistan where the collapse of state institutions and economy has pushed the whole nation to the brink. Consequently, fourteen million Afghans (1 in 3 Afghans) face severe hunger; 3.4 million Afghan children suffer from acute malnutrition; 22.8 million

Afghans need immediate relief aid; and 97 per cent of all Afghans live below the poverty line. To better understand the complexity of the causes of the humanitarian crisis in the country, it helps to briefly revisit the humanitarian situation in the pre-war and in-war periods in Afghanistan. This should enable the donor community and international policymakers to collaborate on finding a durable solution to Afghanistan's externally imposed humanitarian crisis and avert its dangerous consequences on regional stability and international security.

Pre-war Afghanistan

The saga of Afghanistan as a vulnerable nation began in the late 1970s. Although Afghans were destitute at the time and thus somewhat reliant on foreign aid, they were a resilient nation. Displacement for protection or food security was rare. Afghans rarely abandoned their villages of origin where they were leading a peaceful, agrarian way of life. Afghanistan was self-sufficient agriculturally, and the country used to export a variety of fresh and dried horticultural products to its neighbourhood and beyond.

This was a time when the then Afghan government was pursuing a "win-win" foreign policy—as did the Islamic Republic of Afghanistan—promoting regional economic cooperation to ensure prosperity across its still poor and under-developed region: South and Central Asia. Afghans understood then that in order for poverty to be reduced to provide mitigation against unexpected natural disasters such as floods, avalanches, droughts, and earthquakes, they needed to continuously, grow their economy, while fostering and maintaining good relations with their neighbourhood for support during times of hardship.

Through this rational, constructive approach, humanitarian crises resulting from natural disasters were largely averted. However, this approach ceased to work when the former Soviet forces invaded and occupied Afghanistan for a decade. Years of war and violence weakened the resilience and coping mechanisms of the Afghan people, as most of them were forced into multiple waves of displacement in and out of Afghanistan.

The Legacy of the 1990s

Today's protracted, complex humanitarian crisis in Afghanistan dates back to the 1990s, when the country's state institutions completely collapsed, and the once resilient nation turned into a handful of extremely vulnerable groups. Like today, the oppressive foreign-installed regime of the Taliban victimized innocent Afghans on a daily basis, denying them, especially women and girls, access to their basic human rights, including education and healthcare.

A day before the tragedy of 9/11, Afghanistan had sadly turned into a no-man's-land. Save for the presence of the International Committee of the Red Cross (ICRC)—to which Afghans remain thankful—and a few other humanitarian organisations in the country, Afghanistan had been completely forgotten and isolated from the rest of the international community.

Human suffering was deplorable, as oppression, poverty, violence, ethnic cleansing, displacement, and other unspeakable atrocities against Afghans were rampant across the country. In addition, it was the international community's negligence towards this tragic humanitarian situation in Afghanistan that allowed the *al-Qaeda* and the Taliban to mastermind the tragedy of 9/11 from Afghan soil.

Post 9/11

However, thanks to international re-engagement in Afghanistan in the wake of the 9/11 attacks, the precarious humanitarian situation began improving fast. After the Taliban regime collapsed in 2001, Afghanistan's formerly dismal socio-economic indicators began improving significantly. Access to education, higher education, healthcare, and electricity multiplied, while improved infrastructure throughout urban and rural Afghanistan enabled the Islamic Republic to respond much more effectively to man-made and natural disasters.

In the meantime, the Islamic Republic initiated major water management projects to help revitalize Afghanistan's agriculture and livestock sectors, providing jobs for the country's rural population. With the support of India, for example, the Salma Dam was constructed in the western province of Herat in 2016, producing 42 MW of power and irrigating 75,000 hectares of farmland. Moreover, the Islamic Republic undertook a number of regional connectivity projects aimed at enabling Afghanistan to achieve economic self-reliance in the long run.

Despite relentless terrorist attacks by the Taliban to disrupt work on internal and external connectivity projects, steady progress continued being made on the following key projects: the TAPI (Turkmenistan-Afghanistan-Pakistan-India) Pipeline; CASA-1000; TAP-500; Lapis Lazuli Transit, Trade, and Transport Route; Chabahar International Transport and Transit Corridor; Five-Nation Railway Corridor; Afghanistan Rail Network; Trans-Hindukush Road Connectivity Project; and Digital Silk Road. The gradual implementation of these projects not only provided the jobs Afghan youth continue to need but it also gave Afghans a sense of hope and optimism about their future.

Indeed, these achievements, which remained works in progress, would have been impossible without the security, development, and humanitarian assistance provided by the international community, including Afghanistan's constructive neighbours. Unfortunately, however, the Taliban's terror campaign—which Pakistan helped maintain and resource—deliberately disrupted and continued undoing the Afghans' hard-earned gains of the past 20 years.

The Doha Deal

This process was accelerated when last April the Biden Administration announced complete withdrawal of the U.S. forces from Afghanistan by September 11, 2021. In effect, the Taliban were encouraged to renege on their commitments under the Doha Agreement—whose negotiation and signing between the Taliban leaders and the Trump Administration in February 2020—excluded the legitimate and democratically elected Afghan government. For instance, in return for the release of over 5,000 of their prisoners, which the Islamic Republic conceded, the Taliban were supposed to reduce violence, engage in result-driven talks, prevent their released prisoners from returning to the battlefield, and commit to a comprehensive ceasefire that would pave the way for a sustainable political settlement.

On the contrary, however, none of the above materialised, as the Taliban escalated terrorist attacks in urban areas and launched major offensives across Afghanistan throughout the months of May and August. During this four-month period, the Taliban—enjoying full-spectrum military, intelligence, and diplomatic support from Pakistan—systematically destroyed Afghanistan's local state institutions, commercial enterprises, critical service-delivery infrastructure, and the growing sources of licit rural livelihoods.

This was done in gross violation of the provisions of Chapter VII of the United Nations (UN) Charter and despite repeated appeals and calls by the international community, including from UN Secretary-General Antonio Guterres to de-escalate acts of aggression and reduce violence significantly. However, a failure on the part of the UN Security Council to take punitive action under the UN Charter against the state perpetrator of the creeping invasion of Afghanistan continued exacerbating the humanitarian crisis in the country.

By mid-2021, five million Afghans had been displaced internally and 18.4 million others needed humanitarian and protection assistance. Against this grim backdrop, increased offensives by the Taliban forced another 600,000 Afghans to abandon their villages, districts, and provinces of origin, seeking safety and survival in Kabul and other urban areas. Moreover, the convergence of COVID-19 and the adverse effects of climate change, especially droughts affecting one-third of Afghanistan, has further added to the suffering of destitute and war-ravaged Afghans.

Situation since August 15

Since August 15, 2021 when the Taliban illegally and forcefully took over the government in Kabul, the humanitarian crisis has further deteriorated across Afghanistan. Competent government employees have abandoned their jobs, leaving Afghanistan with an irreparable brain drain. As a result, key service-delivery institutions no longer function and lack the resources to address the basic needs of an impoverishing population. The banking sector has ground to a halt, and people are unable to withdraw their savings. At the same time, in the wake of August 15, most international aid organisations and diplomatic missions closed down their development programs and evacuated their staff, negatively impacting the humanitarian situation across Afghanistan.

Moreover, since September 7 when the Taliban—following much factional infighting—announced their foreign-installed interim government, three key developments have proven most harmful to the humanitarian situation in Afghanistan. Credible and abundant evidence shows that the Taliban and their external state sponsor are directly responsible for these harmful developments, daily claiming Afghan lives.

First, the formation of an all-male exclusionary interim cabinet with half of its members sanctioned by the UN and one of them blacklisted by the U.S. Federal Bureau of Investigation (FBI) has led to the freezing of $9.5 billion in the Afghan Central Bank's reserves. Moreover, the International Monetary Fund (IMF) has withheld $370, which was supposed to reach Afghanistan on August 23 as part of "a global IMF response to the economic crisis." The state sponsor of the Taliban knows all too well from its own experiences with sanctions regimes that such a totalitarian setup, trampling on all international laws, would hardly ensure continued support from the international community, and that the price of installing such an exclusionary entity that can be remote-controlled from Pakistan would have to be borne by destitute Afghans, who had just been hit hard by months of deadly aggression by proxy.

Second, the enforcement by the Taliban of gender apartheid—banning women from work and girls from education—has ensured an indefinite lack of international recognition, even from their own state-sponsor. This is because Afghanistan is the only country out of over 190 member-states of the UN where women are banned from participation in polity, society, and economy—a situation where none of the globally adopted 2030 sustainable development goals (SDGs) could ever be achieved without women's full inclusion and participation. This has effectively condemned Afghanistan to a perpetual humanitarian crisis, since women's education and health have a direct impact on the overall health and economic productivity of any nation.

Third, the Taliban are least capable of governing, which is far more complex and difficult than carrying out suicide terrorist attacks, targeting innocent civilians, and destroying such soft targets as telephone towers, pylons, roads, bridges, culverts, and so on. Over the past two months, they have learned that—unlike destroying—building, operating, and maintaining anything that is helpful takes technical competence and resources, of which they have remorselessly deprived Afghanistan. As of this writing, the Taliban are busy undoing the hard-won gains of Afghanistan, including the country's free press, with a direct impact on the humanitarian situation. A country ravaged by conflict, climate, COVID-19, and poverty can hardly afford a lack of information that can help impoverished households decide on the right coping mechanisms and survival strategies to make it to the next day.

Life under the Taliban

Consequently, the UN Development Program (UNDP) reported in September that under the Taliban's rule, "97 per cent of Afghans would sink below the poverty line by next year—a staggering increase of 25 per cent." The IMF reported in October that the "Afghan economy would contract by 30 per cent, leaving the whole nation dependent on humanitarian aid for mere survival."

These dismal statistics has hardly shocked the Taliban or persuaded them to reverse their draconian policies, which underpin Afghanistan's widening humanitarian crisis. For example, they have completely disregarded international appeals, including the most recent UN Security Council statement, calling for the formation of an inclusive and representative government—one that embraces and capitalizes on the hard-earned gains of the Afghan people.

Pakistan's Role

Some observers of the region argue that the Taliban's indifference to the dire humanitarian situation affecting all Afghans is by strategic design. This intends to serve the military objective of Pakistan that seeks to keep Afghanistan aid-dependent and on the brink, thereby securing Pakistan's deep influence over Afghan politics. Therefore, one way to achieve this goal would be to manufacture and manage a perpetual humanitarian crisis in Afghanistan, milking the donor community for enough handout resources to prevent mass starvation in the country.

Indeed, Pakistan could prove these credible assumptions wrong by getting the Taliban leadership, which the country recently installed in the interim cabinet, to form an inclusive and broad-based government, including women, that is acceptable to all Afghans. This would immediately help avert the impending humanitarian catastrophe, as Afghanistan's inclusive government would earn international recognition accompanied with development aid, halt the exodus of Afghan professionals, and attract international investment in the country's virgin markets.

International Humanitarian Response

As a reactive and short-term measure, on September 13, UN Secretary-General Guterres convened in Geneva a high-level ministerial conference on Afghanistan's humanitarian situation, in which over one hundred countries and thirty international and regional organisations participated. In all, $1.2 billion—including $606 million for the next four months through the end of December—was pledged. "Urgent aid should reach one in three Afghans, who is experiencing emergency level of food insecurity, as well as more than half of Afghan children under age 5, who are at the brink of acute malnutrition," which the UN Office for the Coordination of Humanitarian Affairs (UNOCHA) warned recently.

However, considering the enormity of the challenges confronting Afghanistan due to the convergence of an ongoing conflict, widening poverty, internal displacement, migration movements, climate-induced floods and droughts, and the still unresolved COVID-19 pandemic, the UN's band-aid approach to averting a catastrophic humanitarian crisis would hardly work. It actually encourages perverse incentives and perpetuates a culture of dependency, while fatiguing the community donors, which is unwilling to provide over $600 million every four months to keep Afghanistan alive. In other words, while relief aid does save lives now, it is self-defeating in the long run, killing more aid-reliant innocents when relief assistance resources have dried up.

The Way Forward

Throughout their terror campaign over the past 20 years, the Taliban promised suffering Afghans "permanent peace, welfare, and prosperity, if Allah wills, once in power." They should now be put to the test to do so. If they are unable or unwilling to govern, secure, and provide for the basic needs of the Afghan people, they should be held accountable under international law so that they rethink their irrational behaviour and make a course correction.

Indeed, the first step they should consider taking without any delay is to embrace and reconcile with the much greater half of Afghanistan—including other ethnic groups, women, and youth—and to allow them adequate and fair representation in a permanent government to be established soon. This can be achieved under the incomplete Doha peace process, which can resume with the continued support of the international community under a robust UN mission with an operational and coercive mandate to enforce peace, if necessary. Unless this fundamental root cause of the widening humanitarian crisis is resolved, Afghanistan's crises would only multiply, the spillover effects of which would not only undermine regional stability but also international peace and security.

Fortunately, the international community vividly recalls the consequences of neglecting the externality of Afghanistan's challenges in the 1990s that brought about the tragedy of 9/11. In addition, the lessons of the past twenty years must never be overlooked. This includes the past six months of well-documented Pakistani aggression by proxy that has brought about the current humanitarian crisis affecting 97 per cent of Afghans. That is why it is in the best long-term interest of all regional and extra-regional stakeholders to learn from the past forty years of their involvement and interventions in Afghanistan to do what is right for them and the Afghan people, consistent with the UN Charter. More of the same would only ensure the continuity and further expansion of the threats of terrorism, extremism, and criminality that have found an enabling environment in Afghanistan again, as they did throughout the 1990s before 9/11.

Indeed, keeping the country on humanitarian life-support or abandoning it altogether is hardly the right solution. However, working together to help form an inclusive government that can look after the long-term protective and human security needs of the Afghan people constitutes a durable solution to the international problem in Afghanistan. This is what the vast majority of the Afghan people need, demand, and deserve, following four decades of imposed deadly and destructive conflicts. The international community must deliver on these basic Afghan expectations. Doing so would automatically help ensure regional stability and maintain international peace and security.

14

ENDANGERED PEACE

Nadeem Shah

Looking at the Taliban, I recall a famous couplet of Mir Taqi Mir, "All the measures were reversed; even some medicines did not work", which interprets the current situation of Taliban. In other words, the Doha Pact has stuck up the Taliban in the middle. Moreover, the peace deal has shamefully defeated the narrative of patronizing proxies and militant groups.

There are two prospects that can appear in the future: If the Taliban does not abide by the Doha Pact, the entire world may rise up against them. The other prospect is that if they abide by it, they will have to face strong opposition and fierce resistance from international terrorist networks in Afghanistan. In both cases, there are serious threats to peace, which may harm the Belt and Road project and the China-Pakistan Economic Corridor.

Let's see what happens next and which action the Taliban may take. The future course of their actions can determine their choices but the fact is that Doha Pact has taken away all the Taliban's arrogance. Now their only safety is to abide by its terms. I believe the real future threats are Islamist States of Khorasan Province, *al-Qaeda* its affiliates and the Tehreek Taliban Pakistan instead of Afghan

Taliban. The situation can take a major turn when the world leaves the Taliban alone and bases are provided to the United States in Balochistan. The peace is still a long way off. Political institutions in Afghanistan are in vulnerable conditions as unsteady efforts were made during the US-led coalition's war in Afghanistan during the last 20 years.

The Doha Pact, which is also known as the Joint Declaration between the Islamist Republic of Afghanistan and the USA comprising four pages, four parts, 18 clauses, four sub-clauses explains the role and commitments of the Taliban and the USA.[1] However, it is pessimistically noted that the Taliban leadership is behaving differently after capturing Kabul on protecting human rights, civil liberties and forming an inclusive government, which are the crux of the Doha Pact. The Taliban's actions go against their commitments and promises made to the world. The female journalists are frightened to perform after Taliban take over and recently a group of women staged demonstration in Kabul demanded protection from Taliban.[2]

Mullah Abdul Ghani Baradar, the head of the Taliban's political office, told *Al Jazeera* they are in the process of forming an inclusive government.[3] The *BBC* reported in the second week of September, highlighting a new order begins under Taliban's governance, and quoted Taliban spokesperson Zabihullah Mujahid as saying they are forming an inclusive government representing all the factions.[4]

Dawn newspapers' monitoring desk reported that Prime Minister Imran Khan had expressed concerns of civil war in Afghanistan after the Taliban failed to form an inclusive government.[5] A well reputed newspaper *Daily Times* reported that Afghan spokesperson Zabihullah Mujahid criticized Pakistan after demanding the creation of an inclusive government in Afghanistan.[6] However, the Taliban remained aloof in forming an inclusive government, giving representation to all factions.

Apart from the Taliban's commitments, ground realities explain a rosy picture of protecting rights of minorities and women. The American Press Agency had reported in the beginning of the second week of September that the Taliban had formed an exclusive male dominated government instead of forming an inclusive government of all factions. The first cabinet lacks a single female representation.[7]

In the backdrop of not keeping promises, serious rights violations have been observed in the Taliban rule since August. The 31st Special Session of UN Human Rights Council expressed concerns one's serious rights violations in Afghanistan and adopted a resolution to strengthen and protect human rights.[8] The *BBC* had reported the fleeing of Afghan singers after the Taliban's takeover of Kabul due to security concerns.[9]

Al-Jazeera had reported the United Nations (UN) condemnation against the Taliban's violent handling of peaceful protests after the Taliban fighters used guns, whips and batons against the protestors. The UN called on the Taliban to immediately cease the use of force and arbitrary detention against those exercising their right to peaceful assembly and journalists covering the protests.[10]

If the Taliban backs out of the Doha Pact and its proxies, regroup and militancy continues, it will invite an endless destructive war in the region. The re-demarcation of the country's maps cannot be ruled out as the result of insurgency. The Taliban's opposition and resistance to the Durand Line agreement cannot be ruled out.

Challenges

The ruling Taliban factions have two key challenges: revival of the economy and the elimination of domestic international terror networks. Currently, they have to face four key groups to eliminate such as Uzbekistan Islamist Movement, East Turkmenistan Islamist Movement, *al-Qaeda*, its affiliates and Islamist State of Khorasan Province.

The Turkmenistan Islamist Movement, formerly known as the East Turkmenistan Islamist Movement (ETIM), is a foreign terror group and one of the Afghan Taliban's allies. Its stated goals are to establish an independent state called East Turkestan in place of the Chinese province of Xingjian. It was founded in western China and based in the Afghan province of Badakhshan.[11] Similarly, the Islamist

Movement of Uzbekistan is another *al-Qaeda* linked highly troubling group, which can retaliate against the Taliban based on their non-Pakhtoon identity and link with international terrorism networks. The highly prestigious institution Stanford University's mapping Militant organisation provides a detailed profile of IMU that the group is active to overthrow Uzbek government and promulgate the Islamist Shariah.[12]

Another threat is the Islamist State Khorasan-Province (ISKP). The *BBC* has reported that ISIS had established the ISKP in January 2015 in Nangarhar close to Pakistan boarders and human trafficking routes. The report says that ISKP recruited both Afghan and Pakistani *jihadists*, particularly defecting members of the Afghan Taliban who do not consider their own organisation to be extreme enough. The *BBC* report links the ISKP with the Haqqani Network.[13] *Al Jazeera* had reported on August 26 that ISKP is making efforts to derail Taliban rule.[14] The ideological base of the ISKP is extremely anti-Shiite and closely associated with militant groups based in Pakistan and the Saraiki region and is dependent upon the Saraiki region in Afghanistan. A meaningful research policy memo of the well reputed research institution Stimson Organization says the anti-Shiite ISKP killed 100 Shiites mostly including children in a Kabul school in May last year. The ISKP had lost six of its top leaders between 2015 and 2021 in Afghanistan. Five of them belonged to Pakistan's Saraiki Region. The terrorists were identified as Hafeez Saeed Khan, Abdul Haseeb Leghari, Abu Sayed, Abu Saad Orakzai, Abu Omar al-Khorasani, and Aslam Farooqi. Three terrorists were previously affiliated with the TTP and one was a Taliban defector. The current leader of the ISKP, identified as Shabab al-Muhajir, is reportedly of Arab descent. Muhajir is reportedly an urban warfare expert. The increasing prevalence of Salafi-jihadist ideas amongst young and educated Afghans in urban areas as a driver for ISKP's recruitment of urban cells and support structure underlies a major security problem. The Stimson Organization research has mentioned 2500-8500 ISKP fighters in Afghanistan. The ISKP had aligned itself with various smaller groups developed in remote areas of Baluchistan and Saraiki region like Lashkar-e-Jhangvi Al-Alami, Lashkar-e-Islam, and Jamaat-ul-Ahrar among others. The policy memo says the Taliban and the ISKP are rivals and there is hardly any scope of accommodation given their differing ideologies as well as objectives.[1]

The emergence of a new coalition among the non-Pakhtoons, international terrorism network including Chechen, Uzbek, Turkmenistan and renegades form the Tehreek-e-Taliban Pakistan cannot be ruled out in coming months in the current situation in Afghanistan. These groups have embraced allegiances to ISIS and have grown rapidly across Afghanistan in the presence of the US-led coalition. The Long War Journal ran a story of reunion between TTP and Afghan Taliban after the TTP emir Noor Wali Mehsood renewed allegiance to Afghan Taliban on August 19.[16]

I believe that in the next few years the region will become a hotbed of war zones. No one knows which country's maps will change. However, the people of the Saraiki region must be organized to protect their national character. An Afghanistan dominated by the fundamentalist Taliban is the second extremist Islamist country in our neighbourhoods after Iran.

The Taliban have seized control of a country bordering six countries, including Turkmenistan, Uzbekistan, China, Iran, Pakistan and Tajikistan. Terrorist groups from Turkmenistan and Uzbekistan, led by the Afghan and Pakistani Taliban, have been involved in terrorist attacks inside Pakistan in the past. The USA came to Afghanistan 20 years ago to eliminate the Taliban and *al-Qaeda*, but they have not been eliminated and have flourished, while a third group in the form of ISKP, a continuation of ISIS has developed rapidly and is present in Afghan territories.

In the current situation we can expect three types of shifts:

First: The Afghan Taliban may pledge allegiance to ISIS and make the ISKP their ally or fight against them as a second option.

Second: Under the Doha Pact, the Afghan Taliban have no alternative but to take action against armed groups, in which case the ISKP and other militant groups that can form a new coalition against it.

Third: The Tehreek-e-Taliban Pakistan may divide into Afghan Taliban and ISKP.

In all the three situations, the dream of peace does not seem to have come to fruition. This situation is not ideal for Pakistan and particularly China. In the present bleak scenario for peace everyone is trying to save their nearest and favourite terror groups in order to protect their vested interests.

My research indicates that peace will remain a dream as long as countries in the region like Pakistan, India and China do not resolve their territorial disputes with each other and find an acceptable solution. Otherwise, the agencies of these countries will continue a proxy war. Therefore, the peace-loving forces in the Saraiki region will have to strengthen their nationalist unity to protect their right of freedom in fight against terror groups emerging in the future scenario; otherwise the region will be engulfed in an unending war. This is the time that civil society and pro-people forces wake up as the future prospects are not optimistic for Pakistan.

Pakistan has announced amnesty for the TTP, which lacks with a De-Radicalization Program (DRP). Only amnesty or pardon is not a solution to end terrorism. Pakistan has a long history of sponsoring militancy and *jihadist* groups. The *madarsa* network and its by-product of *Mujahedeen* were used for the first time against the Afghan Socialist Revolution in partnership with the United States. Pakistan continued sponsoring militant groups after the Geneva accord and exit of Russian troops.

Pakistan President Arif Alvi has made his amnesty offer in a *Dawn News* programme, *'Khabar Se Khabar'*, aired on September 11.[17] It looks like the President issued a vague statement without undermining its serious repercussions. We can find only two Islamist countries across the globe, which had offered an amnesty program for Islamist terrorists. The Kenyan and Nigerian models of amnesty programs need in depth study before Pakistan inks an amnesty deal with TTP. The Federal Republic of Nigeria had offered an unconditional pardon for Islamist terrorists in 2009 with cash payments and entitling them pension rights.[18]

The Nigerian government had announced an unconditional amnesty program in 2009. The Islamist terrorist groups had killed more than 350,000 people. However, a report released in August last has established the amnesty program has invited a rage among the families and victims of Nigerian terror group Boko Haram.[19] Similarly, Kenya offered an amnesty program for Al-Shahbab terrorists in 2015 to stop young Kenyans from joining the Al Shahbab's training camps in neighboring Somalia. Those found eligible for amnesty received support to help them reintegrate in the society. Kenya is also facing serious problems in rehabilitating 'former terrorists'. The amnesty program has been made ineffective practically in Kenya. The Center for Strategic and International Studies' research report published in 2018 identified five loopholes in the ineffectiveness of the Kenyan amnesty program including lack of an operational framework, poor or incomplete execution, and questions around eligibility, uncooperative state security forces and weak monitoring mechanisms.[20] The internal controversies in Pakistan's state actors is the key tussle point in materializing the amnesty deal between TTP and Pakistan.

Senior journalist Mujahid Hussein believes an amnesty deal is unlikely to materialize between Pakistan and TTP due to trust deficiencies after the arrest and escape incidents of former TTP spokesperson Ehsanullah Ehsan. He says the Taliban groups from Khyber, Momand, Bajaur, Dir, Swat, Mardan, Kohat and Peshawar are of the opinion not to negotiate with Pakistan. Ehsanullah Ehsan himself admitted that he was brought to Peshawar after promising to fulfill his demands including money and security. But he said that his demands were never met therefore he fled from their custody. He says a few Taliban factions believe the prime objective of TTP's creation has been achieved after the US-led NATO forces' withdrawal from Afghanistan, so TTP should join mainstream. These TTP factions were supporting negotiations with Pakistan.

Conclusion

In the final crux of the whole situation, it is imperative to mention that the ongoing insurgency in Afghanistan is in fact the result of religious exploitation, which also causes a decline in social consciousness. The theory of Karl Marx argues that religion was constructed by people to calm uncertainty over our role in the universe and in society. The religious insurgency is a tool of social control used by the suppressors to keep the oppressors with an unequal status quo like Taliban are doing.

Afghanistan is a tribal society where religion is the political system and plays a critical role in maintaining an unequal status quo to continue religious exploitation. People in tribal societies have radically more resources and power than other groups of people of non-tribal societies. Tribal chiefs use religion as a tool to keep the less powerful groups pacified.

A complete withdrawal of the US-led coalition forces was not the solution; instead the presence of sufficient troops was mandatory to contain insurgency to a level to ensure protection of the political government. The war torn country has been surviving under grave poverty. The Asian Development Bank statistics show 47.3 per cent of the population was living below the national poverty line in 2020. The proportion of the employed population below $1.90 purchasing power parity a day is 34.3 per cent in 2019. For every 1,000 babies born in Afghanistan in 2019, 60 die before their 5th birthday.[21] An eternal peace, strengthening democratic institutions and addressing the causes of religious insurgency should be a solution to poverty in the war torn country to minimize religious exploitation!

(Article is part of updated version of book Saraiki Region: Roots of Radicalization by author Nadeem Shah)

NOTES

1. https://www.washingtonpost.com/context/u-s-taliban-peace-deal/7aab0f58-dd5c-430d-9557-1b6672d889c3/
2. https://apnews.com/article/afghanistan-taliban-kabul-1d4b052ccef113adc8dc94f965ff23c7
3. https://www.aljazeera.com/news/2021/9/4/afghanistan-mullah-baradar-promises-an-inclusive-government
4. https://www-bbc-com.cdn.ampproject.org/v/s/www.bbc.com/news/world-asia-58495112.amp?amp_gsa=1&amp_js_v=a6&usqp=mq331AQKKAFQArABIIACAw%3D%3D#amp_tf=From% 20%251%24s&aoh=163341131129

26&referrer= https%3A%2F%2Fwww.google.com&ampshare=https%3A%2F%2Fwww.bbc.com%2Fnews%2Fworld-asia-58495112

5. https://www.dawn.com/news/1647706
6. https://dailytimes-com-pk.cdn.ampproject.org/v/s/dailytimes.com.pk/818499/pakistan-has-no-right-to-call-for-inclusive-govt-taliban-leader/amp/?amp_gsa=1&amp_js_v=a6&usqp=mq331AQKKAFQArABIIACAw%3D%3D#amp_tf=From %20%251%24s&aoh=1 6334113112926&referrer=https%3A%2 F%2Fwww.google. com&ampshare=https%3A%2F%2Fdailytimes.com.pk%2F818499%2 Fpakistan-has-no-right-to-call-for-inclusive-govt-taliban-leader%2Famp%2F%23amp_tf%3DFrom%2520%25251%2524s%26aoh%3D16334113112926%26 referrer%3 Dhttps%253A%2 52F%252Fwww.google.com%26ampshare%3 Dhttps%253A%252F%252Fdailytimes.com.pk%252F818499%252Fpakistan-has-no-right-to-call-for-inclusive-govt-taliban-leader%252F.
7. https://apnews.com/article/middle-east-pakistan-afghanistan-arrests-islamabad-d50b1b490d27d32eb20cc11b77c12c87
8. https://www.ohchr.org/EN/HRBodies/HRC/SpecialSessions/Session31/Pages/31stSpecialSession.aspx
9. https://www.bbc.com/news/world-asia-58583217
10. https://www.aljazeera.com/news/2021/9/10/un-condemns-talibans-violence-against-peaceful-protesters
11. https://gandhara.rferl.org/a/afghanistan-badakhshan-taliban-chian-uighur/29035817.html
12. http://web.stanford.edu/group/mappingmilitants/cgi-bin/maps/view/islamic-state
13. https://www-bbc-com.cdn.ampproject.org/v/s/www.bbc.com/news/world-asia-58333533.amp?amp_js_v=a6&amp_gsa=1&usqp=mq331AQKKAFQArABIIACAw%3 D%3D#aoh=1 6300393407774&referrer=ht tps%3A%2F%2Fwww.google.com &amp_tf=From%20%251%24s&ampshare=https%3A%2F%2Fwww.bbc.com%2Fnews%2Fworld-asia-58333533
14. https://www.aljazeera.com/opinions/2021/8/27/the-threat-of-iskp-in-afghanistan-has-been-underestimated
15. https://www.stimson.org/2021/https-www-stimson-org-2021-iskp-and-afghanistans-future-security/
16. https://www.longwarjournal.org/archives/2021/08/pakistani-talibans-emir-renews-allegiance-to-afghan-taliban.php
17. https://www.dawn.com/news/1645439
18. https://www.csis.org/analysis/kenyas-struggling-amnesty-experiment-policy-challenge-rehabilitating-former-terrorists
19. https://www.theafricareport.com/123114/nigerias-amnesty-for-terrorists-re-opens-old-wounds/
20. https://www.csis.org/analysis/kenyas-struggling-amnesty-experiment-policy-challenge-rehabilitating-former-terrorists
21. https://www.adb.org/countries/afghanistan/poverty

Index

*